CAMBRIDGE TRACTS IN MATHEMATICS

General Editors

B. BOLLOBÁS, W. FULTON, A. KATOK, F. KIRWAN,
P. SARNAK, B. SIMON, B. TOTARO

205   Ridge Functions

CAMBRIDGE TRACTS IN MATHEMATICS

GENERAL EDITORS

B. BOLLOBÁS, W. FULTON, A. KATOK, F. KIRWAN, P. SARNAK,
B. SIMON, B. TOTARO

A complete list of books in the series can be found at www.cambridge.org/mathematics.
Recent titles include the following:

Ridge Functions

ALLAN PINKUS
Technion – Israel Institute of Technology, Haifa

CAMBRIDGE
UNIVERSITY PRESS

CAMBRIDGE
UNIVERSITY PRESS

University Printing House, Cambridge CB2 8BS, United Kingdom

Cambridge University Press is part of the University of Cambridge.

It furthers the University's mission by disseminating knowledge in the pursuit of education, learning and research at the highest international levels of excellence.

www.cambridge.org
Information on this title: www.cambridge.org/9781107124394

© Allan Pinkus 2015

First published 2015

A catalog record for this publication is available from the British Library

Library of Congress Cataloging in Publication data
Pinkus, Allan, 1946–
Ridge functions / Allan Pinkus, Technion, Israel Institute of Technology, Haifa.
pages cm
Includes bibliographical references and indexes.
ISBN 978-1-107-12439-4 (Hardback: alk. paper)
1. Function spaces. 2. Multivariate analysis. 3. Numbers, Real. I. Title.
QA323.P56 2016
515′.73–dc23   2015014539

ISBN 978-1-107-12439-4 Hardback

Contents

v

Preface

This monograph is an attempt to examine and study ridge functions as entities in and of themselves. As such we present what we consider to be various central properties of ridge functions. However, no encyclopedic claims are being made, and the topics chosen are those that we alone considered appropriate. In addition, most chapters contain, either explicitly or implicitly, unresolved questions. It is our hope that this monograph will prove useful and interesting to both researchers and the more casual reader. And, of course, all errors, omissions and other transgressions are totally our responsibility.

No monograph is written in a vacuum, and I would like to especially thank Carl de Boor, Vugar Ismailov and an anonymous referee for various comments and suggestions. Thanks also to Heinz Bauschke, Vitaly Maiorov, Simon Reich and Yuan Xu for their patience, and help with my various inquiries.

Glossary of Selected Symbols

Symbol	Meaning	Page
$J(F)$	$\{\mathbf{x} : \|F(\mathbf{x})\| = \|F\|\}$	92
$P_A G(\mathbf{y})$	$\frac{1}{2}[\max_{\{\mathbf{x}:A\mathbf{x}=A\mathbf{y}\} \cap K} G(\mathbf{x}) + \min_{\{\mathbf{x}:A\mathbf{x}=A\mathbf{y}\} \cap K} G(\mathbf{x})]$	101
$Z(G)$	$\{x : G(x) = 0\}$	139
$\Delta_{\mathbf{x}}$	$\sum_{i=1}^{n} \frac{\partial^2}{\partial x_i^2}$	141
ω_n	$\frac{2\pi^{n/2}}{\Gamma(n/2)}$	141
$\mathcal{N}$	$\{\big(G(\mathbf{x}^1), \ldots, G(\mathbf{x}^k)\big) : G \in \mathcal{M}(A^1, \ldots, A^r)\}$	153
Λ_i	$\{A^i \mathbf{x}^j : j = 1, \ldots, k\}$	154
$\Gamma_A(\mathbf{c})$	$\{\mathbf{x} : A\mathbf{x} = \mathbf{c}\}$	155

1

Introduction

This monograph is about *Ridge Functions*. A ridge function is any multivariate real-valued function

$$F : \mathbb{R}^n \to \mathbb{R}$$

of the form

$$F(x_1, \ldots, x_n) = f(a_1 x_1 + \cdots + a_n x_n) = f(\mathbf{a} \cdot \mathbf{x}),$$

where $\mathbf{x} = (x_1, \ldots, x_n) \in \mathbb{R}^n$ are the variables, f is a univariate real-valued function, i.e., $f : \mathbb{R} \to \mathbb{R}$, and $\mathbf{a} = (a_1, \ldots, a_n) \in \mathbb{R}^n \backslash \{\mathbf{0}\}$ is a fixed vector. This vector $\mathbf{a} \in \mathbb{R}^n \backslash \{\mathbf{0}\}$ is generally called the *direction*. In other words, a ridge function is a multivariate function constant on the parallel hyperplanes $\mathbf{a} \cdot \mathbf{x} = c$, $c \in \mathbb{R}$. It is one of the simpler multivariate functions. Namely, it is a superposition of a univariate function with one of the simplest multivariate functions, the inner product.

More generally, we can and will consider, for given d, $1 \leq d \leq n-1$, functions F of the form

$$F(\mathbf{x}) = f(A\mathbf{x}),$$

where A is a fixed $d \times n$ real matrix, and $f : \mathbb{R}^d \to \mathbb{R}$. We call such functions *Generalized Ridge Functions*. For $d = 1$, this reduces to a ridge function.

1.1 Motivation

We see specific ridge functions in numerous multivariate settings without considering them of interest in and of themselves. We find them, for example, as kernels in integral formulæ. They appear in the Fourier transform

$$F(\mathbf{w}) = \int_{\mathbb{R}^n} e^{-i(\mathbf{w} \cdot \mathbf{x})} f(\mathbf{x}) \, d\mathbf{x},$$

1

and its inverse. We see them in the n-dimensional Radon transform

$$(R_{\mathbf{a}}f)(t) = \int_{\mathbf{a}\cdot\mathbf{x}=t} f(\mathbf{x})\, d\sigma(\mathbf{x}),$$

and its inverse. Here the integral is taken with respect to the natural hypersurface measure $d\sigma$. It is possible to generalize the Radon transform still further by integrating over $(n-d)$-dimensional affine subspaces of $\mathbb{R}^n$. In addition, we find them in the Hermite–Genocchi formula for divided differences

$$f[x_0, x_1, \ldots, x_n] = \int_{\Sigma_n} f^{(n)}(\mathbf{t}\cdot\mathbf{x})dt,$$

where Σ_n is the n-simplex in $\mathbb{R}_+^{n+1}$, i.e., $\Sigma_n = \{\mathbf{t} = (t_0, t_1, \ldots, t_n) : t_i \geq 0, \sum_{i=0}^n t_i = 1\}$. See, for example, de Boor [2005] for a discussion and history of this formula. They appear in multivariate Fourier series where the basic functions are of the form $e^{i(\mathbf{n}\cdot\mathbf{x})}$, for $\mathbf{n} \in \mathbb{Z}^n$. And also in partial differential equations where, for example, if P is a constant coefficient polynomial in n variables, then

$$P\left(\frac{\partial}{\partial x_1}, \ldots, \frac{\partial}{\partial x_n}\right) f = 0$$

has a solution of the form $f(\mathbf{x}) = e^{\mathbf{a}\cdot\mathbf{x}}$ if and only if $P(\mathbf{a}) = 0$.

Classes of ridge functions also play a fundamental role in various subjects. The term *ridge function* is rather recent. However, these functions had been considered for many years under the name of *plane waves*. See, for example, the well-known book of John [1955]. In that book are considered representations of multivariate functions using integrals whose kernels are specific "plane waves" and applications thereof to partial differential equations. Plane waves are also discussed by Courant and Hilbert [1962]. In general, linear combinations of ridge functions with fixed directions occur in the study of hyperbolic constant coefficient partial differential equations. As an example, assume that the (a_i, b_i) are pairwise linearly independent vectors in $\mathbb{R}^2$. Then the general "solution" to the homogeneous partial differential equation

$$\prod_{i=1}^r \left(b_i\frac{\partial}{\partial x} - a_i\frac{\partial}{\partial y}\right) F = 0,$$

where the derivatives are understood in the sense of distributions, are all functions of the form

$$F(x, y) = \sum_{i=1}^r f_i(a_i x + b_i y),$$

for (almost) arbitrary univariate functions f_i.

The term *ridge function* was coined in the 1975 paper by Logan and Shepp

[1975]. Seemingly, they were unaware of the previous terminology, and the term "ridge function" has now been fairly universally adopted. This was a seminal paper in computerized tomography. In tomography, or at least in tomography as the theory was initially constructed in the early 1980s, ridge functions were basic. The idea there was to try to reconstruct a given, but unknown, function $G(\mathbf{x})$ from the values of its integrals along certain parallel planes or lines. Logan and Shepp considered functions in the unit disk in $\mathbb{R}^2$ with given line integrals along parallel lines and a finite number of equally spaced directions. More generally, consider some nice domain K in $\mathbb{R}^n$, and a function G belonging to $L^2(K)$. Assume that for some fixed directions $\{\mathbf{a}^i\}_{i=1}^r$ we are given the values

$$\int_{K \cap \{\mathbf{a}^i \cdot \mathbf{x} = \lambda\}} G(\mathbf{x}) \, d\sigma(\mathbf{x})$$

for each λ and $i = 1, \ldots, r$, where $d\sigma(\mathbf{x})$ is the natural measure on the hyperplanes $\{\mathbf{x} : \mathbf{a}^i \cdot \mathbf{x} = \lambda\}$. They (mis-)termed these values the *projections* of G along the hyperplanes $K \cap \{\mathbf{a}^i \cdot \mathbf{x} = \lambda\}$. Assume that we are given these values for each λ and $i = 1, \ldots, r$. What is a good method of reconstructing G based only on this information? It easily transpires, from basic orthogonality considerations, that the unique best $L^2(K)$ approximation

$$f^*(\mathbf{x}) = \sum_{i=1}^r f_i^*(\mathbf{a}^i \cdot \mathbf{x})$$

to G from the linear subspace

$$\mathcal{M}(\mathbf{a}^1, \ldots, \mathbf{a}^r) = \left\{ \sum_{i=1}^r f_i(\mathbf{a}^i \cdot \mathbf{x}) : f_i \text{ vary} \right\},$$

if such a best approximation exists, necessarily satisfies

$$\int_{K \cap \{\mathbf{a}^i \cdot \mathbf{x} = \lambda\}} G(\mathbf{x}) \, d\sigma(\mathbf{x}) = \int_{K \cap \{\mathbf{a}^i \cdot \mathbf{x} = \lambda\}} f^*(\mathbf{x}) \, d\sigma(\mathbf{x})$$

for each λ and $i = 1, \ldots, r$. That is, it has the same projections as G. Furthermore, since it is a best approximation from a linear subspace in a Hilbert space, its norm is strictly less than the norm of G, unless $f^* = G$. Thus, among all functions with the same data (projections) as G, this specific linear combination of ridge functions is the one of minimal $L^2(K)$ norm. In the unit disk in $\mathbb{R}^2$ with equally spaced directions, Logan and Shepp also give a more closed-form expression for f^*.

Ridge functions and ridge function approximations are also studied in statistics in the analysis of large multivariate data sets. There they often go under the name of *projection pursuit*, see, for example, Friedman and Stuetzle [1981],

Huber [1985] and Donoho and Johnstone [1989]. Projection pursuit algorithms approximate a function G of n variables by functions of the form

$$\sum_{i=1}^{r} f_i(\mathbf{a}^i \cdot \mathbf{x}),$$

where both the directions $\mathbf{a}^i$ and the univariate functions f_i are variables. The idea here is to "reduce dimension" and thus bypass the "curse of dimensionality". Each $\mathbf{a}^i \cdot \mathbf{x}$ is considered as a projection of $\mathbf{x}$. The directions $\mathbf{a}^i$ are chosen to "pick out the salient features". The method of approximation, introduced by Friedman and Stuetzle [1981] and called projection pursuit regression (PPR), is essentially a stepwise greedy algorithm that, at its kth step, looks for a best (or good) approximation of the form $f_k(\mathbf{a}^k \cdot \mathbf{x})$ to the function $G(\mathbf{x}) - \sum_{i=1}^{k-1} f_i(\mathbf{a}^i \cdot \mathbf{x})$, as we vary over both the univariate function f_k and the direction $\mathbf{a}^k$.

Ridge functions appear in many neural network models. One of the popular models in the theory of neural nets is that of a *multilayer feedforward perceptron* (MLP) neural net with input, hidden and output layers. The simplest case (which is that of one hidden layer, r processing units and one output) considers, in mathematical terms, functions of the form

$$\sum_{i=1}^{r} \alpha_i \sigma(\mathbf{w}^i \cdot \mathbf{x} + \theta_i),$$

where $\sigma : \mathbb{R} \to \mathbb{R}$ is some given fixed univariate function, $\theta_i \in \mathbb{R}$, and $\mathbf{w}^i \in \mathbb{R}^n \setminus \{\mathbf{0}\}$. In this model, which is just one of many, we are in general permitted to vary over the $\mathbf{w}^i$ and θ_i, in order to approximate an unknown function. Note that for each $\mathbf{w}$ and θ the function

$$\sigma(\mathbf{w} \cdot \mathbf{x} + \theta)$$

is a ridge function. Thus, a lower bound on the degree of approximation by such functions is given by the degree of approximation by linear combinations of ridge functions. See, for example, Pinkus [1999] and references therein for more on this problem.

Motivated by the previous two topics, and other considerations, Candès in his thesis Candès [1998], see also Candès [1999], introduced the theory of ridgelets. In essence, the set

$$\{\sigma(\mathbf{w} \cdot \mathbf{x} + \theta) : \mathbf{w} \in \mathbb{R}^n, \theta \in \mathbb{R}\}$$

is called the set of *ridgelets* generated by σ. Ridgelets generated by a σ are a subset of ridge functions. For a class of σ, Candès [1998], [1999], provides an integral representation for functions with an associated ridgelet kernel. He then discretizes this representation with an eye towards obtaining approximations that are constructive, qualitative and stable.

Even the restriction of ridge functions to polynomials leads to interesting questions. *Waring's Problem* asks whether every positive integer can be expressed as a sum of at most $h(m)$ mth powers of positive integers, where $h(m)$ depends only upon m. This problem was solved in the affirmative by Hilbert [1909]. The key result in his proof was the following: for given m and n, and $N = \binom{n-1+2m}{n-1}$, there exist $\mathbf{a}^i \in \mathbb{Z}^n$, $i = 1, \ldots, N+1$, and λ_i positive rationals, $i = 1, \ldots, N+1$, such that

$$(x_1^2 + \cdots + x_n^2)^m = \sum_{i=1}^{N+1} \lambda_i (\mathbf{a}^i \cdot \mathbf{x})^{2m},$$

see also Stridsberg [1912]. A lucid exposition of Waring's Problem, and elementary proof of this result may be found in Ellison [1971]. Waring's Problem has various generalizations. One of them, for example, is the following. Can each homogeneous polynomial of degree m in n variables be written as a linear combination of mth powers of r linear homogeneous polynomials, where r depends only on n and m, i.e., linear combinations of $(\mathbf{a} \cdot \mathbf{x})^m$, where $\mathbf{a} \in \mathbb{R}^n \backslash \{\mathbf{0}\}$? And if it can, what is then the minimal number $h(m, n)$ such that each homogeneous polynomial of degree m in n variables can be written as a linear combination of mth powers of $h(m, n)$ linear homogeneous polynomials? And what about the same question for general algebraic polynomials of degree at most m in n variables? That is, we wish to express each algebraic polynomial of degree at most m in n variables in the form

$$p(\mathbf{x}) = \sum_{i=1}^{r} q_i (\mathbf{a}^i \cdot \mathbf{x}),$$

where the q_i are univariate algebraic polynomials, and r is minimal. There is a rich literature, mainly in number theory, on this and related issues.

Ridge functions are also of interest to researchers and students of approximation theory. The basic goal in approximation theory is straightforward and fundamental. Approximate complicated objects by simpler objects. Recent years have witnessed a flurry of interest in approximation from different classes of multivariate functions. We have, for example, multivariate spline functions, wavelets, radial basis functions, and many other such classes. Among the class of multivariate functions, linear combinations of ridge functions are a class of simpler functions. The questions one asks are the fundamental questions of approximation theory. Can one approximate arbitrarily well (density)? How well can one approximate (degree of approximation)? How does one approximate (algorithms)?

In this monograph we review much of what is today known about ridge functions. We hope this whets the reader's appetite, as much still remains unknown.

1.2 Organization

These notes are organized as follows. In Chapters 2–4 we consider some of the very basic properties of finite linear combinations of ridge and generalized ridge functions. In Chapter 2 we ask what can be said about the smoothness of each ridge function component if a finite linear combination of them is smooth. For example, assume

$$F(\mathbf{x}) = \sum_{i=1}^{r} f_i(\mathbf{a}^i \cdot \mathbf{x}) \tag{1.1}$$

and $F \in C^k(\mathbb{R}^n)$. What, if anything, does this imply with regard to the smoothness of the f_i? In Chapter 3 we consider to what extent the representation of a function as a finite linear combination of ridge functions is unique. That is, how many fundamentally different ways are there to represent an F of the form (1.1) as a linear combination of a finite number of ridge functions? In Chapter 4 we study an inverse problem. Namely, given an F of the form (1.1) with known or unknown directions and unknown functions, is it possible to identify associated unknown directions and functions in the finite sum based on our knowledge of F? Definitive answers to all these questions are not known.

Algebraic and homogeneous polynomials are important in the study of ridge functions. In Chapter 5 we consider ridge functions that are polynomials and discuss a wide variety of associated problems. In particular, we study questions of linear independence, interpolation and spanning by linear combinations of $(\mathbf{a}\cdot\mathbf{x})^m$ in the space of homogeneous polynomials of degree m, as we vary over a subset of directions, ask similar questions for algebraic polynomials of degree m, and discuss Waring's Problem for real homogeneous and algebraic polynomials.

In Chapter 6 we consider various questions associated with the density of linear combinations of ridge functions with fixed and variable directions in the set of continuous functions on $\mathbb{R}^n$, in the topology of uniform convergence on compact subsets of $\mathbb{R}^n$.

Chapter 7 contains a discussion of the closure properties of finite linear combinations of ridge functions with given directions in different norms and domains, while Chapter 8 is concerned with the existence and characterization of best approximations from these same subspaces.

In Chapter 9 we survey approximation algorithms for finding best approximations from spaces of linear combinations of ridge functions. We consider approximations in the cases of both fixed and variable directions. The algorithms considered are all predicated on the notion that it is possible to find a best approximation from each of its component subspaces, i.e., sets of ridge functions with one direction.

In Chapter 10 we look at integral representations of functions where the kernel is a ridge function. In particular we consider an integral representation using an orthogonal decomposition in terms of Gegenbauer polynomials (from Petrushev [1998]), and an integral representation based upon ridgelets (as presented by Candès [1998]).

Chapters 11 and 12 are concerned with the problem of interpolation by finite linear combinations of ridge functions. In Chapter 11 we look at point interpolation, while in Chapter 12 we consider interpolation to data given on straight lines.

In most of the chapters we also consider the extent to which the results reported on can extend to generalized ridge functions.

Finally, the reference section is divided into two parts. The first section contains all works that are actually referenced in the text. In a futile attempt to provide the interested researcher with a complete overview of the subject we have included a supplemental list of references on ridge functions.

There are topics related to ridge functions that are not presented here. The most glaring omission is that of degree of approximation, i.e., estimates on the error of approximation when using linear combinations of ridge functions, and the understanding of which classes of functions are well approximated by linear combinations of ridge functions, and which classes are not well approximated by linear combinations of ridge functions. Different papers are devoted to various aspects of this problem. We wish to mention Oskolkov [1997], [1999a], Petrushev [1998], Maiorov [1999], Maiorov, Meir and Ratsaby [1999], Maiorov, Oskolkov and Temlyakov [2002] and Maiorov [2010a]. Most known error estimates for approximating by linear combinations of ridge functions do not provide for bounds that are better than those provided by the full space of algebraic polynomials they contain. That is, in $\mathbb{R}^n$ there are many choices of m directions for which the space of linear combinations of ridge functions with these directions are easily seen to contain all algebraic polynomials of degree $c_n m^{1/(n-1)}$, with a constant c_n independent of m. The error estimates for many different classical function spaces, when approximating by either linear combinations of m ridge functions or the algebraic polynomials they contain, are comparable. As this is the case, then why bother approximating by ridge functions? Ridge functions are undoubtedly better approximants for certain classes of functions. But for which classes of functions? An interesting example is due to Oskolkov [1999a]. He proved therein that, for harmonic functions in $\mathbb{R}^2$, approximation by ridge functions gives significantly better bounds than those provided by the associated algebraic polynomials. In ad-

dition, as has been pointed out by Candès and Donoho, see, for example, Candès
and Donoho [1999], ridge functions with varying directions are well-adapted to
handle singularities along $(n-1)$-dimensional hyperplanes. Nevertheless the full
theory, in the opinion of the author, is still very much lacking. This is unfortunate
as the problems are both interesting and important.

1.3 Notation

In this section we review some of the notation that will be used repeatedly in
these notes. A *direction* is any non-zero vector in $\mathbb{R}^n$. For a given direction
$\mathbf{a} = (a_1, \ldots, a_n)$, set

$$\mathcal{M}(\mathbf{a}) := \{f(\mathbf{a} \cdot \mathbf{x}) : f : \mathbb{R} \to \mathbb{R}\},$$

where $\mathbf{x} = (x_1, \ldots, x_n) \in \mathbb{R}^n$ are the variables and

$$\mathbf{a} \cdot \mathbf{x} = \sum_{i=1}^{n} a_i x_i$$

is the standard inner product on $\mathbb{R}^n$. Note that $\mathcal{M}(\mathbf{a})$ is an infinite-dimensional
linear subspace, and since we are varying over all univariate functions f it immediately follows that

$$\mathcal{M}(\mathbf{a}) = \mathcal{M}(\mathbf{b})$$

for directions $\mathbf{a}$ and $\mathbf{b}$ if and only if $\mathbf{a} = \lambda \mathbf{b}$ for some $\lambda \in \mathbb{R}$, $\lambda \neq 0$. Thus we
could assume that the directions $\mathbf{a}$ are chosen to be of norm 1 and also identify $\mathbf{a}$
with $-\mathbf{a}$. But there seems to be no particular advantage in such an assumption.

Given directions $\mathbf{a}^i$, $i = 1, \ldots, r$, we set

$$\mathcal{M}(\mathbf{a}^1, \ldots, \mathbf{a}^r) := \mathcal{M}(\mathbf{a}^1) + \cdots + \mathcal{M}(\mathbf{a}^r)$$

$$= \left\{ \sum_{i=1}^{r} f_i(\mathbf{a}^i \cdot \mathbf{x}) : f_i : \mathbb{R} \to \mathbb{R}, \ i = 1, \ldots, r \right\}.$$

We will sometimes also use the following notation. For a set $\Omega \subseteq \mathbb{R}^n$ we let

$$\mathcal{M}(\Omega) := \operatorname{span}\{f(\mathbf{a} \cdot \mathbf{x}) : f : \mathbb{R} \to \mathbb{R}, \ \mathbf{a} \in \Omega\}.$$

These are all linear spaces.

Similarly, for a given d, $1 \leq d \leq n-1$, and $d \times n$ matrices $A^1, \ldots, A^r$, we let

$$\mathcal{M}(A^1, \ldots, A^r) := \left\{ \sum_{i=1}^{r} f_i(A^i \mathbf{x}) : f_i : \mathbb{R}^d \to \mathbb{R}, \ i = 1, \ldots, r \right\}.$$

Sometimes we will also let Ω_d denote a subset of $d \times n$ real matrices, and set

$$\mathcal{M}(\Omega_d) := \text{span}\{f(A\mathbf{x}) : A \in \Omega_d, \ f : \mathbb{R}^d \to \mathbb{R}\}.$$

In $\mathbb{R}^n$ we let B^n and S^{n-1} denote the unit ball and unit sphere, respectively. That is,

$$B^n := \{\mathbf{x} : \|\mathbf{x}\|_2 \le 1\}$$

and

$$S^{n-1} := \{\mathbf{x} : \|\mathbf{x}\|_2 = 1\},$$

where $\|\cdot\|_2$ is the usual Euclidean (ℓ_2) norm on $\mathbb{R}^n$.

We recall some standard multi-index notation. For $\mathbf{k} = (k_1, \ldots, k_n) \in \mathbb{Z}_+^n$, let $|\mathbf{k}| = k_1 + \cdots + k_n$ and $\mathbf{k}! = k_1! \cdots k_n!$. We have that

$$\binom{|\mathbf{k}|}{\mathbf{k}} := \frac{|\mathbf{k}|!}{\mathbf{k}!} = \frac{(k_1 + \cdots + k_n)!}{k_1! \cdots k_n!}$$

are the usual multinomial coefficients. Given $\mathbf{x} \in \mathbb{R}^n$ and $\mathbf{k} \in \mathbb{Z}_+^n$, we set

$$\mathbf{x}^{\mathbf{k}} := x_1^{k_1} \cdots x_n^{k_n}.$$

Let H_m^n denote the set of real homogeneous polynomials of degree m in n variables, i.e.,

$$H_m^n := \left\{ \sum_{|\mathbf{k}|=m} b_{\mathbf{k}} \mathbf{x}^{\mathbf{k}} : b_{\mathbf{k}} \in \mathbb{R} \right\}.$$

It is well-known that $\dim H_m^n = \binom{n-1+m}{n-1}$. In addition, let Π_m^n denote the set of all real algebraic polynomials of total degree at most m in n variables, i.e.,

$$\Pi_m^n := \left\{ \sum_{|\mathbf{k}|\le m} b_{\mathbf{k}} \mathbf{x}^{\mathbf{k}} : b_{\mathbf{k}} \in \mathbb{R} \right\}$$

or

$$\Pi_m^n = \bigoplus_{r=0}^m H_r^n.$$

It is easily verified that $\dim \Pi_m^n = \dim H_m^{n+1} = \binom{n+m}{n}$. By Π^n we denote the set of all algebraic polynomials of n variables, and by H^n the set of all homogeneous polynomials of n variables, i.e.,

$$H^n = \bigcup_{k=0}^\infty H_k^n.$$

For $\mathbf{k} \in \mathbb{Z}_+^n$, set

$$D^{\mathbf{k}} := \frac{\partial^{|\mathbf{k}|}}{\partial x_1^{k_1} \cdots \partial x_n^{k_n}} .$$

For any polynomial q of the form

$$q(\mathbf{x}) = \sum_{\mathbf{k}} a_{\mathbf{k}} \mathbf{x}^{\mathbf{k}},$$

where $a_{\mathbf{k}} \in \mathbb{R}$, we let

$$q(D) = \sum_{\mathbf{k}} a_{\mathbf{k}} D^{\mathbf{k}}$$

denote the associated constant coefficient partial differential operator. A simple calculation shows that, for $\mathbf{k} \in \mathbb{Z}_+^n$, $|\mathbf{k}| = m$, we have

$$D^{\mathbf{k}}(\mathbf{a} \cdot \mathbf{x})^\ell = \begin{cases} 0, & m > \ell \\ \frac{\ell!}{(\ell-m)!} \mathbf{a}^{\mathbf{k}} (\mathbf{a} \cdot \mathbf{x})^{\ell-m}, & m \le \ell. \end{cases}$$

Thus, if $q \in H_m^n$, then

$$q(D)(\mathbf{a} \cdot \mathbf{x})^\ell = \begin{cases} 0, & m > \ell \\ \frac{\ell!}{(\ell-m)!} q(\mathbf{a}) (\mathbf{a} \cdot \mathbf{x})^{\ell-m}, & m \le \ell \end{cases} \tag{1.2}$$

and, in particular, for $q \in H_m^n$ we have

$$q(D)(\mathbf{a} \cdot \mathbf{x})^m = m! \, q(\mathbf{a}). \tag{1.3}$$

Furthermore, for $\mathbf{k}, \mathbf{j} \in \mathbb{Z}_+^n$, $|\mathbf{k}| = |\mathbf{j}| = m$, we also have

$$D^{\mathbf{k}} \mathbf{x}^{\mathbf{j}} = \delta_{\mathbf{k}, \mathbf{j}} \mathbf{k}!, \tag{1.4}$$

where δ denotes the usual Dirac delta function. Finally, for $\mathbf{c} \in \mathbb{R}^n$, $\mathbf{c} = (c_1, \ldots, c_n)$, let

$$D_{\mathbf{c}} := \sum_{k=1}^n c_k \frac{\partial}{\partial x_k}$$

denote differentiation in the direction $\mathbf{c}$. For any univariate function $f \in C^1(\mathbb{R})$ we have

$$D_{\mathbf{c}} f(\mathbf{a} \cdot \mathbf{x}) = (\mathbf{a} \cdot \mathbf{c}) f'(\mathbf{a} \cdot \mathbf{x}). \tag{1.5}$$

Notation is often a compromise and is not necessarily unconditionally exact. For example, in this monograph we will use $\mathbf{a}^i$ for vectors and A^i for matrices. The former is in boldface, while the latter is in italics. In addition the i is here an index and in neither case does it indicate a power. (The A^i are also not square matrices.) We also do not always differentiate between a function and its value at a point. We tried different notations. But the inconvenience far outweighed the added rigor. We hope that the exact meaning will be evident from the context and apologize for these imprecisions.

2

Smoothness

In this chapter we study one of the basic properties of ridge function decomposition, namely smoothness. In the first section we ask the following question. If

$$\sum_{i=1}^{r} f_i(\mathbf{a}^i \cdot \mathbf{x})$$

is smooth, does this imply that each of the f_i is also smooth? In the second section we ask this same question with regard to generalized ridge functions, i.e., linear combinations of functions of the form $f(A\mathbf{x})$, where the A are $d \times n$ real matrices, and $f : \mathbb{R}^d \to \mathbb{R}$.

2.1 Ridge Function Smoothness

Let $C^k(\mathbb{R}^n)$, $k \in \mathbb{Z}_+$, denote the usual class of real-valued functions with all derivatives of order up to and including k being continuous. Assume $F \in C^k(\mathbb{R}^n)$ is of the form

$$F(\mathbf{x}) = \sum_{i=1}^{r} f_i(\mathbf{a}^i \cdot \mathbf{x}), \tag{2.1}$$

where r is finite, i.e., $F \in \mathcal{M}(\mathbf{a}^1, \ldots, \mathbf{a}^r)$, and the $\mathbf{a}^i$ are given pairwise linearly independent vectors in $\mathbb{R}^n$. What can we say about the smoothness of the f_i? Do the f_i necessarily inherit all the smoothness properties of the F?

When $r = 1$ the answer is yes, and there is essentially nothing to prove. That is, if

$$F(\mathbf{x}) = f_1(\mathbf{a}^1 \cdot \mathbf{x})$$

is in $C^k(\mathbb{R}^n)$ for some $\mathbf{a}^1 \neq \mathbf{0}$, then for $\mathbf{c} \in \mathbb{R}^n$ satisfying $\mathbf{a}^1 \cdot \mathbf{c} = 1$ and all $t \in \mathbb{R}$ we have that $F(t\mathbf{c}) = f_1(t)$ is in $C^k(\mathbb{R})$. This same result holds when $r = 2$.

12

As the $\mathbf{a}^1$ and $\mathbf{a}^2$ are linearly independent, there exists a vector $\mathbf{c} \in \mathbb{R}^n$ satisfying $\mathbf{a}^1 \cdot \mathbf{c} = 0$ and $\mathbf{a}^2 \cdot \mathbf{c} = 1$. Thus

$$F(t\mathbf{c}) = f_1(\mathbf{a}^1 \cdot t\mathbf{c}) + f_2(\mathbf{a}^2 \cdot t\mathbf{c}) = f_1(0) + f_2(t).$$

Since $F(t\mathbf{c})$ is in $C^k(\mathbb{R})$, as a function of t, so is f_2. The same result holds for f_1.

However, this result is no longer valid when $r \geq 3$, without some further assumptions on the f_i. To see this, recall that the Cauchy Functional Equation

$$h(x + y) = h(x) + h(y) \tag{2.2}$$

has, as proved in Hamel [1905], very badly behaved solutions, see, for example, Aczél [1966] for a discussion of the solutions of this equation. As such, setting $f_1 = f_2 = -f_3 = h$, we have very badly behaved (and certainly not in $C^k(\mathbb{R})$) f_i, $i = 1, 2, 3$, that satisfy

$$0 = f_1(x_1) + f_2(x_2) + f_3(x_1 + x_2)$$

for all $(x_1, x_2) \in \mathbb{R}^2$. That is, the very smooth function on the left-hand side of this equation is a sum of three unruly ridge functions. As will shortly become evident, this Cauchy Functional Equation is critical in the analysis of our problem for all $r \geq 3$.

We also recall, see, for example, Aczél [1966], that if a real-valued function f, defined on $\mathbb{R}$, satisfies the Cauchy Functional Equation (2.2) and, in addition, is any of continuous at a point, or monotonic on an interval, or bounded on one side on a set of positive measure, or Lebesgue measurable, then f must be a linear function, i.e., $f(x) = cx$ for some constant c, and all $x \in \mathbb{R}$.

Let $\mathcal{B}$ denote any linear space of real-valued functions defined on $\mathbb{R}$ that is closed under translation, i.e., $f(\cdot) \in \mathcal{B}$ implies $f(\cdot + \alpha) \in \mathcal{B}$ for every $\alpha \in \mathbb{R}$, and has the property that if $f \in \mathcal{B}$ and there is a function $g \in C(\mathbb{R})$ for which $f - g$ satisfies the Cauchy Functional Equation, then $f - g$ is necessarily a linear function. Assuming each $f_i \in \mathcal{B}$, $i = 1, \ldots, r$, we have the following.

Theorem 2.1 *Assume $F \in C^k(\mathbb{R}^n)$ is of the form (2.1), i.e.,*

$$F(\mathbf{x}) = \sum_{i=1}^{r} f_i(\mathbf{a}^i \cdot \mathbf{x}),$$

where r is finite, and the $\mathbf{a}^i$ are given pairwise linearly independent vectors in $\mathbb{R}^n$. Assume, in addition, that each $f_i \in \mathcal{B}$. Then, necessarily, $f_i \in C^k(\mathbb{R})$ for $i = 1, \ldots, r$.

Proof The proof will be by induction on r. As we have seen, this result is valid when $r = 1$. Let $\mathbf{c} \in \mathbb{R}^n$ satisfy $(\mathbf{c} \cdot \mathbf{a}^r) = 0$ and $(\mathbf{c} \cdot \mathbf{a}^i) =: b_i \neq 0$ for $i = 1, \ldots, r - 1$. Such $\mathbf{c}$ exist. Now

$$F(\mathbf{x} + t\mathbf{c}) - F(\mathbf{x}) = \sum_{i=1}^{r} f_i(\mathbf{a}^i \cdot \mathbf{x} + t\mathbf{a}^i \cdot \mathbf{c}) - f_i(\mathbf{a}^i \cdot \mathbf{x}).$$

By construction we have $f_r(\mathbf{a}^r \cdot \mathbf{x} + t\mathbf{a}^r \cdot \mathbf{c}) - f_r(\mathbf{a}^r \cdot \mathbf{x}) = f_r(\mathbf{a}^r \cdot \mathbf{x}) - f_r(\mathbf{a}^r \cdot \mathbf{x}) = 0$, while $f_i(\mathbf{a}^i \cdot \mathbf{x} + t\mathbf{a}^i \cdot \mathbf{c}) - f_i(\mathbf{a}^i \cdot \mathbf{x}) = f_i(\mathbf{a}^i \cdot \mathbf{x} + tb_i) - f_i(\mathbf{a}^i \cdot \mathbf{x})$ for $i = 1, \ldots, r-1$. Thus, for each fixed $t \in \mathbb{R}$,

$$H(\mathbf{x}) := F(\mathbf{x} + t\mathbf{c}) - F(\mathbf{x}) = \sum_{i=1}^{r-1} h_i(\mathbf{a}^i \cdot \mathbf{x}),$$

where $h_i(y) := f_i(y + tb_i) - f_i(y)$. Now $H \in C^k(\mathbb{R}^n)$ and $h_i \in \mathcal{B}$, since $\mathcal{B}$ is a linear space closed under translation. Thus by our induction assumption we have $h_i \in C^k(\mathbb{R})$. Note that this is valid for each and every $t \in \mathbb{R}$.

We have reduced our problem to the following. Assume $b \neq 0$, and for every $t \in \mathbb{R}$

$$h(y) := f(y + tb) - f(y)$$

is in $C^k(\mathbb{R})$. Are there conditions implying that $f \in C^k(\mathbb{R})$? A detailed answer is contained in the paper de Bruijn [1951]. What is proved therein is that if $h \in C^k(\mathbb{R})$, then f is necessarily of the form $f = g + v$, where $g \in C^k(\mathbb{R})$ and v satisfies the Cauchy Functional Equation (2.2). Thus each of our f_i is of the form $f_i = g_i + v_i$, with g_i and v_i as above. However, by assumption, each f_i is in $\mathcal{B}$. From our definition of $\mathcal{B}$ it therefore follows that $f_i - g_i = v_i$ is a linear function, i.e., $v_i(t) = c_i t$ for some constant c_i. Thus $f_i = g_i + v_i$, where both $g_i, v_i \in C^k(\mathbb{R})$, implying that $f_i \in C^k(\mathbb{R})$. This is valid for $i = 1, \ldots, r-1$, and hence also for $i = r$. $\qquad\square$

Theorem 2.1 does not provide an answer to the following open question.

Question Assume $F(\mathbf{x}) = \sum_{i=1}^{r} f_i(\mathbf{a}^i \cdot \mathbf{x})$, where $F \in C^k(\mathbb{R}^n)$, but nothing is known regarding the functions f_i. What can be said regarding these f_i? And is it true that there will always exist $g_i \in C^k(\mathbb{R})$ such that

$$F(\mathbf{x}) = \sum_{i=1}^{r} g_i(\mathbf{a}^i \cdot \mathbf{x})?$$

Remark 2.2 In de Bruijn [1951], [1952] are delineated various classes $\mathcal{D}$ of real-valued functions with the property that if

$$h_t := \Delta_t f = f(\cdot + t) - f(\cdot) \in \mathcal{D}$$

for all $t \in \mathbb{R}$, then f is necessarily of the form $f = g + v$, where $g \in \mathcal{D}$ and v satisfies the Cauchy Functional Equation. Some of these classes $\mathcal{D}$ are: $C^k(\mathbb{R})$, functions with k continuous derivatives; $\widetilde{C}^k(\mathbb{R})$, functions that are k times differentiable (but their kth derivative need not be continuous); $C^\infty(\mathbb{R})$ functions; analytic functions; functions that are absolutely continuous on any finite interval; functions having bounded variation over every finite interval; algebraic polynomials; trigonometric polynomials; and Riemann integrable functions. Theorem 2.1 can be suitably restated for any of these classes $\mathcal{D}$.

Remark 2.3 Most of the material in this chapter is to be found in Pinkus [2013]. It was also proved in Buhmann and Pinkus [1999] that if F is of the form (2.1), $F \in C^k(\mathbb{R}^n)$, $k \geq r - 1$, and $f_i \in L^1_{loc}(\mathbb{R})$ for each i, then $f_i \in C^k(\mathbb{R})$ for each i. The method of proof therein used smoothing and generalized functions.

2.2 Smoothness in the Multivariate Setting

We consider in this section the same problem as that in the previous section, but for generalized ridge functions, i.e., linear combinations of functions of the form $f(A\mathbf{x})$ where A is a fixed $d \times n$ real matrix, $1 \leq d < n$, and f is a real-valued function defined on $\mathbb{R}^d$. For $d = 1$, this reduces to a ridge function.

As previously, assume we are given a function F of the form

$$F(\mathbf{x}) = \sum_{i=1}^{r} f_i(A^i \mathbf{x}), \tag{2.3}$$

where r is finite, the A^i are $d \times n$ matrices, for some fixed d, $1 \leq d < n$, and each $f_i : \mathbb{R}^d \to \mathbb{R}$. (In fact we could also consider A^i whose number of rows depends on i. The analysis would be much the same.) We again ask what the smoothness of F implies regarding the smoothness of the f_i.

The situation here is slightly more problematic, as redundancies can easily occur. Consider, for example, the case $n = 3, r = 2, d = 2$, and

$$A^1 = \begin{bmatrix} 1 & 0 & 0 \\ 0 & 1 & 0 \end{bmatrix}, \quad A^2 = \begin{bmatrix} 0 & 1 & 0 \\ 0 & 0 & 1 \end{bmatrix}.$$

Thus

$$F(x_1, x_2, x_3) = f_1(x_1, x_2) + f_2(x_2, x_3).$$

Setting $f_1(x_1, x_2) = g(x_2)$ and $f_2(x_2, x_3) = -g(x_2)$ for any arbitrary univariate function g, we have

$$0 = f_1(x_1, x_2) + f_2(x_2, x_3),$$

and yet f_1 and f_2 do not exhibit any of the smoothness or polynomial properties of the left-hand side of this equation.

This simple example is easily generalized. For convenience we will, in what follows, always assume that the A^i are of full rank d.

Proposition 2.4 *Assume there exist* $i, j \in \{1, \ldots, r\}$, $i \neq j$, *such that the* $2d$ *rows of* A^i *and* A^j *are linearly dependent. Then there exist non-smooth functions* f_i *and* f_j *such that*

$$f_i(A^i\mathbf{x}) + f_j(A^j\mathbf{x}) = 0$$

for all $\mathbf{x} \in \mathbb{R}^n$.

Proof Since the $2d$ rows of A^i and A^j are linearly dependent and, in addition, A^i, A^j are of full rank d, there exist $\mathbf{c}^i, \mathbf{c}^j \in \mathbb{R}^d$ for which

$$\mathbf{c}^i A^i = \mathbf{c}^j A^j \neq \mathbf{0}.$$

Thus for all $\mathbf{x} \in \mathbb{R}^n$, and any arbitrary non-smooth univariate function g we have

$$g(\mathbf{c}^i A^i \mathbf{x}) = g(\mathbf{c}^j A^j \mathbf{x}).$$

Set

$$f_i(A^i\mathbf{x}) := g(\mathbf{c}^i A^i \mathbf{x}),$$

and

$$f_j(A^j\mathbf{x}) := -g(\mathbf{c}^j A^j \mathbf{x}).$$

Thus

$$f_i(A^i\mathbf{x}) + f_j(A^j\mathbf{x}) = 0,$$

and yet f_i and f_j do not exhibit any of the smoothness or polynomial properties of the right-hand side of this equation. $\square$

The condition that the $2d$ rows of A^i and A^j be linearly independent necessarily implies that $d \leq n/2$. Thus for $d > n/2$ we can never make any smoothness claims on the f_i based on the smoothness of F. This is unfortunate, as functions of the form (2.3) with $d = n - 1$ are of particular interest.

When considering ridge functions, i.e., when $d = 1$, we very naturally demanded that the $\mathbf{a}^i$ be pairwise linearly independent, since for linearly dependent directions $\mathbf{a}$ and $\mathbf{b}$ we have $\mathcal{M}(\mathbf{a}) = \mathcal{M}(\mathbf{b})$. In other words, in the case $d = 1$ we demanded the linear independence of the $2d$ rows of A^i and A^j for all $i \neq j$.

What if we assume the linear independence of the $2d$ rows of A^i and A^j for all $i \neq j$? Do the f_i of (2.3) then inherit, under some weak assumptions, smoothness properties from F? The answer is yes. Here we utilize a generalization of the results of de Bruijn [1951], [1952], due to Kemperman [1957]. Paralleling the $\mathcal{B}$ of Section 2.1, we define $\mathcal{B}_d$ to be any linear space of real-valued functions f defined on $\mathbb{R}^d$ that is closed under translation, with the property that if there is a function $g \in C(\mathbb{R}^d)$ such that $f - g$ satisfies the multivariate Cauchy Functional Equation

$$h(\mathbf{s} + \mathbf{t}) = h(\mathbf{s}) + h(\mathbf{t}) \tag{2.4}$$

for all $\mathbf{s}, \mathbf{t} \in \mathbb{R}^d$, then $f - g$ is necessarily a linear function, i.e., $(f - g)(\mathbf{s}) = \mathbf{c} \cdot \mathbf{s}$ for some constant vector $\mathbf{c} \in \mathbb{R}^d$, and all $\mathbf{s} \in \mathbb{R}^d$. We now prove the multivariate analog of Theorem 2.1.

Theorem 2.5 *Assume $F \in C^k(\mathbb{R}^n)$ is of the form (2.3), where the $2d$ rows of A^i and A^j are linearly independent, for all $i \neq j$. Assume, in addition, that each $f_i \in \mathcal{B}_d$. Then, necessarily, $f_i \in C^k(\mathbb{R}^d)$ for $i = 1, \ldots, r$.*

Proof The proof is much the same as the proof of Theorem 2.1, with slight modifications. Our proof will again be by induction. The result is obviously valid for $r = 1$.

For given A^1 and A^r, let $\mathbf{d}^1, \ldots, \mathbf{d}^d \in \mathbb{R}^n$ satisfy

$$A^r \mathbf{d}^j = \mathbf{0}, \qquad j = 1, \ldots, d, \tag{2.5}$$

and

$$A^1 \mathbf{d}^j = \mathbf{e}^j, \qquad j = 1, \ldots, d, \tag{2.6}$$

where $\mathbf{e}^j$ denotes the jth unit vector in $\mathbb{R}^d$. Such $\mathbf{d}^j$ exist by our assumption that the $2d$ rows of A^1 and A^r are linearly independent.

For each choice of reals $p_1, \ldots, p_d$, consider

$$H(\mathbf{x}) := F(\mathbf{x} + \sum_{j=1}^{d} p_j \mathbf{d}^j) - F(\mathbf{x}) = \sum_{i=1}^{r} f_i(A^i \mathbf{x} + A^i(\sum_{j=1}^{d} p_j \mathbf{d}^j)) - f_i(A^i \mathbf{x}).$$

Set

$$h_i(\mathbf{y}) := f_i(\mathbf{y} + \sum_{j=1}^{d} p_j A^i \mathbf{d}^j) - f_i(\mathbf{y}), \qquad i = 1, \ldots, r,$$

for $\mathbf{y} \in \mathbb{R}^d$. From (2.5)

$$h_r(\mathbf{y}) = 0,$$

and from (2.6)

$$h_1(\mathbf{y}) = f_1(\mathbf{y} + \mathbf{p}) - f_1(\mathbf{y}),$$

where $\mathbf{p} = (p_1, \ldots, p_d)$.

Thus,

$$H(\mathbf{x}) = \sum_{i=1}^{r-1} h_i(A^i \mathbf{x}),$$

with $H \in C^k(\mathbb{R}^n)$ and $h_i \in \mathcal{B}_d$. By the induction hypothesis we may therefore infer that $h_i \in C^k(\mathbb{R}^d)$ for each $i = 1, \ldots, r - 1$. In particular, we have that for each and every $\mathbf{p} \in \mathbb{R}^d$, the function

$$h_1(\mathbf{y}) = f_1(\mathbf{y} + \mathbf{p}) - f_1(\mathbf{y})$$

is in $C^k(\mathbb{R}^d)$. From Kemperman [1957], Section 5, see also de Bruijn [1951], p. 196, it follows that $f_1 = g_1 + v_1$, where $g_1 \in C^k(\mathbb{R}^d)$ and v_1 satisfies the Cauchy Functional Equation (2.4). Since $f_1 \in \mathcal{B}_d$ we have $v_1(\mathbf{s}) = \mathbf{c} \cdot \mathbf{s}$ for some constant vector $\mathbf{c} \in \mathbb{R}^d$, and therefore $f_1 \in C^k(\mathbb{R}^d)$. Thus

$$F(\mathbf{x}) - f_1(A^1 \mathbf{x}) = \sum_{i=2}^{r} f_i(A^i \mathbf{x})$$

is in $C^k(\mathbb{R}^n)$, and again by our induction assumption we have that $f_i \in C^k(\mathbb{R}^d)$ for $i = 2, \ldots, r$. $\qquad\square$

Question What happens if the rows of A^i and A^j are not linearly independent, and/or the f_i are not assumed to be in $\mathcal{B}_d$? In particular, if $F \in C^k(\mathbb{R}^d)$ is of the form (2.3) do there always exist $g_i \in C^k(\mathbb{R}^d)$ such that

$$F(\mathbf{x}) = \sum_{i=1}^{r} g_i(A^i \mathbf{x})?$$

Remark 2.6 For the sake of convenience we stated the results of this chapter over $\mathbb{R}^n$. They in fact hold, *mutatis mutandis*, over any open set in $\mathbb{R}^n$. However, these results are not necessarily valid over closed sets with no interior. In Example 12.1, see also Ismailov and Pinkus [2013], we present an example of a function F of the form

$$F(\mathbf{x}) = f_1(\mathbf{a}^1 \cdot \mathbf{x}) + f_2(\mathbf{a}^2 \cdot \mathbf{x}),$$

that is bounded and continuous on the union of two straight lines in $\mathbb{R}^2$, but such that both f_1 and f_2 are necessarily not continuous (and in fact unbounded) in the neighborhood of a point.

3

Uniqueness

In this chapter we consider the problem of the uniqueness of the representation of a linear combination of a finite number of ridge functions. That is, assume we have two distinct representations for F of the form

$$F(\mathbf{x}) = \sum_{i=1}^{k} g_i(\mathbf{b}^i \cdot \mathbf{x}) = \sum_{j=1}^{\ell} h_j(\mathbf{c}^j \cdot \mathbf{x}) \tag{3.1}$$

where both k and ℓ are finite. What can we say about these two representations? From linearity (3.1) is effectively equivalent to asking the following. Assume

$$\sum_{i=1}^{r} f_i(\mathbf{a}^i \cdot \mathbf{x}) = 0 \tag{3.2}$$

for all $\mathbf{x} \in \mathbb{R}^n$, where r is finite, and the $\mathbf{a}^i$ are pairwise linearly independent vectors in $\mathbb{R}^n$. What does this imply regarding the f_i?

The main result of the first section of this chapter is that, with minimal requirements, the f_i satisfying (3.2) must be polynomials of degree $\leq r - 2$. That is, we essentially have uniqueness of the representation of a finite linear combination of ridge functions up to polynomials of a certain degree. We extend this result, in the second section, to generalized ridge functions. Much of the material of this chapter is taken from Pinkus [2013], and generalizes a result of Buhmann and Pinkus [1999].

3.1 Ridge Function Uniqueness

We recall from Chapter 2 that $\mathcal{B}$ is any linear space, closed under translation, of real-valued functions f defined on $\mathbb{R}$ such that if there is a function $g \in C(\mathbb{R})$ for which $f - g$ satisfies the Cauchy Functional Equation (2.2), then $f - g$ is necessarily a linear function.

As in Section 1.3, let Π_m^n denote the set of algebraic polynomials of total degree at most m in n variables. That is,

$$\Pi_m^n = \left\{ \sum_{|\mathbf{k}| \leq m} b_{\mathbf{k}} \mathbf{x}^{\mathbf{k}} : b_{\mathbf{k}} \in \mathbb{R} \right\}.$$

Theorem 3.1 *Assume (3.2) holds where r is finite, and the $\mathbf{a}^i$ are pairwise linearly independent vectors in $\mathbb{R}^n$. Assume, in addition, that $f_i \in \mathcal{B}$ for $i = 1, \ldots, r$. Then f_i is a univariate polynomial of degree at most $r - 2$, $i = 1, \ldots, r$.*

For $\mathbf{c} \in \mathbb{R}^n$ let

$$D_{\mathbf{c}} := \sum_{i=1}^{n} c_i \frac{\partial}{\partial x_i}$$

denote differentiation in the direction $\mathbf{c}$. For $f \in C^1(\mathbb{R})$ we have, see (1.5),

$$D_{\mathbf{c}} f(\mathbf{a} \cdot \mathbf{x}) = (\mathbf{a} \cdot \mathbf{c}) f'(\mathbf{a} \cdot \mathbf{x}).$$

Using Theorem 2.1 and this formula we easily prove Theorem 3.1.

Proof From Remark 2.2 it follows that each f_i in (3.2) is a polynomial. In fact we need only the sufficient smoothness of each f_i which is a direct consequence of Theorem 2.1. We apply an elementary argument using directional derivatives as may be found, for example, in Diaconis and Shahshahani [1984], see also Buhmann and Pinkus [1999].

Fix $k \in \{1, \ldots, r\}$. For each $j \in \{1, \ldots, r\} \setminus \{k\}$, choose a $\mathbf{c}^j \in \mathbb{R}^n$ to satisfy

$$\mathbf{c}^j \cdot \mathbf{a}^j = 0 \quad \text{and} \quad \mathbf{c}^j \cdot \mathbf{a}^k \neq 0.$$

This is possible since the $\mathbf{a}^i$ are pairwise linearly independent. From (3.2), and as each f_i is sufficiently smooth, we have

$$
\begin{aligned}
0 &= \prod_{\substack{j=1 \\ j \neq k}}^{r} D_{\mathbf{c}^j} \sum_{i=1}^{r} f_i(\mathbf{a}^i \cdot \mathbf{x}) \\
&= \sum_{i=1}^{r} \left(\prod_{\substack{j=1 \\ j \neq k}}^{r} (\mathbf{c}^j \cdot \mathbf{a}^i) \right) f_i^{(r-1)}(\mathbf{a}^i \cdot \mathbf{x}) \\
&= \prod_{\substack{j=1 \\ j \neq k}}^{r} (\mathbf{c}^j \cdot \mathbf{a}^k) f_k^{(r-1)}(\mathbf{a}^k \cdot \mathbf{x}),
\end{aligned}
$$

since $\prod_{\substack{j=1 \\ j \neq k}}^{r} (\mathbf{c}^j \cdot \mathbf{a}^i) = 0$ for $i \neq k$. As $\prod_{\substack{j=1 \\ j \neq k}}^{r} (\mathbf{c}^j \cdot \mathbf{a}^k) \neq 0$ we obtain

$$f_k^{(r-1)}(\mathbf{a}^k \cdot \mathbf{x}) = 0$$

for all $\mathbf{x} \in \mathbb{R}^n$. Therefore

$$f_k^{(r-1)}(y) = 0$$

for all $y \in \mathbb{R}$, and f_k is a polynomial of degree at most $r - 2$. $\qquad\square$

By the same method of proof we in fact have the following.

Corollary 3.2 *Assume $F \in \Pi_m^n$ has the form*

$$F(\mathbf{x}) = \sum_{i=1}^{r} f_i(\mathbf{a}^i \cdot \mathbf{x}),$$

where r is finite, and the $\mathbf{a}^i$ are pairwise linearly independent vectors in $\mathbb{R}^n$. Assume, in addition, that $f_i \in \mathcal{B}$ for $i = 1, \ldots, r$. Then $f_i \in \Pi_s^1$, $i = 1, \ldots, r$, where $s = \max\{m, r - 2\}$.

One immediate consequence of Theorem 3.1 is the following, which easily follows by taking $f_i = f$ for $i = 1, \ldots, r$.

Proposition 3.3 *Assume $f \in \mathcal{B}$ and f is not a polynomial. Then for any finite r, and pairwise linearly independent vectors $\mathbf{a}^1, \ldots, \mathbf{a}^r$ in $\mathbb{R}^n$, the functions*

$$f(\mathbf{a}^1 \cdot \mathbf{x}), \ldots, f(\mathbf{a}^r \cdot \mathbf{x})$$

are linearly independent.

Proposition 3.3 generalizes a result in Dahmen and Micchelli [1987], where they prove, by different methods, that if the dimension of the span of the space $\{f(\mathbf{a} \cdot \mathbf{x}) : \mathbf{a} \in \mathbb{R}^n\}$ is finite, and f is Lebesgue measurable, then f is a polynomial.

Remark 3.4 Is the $r - 2$ in Theorem 3.1 minimal? It is often the case that the result of Theorem 3.1 can be obtained with $f_i \in \Pi_\ell^1$, where ℓ is significantly smaller than $r - 2$. Recall that we took, for each $k \in \{1, \ldots, r\}$, a collection of $r - 1$ vectors $\mathbf{c}^j \in \mathbb{R}^n$, $j \in \{1, \ldots, r\} \backslash \{k\}$, such that $\mathbf{c}^j \cdot \mathbf{a}^j = 0$, $\mathbf{c}^j \cdot \mathbf{a}^k \neq 0$, for $j \neq k$, so that

$$\prod_{\substack{j=1 \\ j \neq k}}^{r} (\mathbf{c}^j \cdot \mathbf{a}^i) = 0$$

for all $i \neq k$. This then implied that $f_k^{(r-1)} = 0$, whence f_k is a polynomial of degree at most $r - 2$. If the $\mathbf{a}^j$ are in generic position, i.e., any n of them are linearly independent, then we can take $\mathbf{c}$ to be orthogonal to any $n - 1$ of the $\mathbf{a}^j$, $j \neq k$, and satisfy $\mathbf{c} \cdot \mathbf{a}^k \neq 0$. In this case we will need only $\lfloor (r-2)/(n-1) \rfloor + 1$ vectors $\mathbf{c}$ to obtain the same desired result, and thus each f_k will be a polynomial of degree at most $\lfloor (r-2)/(n-1) \rfloor$. However, as the $\mathbf{a}^j$ are only pairwise linearly independent, they can all lie in a subspace of dimension 2, and if this is the case (which is the same as taking $n = 2$) then we do need $r - 1$ $\mathbf{c}^j$s in the above proof. Moreover this is not just an artifact of the method of proof. For each r there exist pairwise linearly independent $\mathbf{a}^i \in \mathbb{R}^n$, $i = 1, \ldots, r$, and polynomials f_i of exact degree $r - 2$ such that $\sum_{i=1}^r f_i(\mathbf{a}^i \cdot \mathbf{x}) = 0$. To see that this holds, simply consider pairwise linearly independent $\mathbf{a}^i$ of the form $\mathbf{a}^i = (a_1^i, a_2^i, 0, \ldots, 0)$, $i = 1, \ldots, r$. The polynomials $(\mathbf{a}^i \cdot \mathbf{x})^{r-2}$, $i = 1, \ldots, r$, are homogeneous of degree $r - 2$. The space of homogeneous polynomials of degree $r - 2$ in two variables is of dimension $r - 1$. Thus some non-trivial linear combination of these $(\mathbf{a}^i \cdot \mathbf{x})^{r-2}$, $i = 1, \ldots, r$, vanishes identically.

Let us consider this uniqueness result in more detail. What more can be said apropos the polynomials f_i satisfying (3.2)? To this end, let H_m^n denote the set of homogeneous polynomials of degree m in n variables, i.e.,

$$H_m^n = \left\{ \sum_{|\mathbf{k}|=m} b_{\mathbf{k}} \mathbf{x}^{\mathbf{k}} : b_{\mathbf{k}} \in \mathbb{R} \right\}.$$

Then we have the following.

Proposition 3.5 *Assume r is finite, $f, f_i \in \mathcal{B}$, $i = 1, \ldots, r - 1$, the $\mathbf{a}^i$ are pairwise linearly independent vectors in $\mathbb{R}^n$, and $\mathbf{a} \neq \alpha \mathbf{a}^i$ for any $\alpha \in \mathbb{R}$ and $i \in \{1, \ldots, r - 1\}$. Then*

$$f(\mathbf{a} \cdot \mathbf{x}) = \sum_{i=1}^{r-1} f_i(\mathbf{a}^i \cdot \mathbf{x}) \tag{3.3}$$

if and only if f is a polynomial of exact degree m and for every $q \in H_m^n$ satisfying $q(\mathbf{a}^i) = 0$, $i = 1, \ldots, r - 1$, we have $q(\mathbf{a}) = 0$.

Remark 3.6 Equation (3.3) is, of course, a rewrite of (3.2) where $f(\mathbf{a} \cdot \mathbf{x}) = -f_r(\mathbf{a}^r \cdot \mathbf{x})$. Thus we necessarily have $m \leq r - 2$. However, this automatically follows since for $m \geq r - 1$ we can construct a $q \in H_m^n$ satisfying $q(\mathbf{a}^i) = 0$, $i = 1, \ldots, r - 1$, and $q(\mathbf{a}) \neq 0$. Namely, choose $\mathbf{c}^i \in \mathbb{R}^n$, $i = 1, \ldots, r - 1$, satisfying $\mathbf{c}^i \cdot \mathbf{a}^i = 0$ and $\mathbf{c}^i \cdot \mathbf{a} \neq 0$, and set $q(\mathbf{x}) = \prod_{i=1}^{r-1} (\mathbf{c}^i \cdot \mathbf{x})$.

Proof Assume (3.3) holds. Then from Theorem 3.1 it follows that $f, f_i \in \Pi^1_{r-2}$, $i = 1, \ldots, r-1$. Let

$$f(t) = \sum_{j=0}^{m} d_j t^j, \qquad d_m \neq 0,$$

and

$$f_i(t) = \sum_{j=0}^{m_i} d_{ij} t^j, \qquad i = 1, \ldots, r-1,$$

where $m, m_i \leq r-2$. We rewrite (3.3) as

$$\sum_{j=0}^{m} d_j (\mathbf{a} \cdot \mathbf{x})^j = \sum_{i=1}^{r-1} \sum_{j=0}^{m_i} d_{ij} (\mathbf{a}^i \cdot \mathbf{x})^j.$$

A polynomial is identically zero if and only if each of its homogeneous components are zero. Thus

$$d_m (\mathbf{a} \cdot \mathbf{x})^m = \sum_{i=1}^{r-1} d_{im} (\mathbf{a}^i \cdot \mathbf{x})^m, \tag{3.4}$$

where we set $d_{im} = 0$ if $m > m_i$.

We claim that (3.4) can hold if and only if for every polynomial $q \in H^n_m$ satisfying $q(\mathbf{a}^i) = 0$ at those i for which $d_{im} \neq 0$, we have $q(\mathbf{a}) = 0$. To prove this fact we use a variant of an argument in Lin and Pinkus [1993].

We recall, see Section 1.3, (1.3) and (1.4), that for $q \in H^n_m$

$$q(D)(\mathbf{a} \cdot \mathbf{x})^m = m! \, q(\mathbf{a}),$$

and for $\mathbf{k}, \mathbf{j} \in \mathbb{Z}^n_+$, $|\mathbf{k}| = |\mathbf{j}| = m$, we have

$$D^{\mathbf{k}} \mathbf{x}^{\mathbf{j}} = \delta_{\mathbf{k}, \mathbf{j}} \mathbf{k}!,$$

where δ denotes the usual Dirac delta function. This implies that every non-trivial linear functional ℓ on the finite-dimensional linear space H^n_m may be represented by some $q \in H^n_m$ via

$$\ell(p) = q(D)p$$

for each $p \in H^n_m$. Thus

$$(\mathbf{a} \cdot \mathbf{x})^m \in \text{span}\{(\mathbf{a}^i \cdot \mathbf{x})^m : d_{im} \neq 0\}$$

if and only if every linear functional on H^n_m that annihilates the $(\mathbf{a}^i \cdot \mathbf{x})^m$, where $d_{im} \neq 0$, i.e., every $q \in H^n_m$ satisfying $q(\mathbf{a}^i) = 0$ for all i with $d_{im} \neq 0$, also annihilates $(\mathbf{a} \cdot \mathbf{x})^m$, i.e., satisfies $q(\mathbf{a}) = 0$. Thus, if (3.4) holds, then for every $q \in H^n_m$ satisfying $q(\mathbf{a}^i) = 0$, $i = 1, \ldots, r-1$, we have $q(\mathbf{a}) = 0$.

Assume the converse, i.e., f is a polynomial of degree m and for every $q \in H_m^n$ satisfying $q(\mathbf{a}^i) = 0$, $i = 1, \ldots, r - 1$, we have $q(\mathbf{a}) = 0$. Let

$$f(t) = \sum_{j=0}^{m} d_j t^j, \qquad d_m \neq 0.$$

By the argument of the previous paragraph we have that

$$d_m(\mathbf{a} \cdot \mathbf{x})^m = \sum_{i=1}^{r-1} d_{im}(\mathbf{a}^i \cdot \mathbf{x})^m,$$

for some sequence of $\{d_{im}\}_{i=1}^{r-1}$. We claim that a similar formula holds for all other (lower) powers. This follows by suitable differentiation. Alternatively, based on the above, assume that for some $s < m$ we have a $\widetilde{q} \in H_s^n$ satisfying $\widetilde{q}(\mathbf{a}^i) = 0$, $i = 1, \ldots, r - 1$, and $\widetilde{q}(\mathbf{a}) \neq 0$. Choose any $\mathbf{c} \in \mathbb{R}^n$ such that $\mathbf{c} \cdot \mathbf{a} \neq 0$. Then $q(\mathbf{x}) = (\mathbf{c} \cdot \mathbf{x})^{m-s} \widetilde{q}(\mathbf{x}) \in H_m^n$ satisfies $q(\mathbf{a}^i) = 0$, $i = 1, \ldots, r-1$, and $q(\mathbf{a}) \neq 0$, contradicting our assumptions. Thus, for each $j = 0, 1, \ldots, m$, we have

$$d_j(\mathbf{a} \cdot \mathbf{x})^j = \sum_{i=1}^{r-1} d_{ij}(\mathbf{a}^i \cdot \mathbf{x})^j,$$

for some sequence of $\{d_{ij}\}$, proving that (3.3) holds.   □

Based on Proposition 3.5 we can now present a strengthened version of Theorem 3.1.

Corollary 3.7 *Assume that r is finite, $f_i \in \mathcal{B}$, $i = 1, \ldots, r$, and the $\mathbf{a}^i$ are pairwise linearly independent vectors in $\mathbb{R}^n$. Then we have*

$$\sum_{i=1}^{r} f_i(\mathbf{a}^i \cdot \mathbf{x}) = 0$$

if and only if for each i, f_i is a polynomial of exact degree m_i and if $q_i \in H_{m_i}^n$ satisfies $q_i(\mathbf{a}^j) = 0$, $j \in \{1, \ldots, r\} \setminus \{i\}$, then $q_i(\mathbf{a}^i) = 0$.

For a different approach to this problem, see Petersen, Smith and Solmon [1979], and Falconer [1979].

3.2 Uniqueness in the Multivariate Setting

In this section we consider generalized ridge functions, i.e., linear combinations of functions of the form $f(A\mathbf{x})$ where A is a fixed $d \times n$ real matrix, $1 \leq d < n$, and f is a real-valued function defined on $\mathbb{R}^d$. The multivariate version of Theorem 3.1 is the following result.

Theorem 3.8 *Assume*

$$\sum_{i=1}^{r} f_i(A^i\mathbf{x}) = 0 \tag{3.5}$$

for all $\mathbf{x} \in \mathbb{R}^n$, *where* r *is finite, and the* $2d$ *rows of* A^i *and* A^j *are linearly independent, for all* $i \neq j$. *Assume, in addition, that each* $f_i \in \mathcal{B}_d$. *Then* $f_i \in \Pi_{r-2}^d$, $i = 1, \ldots, r$.

Note that based on the results of Section 2.2, the only possibility of obtaining some sort of uniqueness result occurs when the $2d$ rows of A^i and A^j are linearly independent, for all $i \neq j$.

Proof From Theorem 2.5 it follows that each of the f_i is infinitely smooth. Recall that for $\mathbf{c} = (c_1, \ldots, c_n) \in \mathbb{R}^n$

$$D_{\mathbf{c}} = \sum_{i=1}^{n} c_i \frac{\partial}{\partial x_i}.$$

Furthermore, if A is a $d \times n$ matrix with row vectors $\mathbf{a}^1, \ldots, \mathbf{a}^d$, then as is easily verified,

$$D_{\mathbf{c}} f(A\mathbf{x}) = \sum_{k=1}^{d} (\mathbf{a}^k \cdot \mathbf{c}) \frac{\partial f}{\partial y_k}(A\mathbf{x}), \tag{3.6}$$

where by $\frac{\partial f}{\partial y_k}$ we mean the derivative of f with respect to its kth argument.

For $r = 1$ the result of the theorem is obviously true, where we define $\Pi_{-1}^d = \{0\}$. As the proof is somewhat notationally messy let us first detail the case $r = 2$. Let $\mathbf{c}^j \in \mathbb{R}^n$, $j = 1, \ldots, d$, satisfy

$$A^1 \mathbf{c}^j = \mathbf{0}, \qquad j = 1, \ldots, d,$$

and

$$A^2 \mathbf{c}^j = \mathbf{e}^j, \qquad j = 1, \ldots, d,$$

where $\mathbf{e}^j$ denotes the jth unit vector in $\mathbb{R}^d$. Such $\mathbf{c}^j$ exist since the $2d$ rows of A^1 and A^2 are linearly independent. Now, applying (3.6), we obtain

$$0 = D_{\mathbf{c}^j}[f_1(A^1\mathbf{x}) + f_2(A^2\mathbf{x})] = \frac{\partial f_2}{\partial y_j}(A^2\mathbf{x}), \qquad j = 1, \ldots, d.$$

Since A^2 is of full rank,

$$\mathbb{R}^d = \{A^2\mathbf{x} : \mathbf{x} \in \mathbb{R}^n\}$$

and thus

$$\frac{\partial f_2}{\partial y_j} = 0, \qquad j = 1, \ldots, d,$$

whence $f_2 \in \Pi_0^d$ (a constant function). This same result holds for f_1, proving the case $r = 2$.

For general r, let $j_1, \ldots, j_{r-1}$ be arbitrary values (not necessarily distinct) in $\{1, \ldots, d\}$. We will prove that for all such $j_1, \ldots, j_{r-1}$ we have

$$\frac{\partial^{r-1} f_i}{\partial y_{j_1} \cdots \partial y_{j_{r-1}}} = 0, \qquad i = 1, \ldots, r.$$

This implies that $f_i \in \Pi_{r-2}^d$, $i = 1, \ldots, r$. We prove this result for $i = r$.

For each $k = 1, \ldots, r-1$, and $j_1, \ldots, j_{r-1} \in \{1, \ldots, d\}$, let $\mathbf{c}^{j_k,k} \in \mathbb{R}^n$ satisfy

$$A^k \mathbf{c}^{j_k,k} = \mathbf{0},$$

and

$$A^r \mathbf{c}^{j_k,k} = \mathbf{e}^{j_k}.$$

Such vectors exist since the $2d$ rows of A^k and A^r are linearly independent. From (3.6) we have that

$$D_{\mathbf{c}^{j_k,k}} g_k(A^k \mathbf{x}) = 0, \qquad k = 1, \ldots, r-1,$$

for every choice of sufficiently smooth g_k. Since the differential operators $D_{\mathbf{c}^{j_k,k}}$ commute, it therefore follows that

$$\prod_{k=1}^{r-1} D_{\mathbf{c}^{j_k,k}} f_i(A^i \mathbf{x}) = 0, \qquad i = 1, \ldots, r-1.$$

Furthermore

$$D_{\mathbf{c}^{j_k,k}} f_r(A^r \mathbf{x}) = \frac{\partial f_r}{\partial y_{j_k}}(A^r \mathbf{x}).$$

Thus

$$\begin{aligned}
0 &= \prod_{k=1}^{r-1} D_{\mathbf{c}^{j_k,k}} \sum_{i=1}^{r} f_i(A^i \mathbf{x}) \\
&= \prod_{k=1}^{r-1} D_{\mathbf{c}^{j_k,k}} f_r(A^r \mathbf{x}) \\
&= \frac{\partial^{r-1} f_r}{\partial y_{j_1} \cdots \partial y_{j_{r-1}}}(A^r \mathbf{x}).
\end{aligned}$$

As A^r is of full rank, and the above holds for all $j_1, \ldots, j_{r-1} \in \{1, \ldots, d\}$ this implies that $f_r \in \Pi_{r-2}^d$. $\qquad\square$

Question What may be said if the rows of A^i and A^j are not linearly independent? Are the solutions to (3.5) then polynomials of the correct degree modulo, in some manner, functions over the dependent rows?

Remark 3.9 As in Chapter 2, the results of this chapter hold over any open set in $\mathbb{R}^n$.

4

Identifying Functions and Directions

In this chapter we consider the following inverse problem. Assume that we are given a function F that we know is of the form

$$F(\mathbf{x}) = \sum_{i=1}^{r} f_i(\mathbf{a}^i \cdot \mathbf{x}) \tag{4.1}$$

for some choice of positive integer r, unknown functions f_i, and either known or unknown directions $\mathbf{a}^i$. The question we ask is how to determine these unknowns parameters based on our knowledge of F. In the first section we assume that we know the directions $\mathbf{a}^i$, while in the second section we assume they are unknown. In Section 4.3 we pose these same questions for generalized ridge functions. In the case of unknown A^i we are able only to analyze the case $r = 1$. The material of Sections 4.1 and 4.2 may be found in Buhmann and Pinkus [1999].

4.1 Known Directions

Assume that we know an F of the form (4.1) with given directions $\mathbf{a}^i$. How can we theoretically identify the functions f_i? (We will, of course, assume that the directions $\mathbf{a}^i$ are pairwise linearly independent.) As we have seen, from the previous chapters, we have a degree of non-unicity. However, assuming that F is smooth and $f_i \in \mathcal{B}$ for all i, then from Theorem 3.1 the f_i are determined, at the very least, up to polynomials of degree at most $r - 2$.

Let us now detail how we might determine the f_i. When $r = 1$ we need make no assumptions as

$$F(\mathbf{x}) = f_1(\mathbf{a}^1 \cdot \mathbf{x}).$$

Choosing $\mathbf{c} \in \mathbb{R}^n$ such that $\mathbf{a}^1 \cdot \mathbf{c} = 1$, we have

$$F(t\mathbf{c}) = f_1(t),$$

28

which gives us f_1. Similarly, for $r = 2$ we can find a $\mathbf{c} \in \mathbb{R}^n$ satisfying $\mathbf{a}^1 \cdot \mathbf{c} = 1$ and $\mathbf{a}^2 \cdot \mathbf{c} = 0$, and thus

$$F(t\mathbf{c}) = f_1(t) + f_2(0),$$

which determines f_1 up to a constant. In this same manner we determine f_2 up to a constant.

For $r \geq 3$ the situation is more complicated. We present two different "theoretical methods" of determining the f_i, based on techniques we used in the previous chapters.

The first method, using induction on r, is the following. Let $\mathbf{c} \in \mathbb{R}^n$ satisfy $\mathbf{c} \cdot \mathbf{a}^r = 0$ and $\mathbf{c} \cdot \mathbf{a}^i =: b_i \neq 0$ for $i = 1, \ldots, r - 1$. Such $\mathbf{c}$ exist. Then, as is easily calculated, for each $t \in \mathbb{R}$ we have

$$H_t(\mathbf{x}) := F(\mathbf{x} + t\mathbf{c}) - F(\mathbf{x}) = \sum_{i=1}^{r-1} h_{i,t}(\mathbf{a}^i \cdot \mathbf{x}),$$

where

$$h_{i,t}(y) := f_i(y + tb_i) - f_i(y).$$

By induction we can find the $h_{i,t}$ for each t, and since

$$h_{i,t}(0) = f_i(tb_i) - f_i(0),$$

and b_i is known, we have found f_i at tb_i (up to a constant independent of t). A major drawback to this method is that for each specific t we have to solve the full problem.

A second, possibly more reasonable method of determining the f_i, is the following. Assume, in addition to the above, that $F \in C^{r-1}(\mathbb{R}^n)$, and $f_i \in \mathcal{B}$ for all i. Thus from Theorem 2.1 we have that $f_i \in C^{r-1}(\mathbb{R})$. Let $\mathbf{c}^j \in \mathbb{R}^n$ satisfy

$$\mathbf{c}^j \cdot \mathbf{a}^j = 0 \quad \text{and} \quad \mathbf{c}^j \cdot \mathbf{a}^k \neq 0,$$

for $j \in \{1, \ldots, r\} \backslash \{k\}$. Such $\mathbf{c}^j$ exist since the $\mathbf{a}^i$ are pairwise linearly independent. Now, as each f_i is sufficiently smooth,

$$
\begin{aligned}
\prod_{\substack{j=1 \\ j \neq k}}^{r} D_{\mathbf{c}^j} F(\mathbf{x}) &= \prod_{\substack{j=1 \\ j \neq k}}^{r} D_{\mathbf{c}^j} \sum_{i=1}^{r} f_i(\mathbf{a}^i \cdot \mathbf{x}) \\
&= \sum_{i=1}^{r} \left(\prod_{\substack{j=1 \\ j \neq k}}^{r} (\mathbf{c}^j \cdot \mathbf{a}^i) \right) f_i^{(r-1)}(\mathbf{a}^i \cdot \mathbf{x}) \\
&= \prod_{\substack{j=1 \\ j \neq k}}^{r} (\mathbf{c}^j \cdot \mathbf{a}^k) f_k^{(r-1)}(\mathbf{a}^k \cdot \mathbf{x}).
\end{aligned}
$$

Note that $\prod_{\substack{j=1 \\ j \neq k}}^{r} (\mathbf{c}^j \cdot \mathbf{a}^k) \neq 0$. Thus we have obtained a formula for $f_k^{(r-1)}$ that determines f_k, up to a polynomial of degree $r - 2$. So we have that the unknown f_k is given by

$$f_k = g_k + p_k$$

for known g_k, and unknown $p_k \in \Pi_{r-2}^1$. Thus

$$F(\mathbf{x}) = \sum_{i=1}^{r} f_i(\mathbf{a}^i \cdot \mathbf{x}) = \sum_{i=1}^{r} g_i(\mathbf{a}^i \cdot \mathbf{x}) + \sum_{i=1}^{r} p_i(\mathbf{a}^i \cdot \mathbf{x}),$$

i.e.,

$$F(\mathbf{x}) - \sum_{i=1}^{r} g_i(\mathbf{a}^i \cdot \mathbf{x}) = \sum_{i=1}^{r} p_i(\mathbf{a}^i \cdot \mathbf{x}).$$

The left-hand side of the second equation is known. The right-hand side lies in the finite-dimensional subspace Π_{r-2}^n. It is easy to find p_i (not necessarily unique) satisfying the above, and thus we have determined associated f_i.

4.2 Unknown Directions

The more interesting problem is when the directions are unknown. So let us assume that we are given F of the form (4.1), we know r and assume that the f_i are sufficiently smooth. However, we do not know either the f_i or the $\mathbf{a}^i$. We wish to determine f_i and $\mathbf{a}^i$ satisfying equation (4.1). Our immediate objective will be to find appropriate $\mathbf{a}^i$. We can then apply the methods of Section 4.1 to find associated f_i. Note that there is a further non-uniqueness here in that if we "know" $f(\mathbf{a} \cdot \mathbf{x})$, we still do not know either $\mathbf{a}$ or f precisely, since we can multiply $\mathbf{a}$ by any non-zero constant and redefine f accordingly.

We start with the simplest case of $r = 1$, i.e.,

$$F(\mathbf{x}) = f_1(\mathbf{a}^1 \cdot \mathbf{x}).$$

Assume $F \in C^1(\mathbb{R}^n)$ and thus $f_1 \in C^1(\mathbb{R})$. Then

$$\frac{\partial F(\mathbf{x})}{\partial x_j} = a_j^1 f_1'(\mathbf{a}^1 \cdot \mathbf{x}), \qquad j = 1, \ldots, n,$$

and

$$\left(\frac{\partial F(\mathbf{x})}{\partial x_1}, \ldots, \frac{\partial F(\mathbf{x})}{\partial x_n} \right) = (a_1^1, \ldots, a_n^1) f_1'(\mathbf{a}^1 \cdot \mathbf{x}).$$

At any $\mathbf{x}$ for which $f_1'(\mathbf{a}^1 \cdot \mathbf{x}) \neq 0$ we have found $\mathbf{a}^1$, up to multiplication by a non-zero constant. We can now determine f_1.

What if $r > 1$? In the method to be presented we assume that $F \in C^{2r-1}$ in a neighborhood of some $\mathbf{x}$, where $f_i^{(2r-1)}(\mathbf{a}^i \cdot \mathbf{x}) \neq 0$, $i = 1, \ldots, r$. In addition, we assume we have chosen a $\mathbf{c} \in \mathbb{R}^n$ for which $\mathbf{c} \cdot \mathbf{a}^i \neq 0$, $i = 1, \ldots, r$.

Recall, from (1.5), that for $\mathbf{c} \in \mathbb{R}^n$ and $f \in C^1$ in a neighborhood of $\mathbf{a} \cdot \mathbf{x}$, we have

$$D_{\mathbf{c}} f(\mathbf{a} \cdot \mathbf{x}) = (\mathbf{a} \cdot \mathbf{c}) f'(\mathbf{a} \cdot \mathbf{x}).$$

Thus for any $\mathbf{d} \in \mathbb{R}^n \backslash \{\mathbf{0}\}$ and $k \in \{0, 1, \ldots, 2r - 1\}$, we have

$$
\begin{aligned}
(D_{\mathbf{c}}^{2r-1-k} D_{\mathbf{d}}^k F)(\mathbf{x}) &= \sum_{i=1}^r (\mathbf{c} \cdot \mathbf{a}^i)^{2r-1-k} (\mathbf{d} \cdot \mathbf{a}^i)^k f_i^{(2r-1)}(\mathbf{a}^i \cdot \mathbf{x}) \\
&= \sum_{i=1}^r \left[(\mathbf{c} \cdot \mathbf{a}^i)^{2r-1} f_i^{(2r-1)}(\mathbf{a}^i \cdot \mathbf{x}) \right] \left[\frac{(\mathbf{d} \cdot \mathbf{a}^i)}{(\mathbf{c} \cdot \mathbf{a}^i)} \right]^k.
\end{aligned}
$$

Set

$$c_i := (\mathbf{c} \cdot \mathbf{a}^i)^{2r-1} f_i^{(2r-1)}(\mathbf{a}^i \cdot \mathbf{x}), \qquad i = 1, \ldots, r,$$

$$d_i := \frac{(\mathbf{d} \cdot \mathbf{a}^i)}{(\mathbf{c} \cdot \mathbf{a}^i)}, \qquad i = 1, \ldots, r,$$

and

$$h_k := (D_{\mathbf{c}}^{2r-1-k} D_{\mathbf{d}}^k F)(\mathbf{x}), \qquad k = 0, 1, \ldots, 2r - 1.$$

Rewriting the above we have that

$$h_k = \sum_{i=1}^r c_i d_i^k, \qquad k = 0, 1, \ldots, 2r - 1, \tag{4.2}$$

where the $\{h_k\}_{k=0}^{2r-1}$ are known, whilst the $\{c_i\}_{i=1}^r$ and $\{d_i\}_{i=1}^r$ are unknown.

If the d_i are distinct and the c_i are non-zero (see the above assumptions), then it is well-known that the d_i are the roots of the rth degree polynomial

$$
H(x) = \begin{vmatrix}
h_0 & \cdots & h_{r-1} & h_r \\
\vdots & \ddots & \vdots & \vdots \\
h_{r-1} & \cdots & h_{2r-2} & h_{2r-1} \\
1 & \cdots & x^{r-1} & x^r
\end{vmatrix}.
$$

Here is an elementary proof of this fact.

From (4.2) it follows that

$$
\begin{bmatrix}
h_0 & \cdots & h_{r-1} \\
\vdots & \ddots & \vdots \\
h_{r-1} & \cdots & h_{2r-2}
\end{bmatrix}
=
\begin{bmatrix}
c_1 d_1^0 & \cdots & c_r d_r^0 \\
\vdots & \ddots & \vdots \\
c_1 d_1^{r-1} & \cdots & c_r d_r^{r-1}
\end{bmatrix}
\cdot
\begin{bmatrix}
d_1^0 & \cdots & d_1^{r-1} \\
\vdots & \ddots & \vdots \\
d_r^0 & \cdots & d_r^{r-1}
\end{bmatrix},
$$

and thus

$$
\begin{vmatrix}
h_0 & \cdots & h_{r-1} \\
\vdots & \ddots & \vdots \\
h_{r-1} & \cdots & h_{2r-2}
\end{vmatrix}
= \prod_{i=1}^{r} c_i \cdot \prod_{1 \le i < j \le r} (d_j - d_i)^2 \ne 0.
$$

This implies that $H(x)$ is a polynomial of exact degree r. Now, for each $i \in \{1, \ldots, r\}$

$$
\begin{bmatrix}
h_0 & \cdots & h_{r-1} & h_r \\
\vdots & \ddots & \vdots & \vdots \\
h_{r-1} & \cdots & h_{2r-2} & h_{2r-1} \\
d_i^0 & \cdots & d_i^{r-1} & d_i^r
\end{bmatrix}
$$

$$
=
\begin{bmatrix}
c_1 d_1^0 & \cdots & c_i d_i^0 & \cdots & c_r d_r^0 \\
\vdots & \ddots & \vdots & \ddots & \vdots \\
c_1 d_1^{r-1} & \cdots & c_i d_i^{r-1} & \cdots & c_r d_r^{r-1} \\
0 & \cdots & 1 & \cdots & 0
\end{bmatrix}
\cdot
\begin{bmatrix}
d_1^0 & \cdots & d_1^{r-1} & d_1^r \\
\vdots & \ddots & \vdots & \vdots \\
d_r^0 & \cdots & d_r^{r-1} & d_r^r
\end{bmatrix},
$$

where the last row of the first matrix on the right-hand side is the vector of all 0s except for a 1 in the ith column. As this is a product of an $(r+1) \times r$ and an $r \times (r+1)$ matrix, the left-hand side matrix is singular and thus $H(d_i) = 0$.

Solving, in the above, for the d_i we obtain the

$$
d_i = \frac{(\mathbf{d} \cdot \mathbf{a}^i)}{(\mathbf{c} \cdot \mathbf{a}^i)}, \qquad i = 1, \ldots, r.
$$

If we now solve the above for n linearly independent directions $\mathbf{d}^1, \ldots, \mathbf{d}^n$, then we can determine each of

$$
\frac{\mathbf{a}^i}{(\mathbf{c} \cdot \mathbf{a}^i)}, \qquad i = 1, \ldots, r.
$$

That is, we find in this way the $\mathbf{a}^i$, up to multiplication by constants, which is the best that can be done.

Question The "solution" as presented here is complicated, and various assumptions have been made. It would be preferable to have a simpler method of determining the $\mathbf{a}^i$. In addition, while this "solution" tells us that it is generally theoretically possible to determine the $\mathbf{a}^i$ from a knowledge of F and r, it assumes a certain smoothness of F and the f_i. Can we find the $\mathbf{a}^i$ and f_i, even theoretically, with fewer smoothness assumptions?

4.3 The Multivariate Setting

We would like to generalize the above results to the analogous problems for generalized ridge functions. That is, assume we are given F of the form

$$F(\mathbf{x}) = \sum_{i=1}^{r} f_i(A^i \mathbf{x}), \tag{4.3}$$

where we know r, we have unknown functions $f_i : \mathbb{R}^d \to \mathbb{R}$, and either known or unknown $d \times n$ real matrices A^i of rank d, $1 \le d < n$.

In the case of known A^i we can parallel the analysis in Section 4.1. We will consider only the second method therein that is based on the analysis in Chapter 3. Assume that $F \in C^{r-1}(\mathbb{R}^n)$ is of the form (4.3), where the $2d$ rows of A^i and A^j are linearly independent for all $i \ne j$, and $f_i \in \mathcal{B}_d$, $i = 1, \dots, r$. From Theorem 2.5 we have that $f_i \in C^{r-1}(\mathbb{R}^d)$, $i = 1, \dots, r$.

As in the proof of Theorem 3.8, let $j_1, \dots, j_{r-1}$ be arbitrary values, not necessarily distinct, in $\{1, \dots, d\}$. For each $k = 1, \dots, r-1$ let $\mathbf{c}^{j_k,k} \in \mathbb{R}^n$ satisfy

$$A^k \mathbf{c}^{j_k,k} = \mathbf{0},$$

and

$$A^r \mathbf{c}^{j_k,k} = \mathbf{e}^{j_k}.$$

Such vectors exist since the $2d$ rows of A^k and A^r are linearly independent. From the method of proof of Theorem 3.8 we see that

$$\prod_{k=1}^{r-1} D_{\mathbf{c}^{j_k,k}} F(\mathbf{x}) = \frac{\partial^{r-1} f_r}{\partial y_{j_1} \cdots \partial y_{j_{r-1}}}(A^r \mathbf{x}).$$

The left-hand side of this equation is known for each choice of $j_1, \dots, j_{r-1}$ as above. Since A^r is known this gives us f_r, up to a polynomial in Π_{r-2}^d. In this same manner we determine all the f_i, up to polynomials in Π_{r-2}^d. Thus

$$f_i = g_i + p_i, \qquad i = 1, \dots, r,$$

for known g_i, and unknown $p_i \in \Pi_{r-2}^d$. Since the left-hand side of

$$F(\mathbf{x}) - \sum_{i=1}^{r} g_i(A^i \mathbf{x}) = \sum_{i=1}^{r} p_i(A^i \mathbf{x})$$

is known, we can by various different methods determine $p_i \in \Pi_{r-2}^d$ satisfying the above.

Unfortunately, essentially nothing is known with regards to the more interesting problem of unknown A^i except in the simplest case of $r = 1$. Consider this case $r = 1$, i.e., assume we are given F of the form

$$F(\mathbf{x}) = f(A\mathbf{x}), \tag{4.4}$$

where A is an unknown $d \times n$ real matrix of rank d, $1 \le d < n$. Note that A is not well-defined in this problem. In fact, for two $d \times n$ matrices A and B we have

$$\{f(A\mathbf{x}) : f : \mathbb{R}^d \to \mathbb{R}\} = \{h(B\mathbf{x}) : h : \mathbb{R}^d \to \mathbb{R}\}$$

if and only if the span of the rows of A equals the span of the rows of B, see Proposition 6.5. To see this, note that $\{f(A\mathbf{x}) : f : \mathbb{R}^d \to \mathbb{R}\}$ is simply the space of all functions that are constant on the hyperplanes parallel to the right kernel of A, i.e., to

$$Z_A = \{\mathbf{x} : A\mathbf{x} = \mathbf{0}\}.$$

Thus, if we find Z_A then we can find an appropriate A.

Here are two "methods" for determining A. We first assume that $f \in C^1(\mathbb{R}^d)$. As $F(\mathbf{x}) = f(A\mathbf{x})$ we have for $A = (a_{st})^d_{s=1}{}^n_{t=1}$

$$\frac{\partial F(\mathbf{x})}{\partial x_i} = \sum_{s=1}^{d} \frac{\partial f(A\mathbf{x})}{\partial y_s} a_{si}, \qquad i = 1, \ldots, n. \tag{4.5}$$

Thus

$$\begin{bmatrix} \frac{\partial F(\mathbf{d}^1)}{\partial x_1} & \cdots & \frac{\partial F(\mathbf{d}^1)}{\partial x_n} \\ \vdots & \ddots & \vdots \\ \frac{\partial F(\mathbf{d}^d)}{\partial x_1} & \cdots & \frac{\partial F(\mathbf{d}^d)}{\partial x_n} \end{bmatrix} = \begin{bmatrix} \frac{\partial f(A\mathbf{d}^1)}{\partial y_1} & \cdots & \frac{\partial f(A\mathbf{d}^1)}{\partial y_d} \\ \vdots & \ddots & \vdots \\ \frac{\partial f(A\mathbf{d}^d)}{\partial y_1} & \cdots & \frac{\partial f(A\mathbf{d}^d)}{\partial y_d} \end{bmatrix} A.$$

Assume we have found $\mathbf{d}^1, \ldots, \mathbf{d}^d$ for which

$$\text{rank} \left(\frac{\partial F(\mathbf{d}^j)}{\partial x_i} \right)^d_{j=1,\ i=1}^{\ n} = d.$$

This then implies that

$$\det \left(\frac{\partial f(A\mathbf{d}^j)}{\partial y_s} \right)^d_{j,s=1} \ne 0.$$

It therefore follows that $\mathbf{c} \in \mathbb{R}^n$ satisfies

$$A\mathbf{c} = \mathbf{0}$$

if and only if

$$\begin{bmatrix} \frac{\partial F(\mathbf{d}^1)}{\partial x_1} & \cdots & \frac{\partial F(\mathbf{d}^1)}{\partial x_n} \\ \vdots & \ddots & \vdots \\ \frac{\partial F(\mathbf{d}^d)}{\partial x_1} & \cdots & \frac{\partial F(\mathbf{d}^d)}{\partial x_n} \end{bmatrix} \mathbf{c} = \mathbf{0}. \tag{4.6}$$

Thus the set of all $\mathbf{c} \in \mathbb{R}^n$ satisfying (4.6) spans the $(n-d)$-dimensional subspace of vectors orthogonal to the span of the rows of A. We have found Z_A, and thus can determine an associated matrix A.

The second method is the following. We here assume $f \in C^2(\mathbb{R}^d)$. For any given function $g \in C^2(\mathbb{R}^m)$, let

$$H_g(\mathbf{x}) := \left(\frac{\partial^2 g}{\partial x_i \partial x_j}(\mathbf{x}) \right)_{i,j=1}^m$$

denote the *Hessian* of g at the point $\mathbf{x}$. We claim that for F of the form (4.4)

$$H_F(\mathbf{x}) = A^T H_f(\mathbf{x}) A. \tag{4.7}$$

This follows using (4.5).

Now H_F is an $n \times n$ matrix, A is a $d \times n$ matrix, and H_f is a $d \times d$ matrix. Assuming $\mathbf{d}$ is such that $\det H_f(\mathbf{d}) \neq 0$, then since A is of rank d, it follows that $H_F(\mathbf{d})$ has rank d. Furthermore, at any $\mathbf{d}$ where $\det H_f(\mathbf{d}) \neq 0$, we have

$$H_F(\mathbf{d})\mathbf{c} = \mathbf{0}$$

for $\mathbf{c} \in \mathbb{R}^n$ if and only if

$$A\mathbf{c} = \mathbf{0}.$$

Thus the set of all $\mathbf{c}$ satisfying

$$H_F(\mathbf{d})\mathbf{c} = \mathbf{0}$$

again spans the $(n-d)$-dimensional subspace of vectors orthogonal to the span of the rows of A. We have found Z_A, and thus can determine an associated matrix A.

Question Can we find any method that solves this problem in the case where $r > 1$?

Remark 4.1 There has recently been interest in numerical methods for solving problems of the above type. The interested reader might consult Cohen, Daubechies, DeVore, Kerkyacharian and Picard [2012], Fornasier, Schnass and Vybíral [2012], and Tyagi and Cevher [2014], among others.

5

Polynomial Ridge Functions

In this chapter we consider ridge functions that are algebraic polynomials. While some of the material detailed here is a consequence of more general results, we also present results that are particular to polynomials. We start with a review of some of the basic notions. In Section 5.1 we consider homogeneous polynomials and present results on spanning, linear independence and interpolation by linear combinations of the $(\mathbf{a} \cdot \mathbf{x})^m$ for fixed $m \in \mathbb{Z}_+$, as we vary over a subset Ω of directions in $\mathbb{R}^n$. In Section 5.2 we translate many of these results to the space of algebraic polynomials. Section 5.3 is concerned with what is called Waring's Problem for real polynomials (real linear forms). We consider the minimal number of linear combinations of ridge polynomials needed to represent any algebraic or homogeneous polynomial. Finally, in Section 5.4 we discuss generalized ridge functions that are polynomials. That is, we consider linear combinations of functions of the form $p(A\mathbf{x})$, where the A are fixed $d \times n$ matrices, and the p are d-variate polynomials.

5.1 Homogeneous Polynomials

As a matter of convenience we will, for a fixed direction $\mathbf{a} \in \mathbb{R}^n \backslash \{\mathbf{0}\}$ and univariate polynomial p of degree m, term $p(\mathbf{a} \cdot \mathbf{x})$ a *ridge polynomial of degree m* with direction $\mathbf{a}$, and the polynomial $(\mathbf{a} \cdot \mathbf{x})^m$ will be called a *ridge monomial of degree m* with direction $\mathbf{a}$.

For a given set $\Omega \subseteq \mathbb{R}^n$ let

$$L(\Omega) := \{\lambda \mathbf{a} : \mathbf{a} \in \Omega, \lambda \in \mathbb{R}\}.$$

The set of ridge polynomials with direction $\mathbf{a}$ is the same as the set of ridge polynomials with direction $\lambda \mathbf{a}$ for any $\lambda \in \mathbb{R}$, $\lambda \neq 0$. Thus $L(\Omega)$ is the set of directions we should or could be considering. Let

$$\mathcal{P}(\Omega) := \{p : p\big|_{L(\Omega)} = 0, \, p \in \Pi^n\}.$$

That is, $\mathcal{P}(\Omega)$ is the set of all polynomials that vanish on $L(\Omega)$. Note that a homogeneous polynomial vanishes on $L(\Omega)$ if and only if it vanishes on Ω.

If $p \in \mathcal{P}(\Omega)$ with

$$p := \sum_{r=0}^{m} p_r,$$

where $p_r \in H_r^n$, i.e., $p \in \Pi_m^n$ and each p_r is its homogeneous component of degree r, then $p_r \in \mathcal{P}(\Omega)$ for each $r = 0, \ldots, m$. To verify this note that

$$p(\lambda \mathbf{a}) = \sum_{r=0}^{m} \lambda^r p_r(\mathbf{a})$$

for each $\lambda \in \mathbb{R}$ and $\mathbf{a} \in \mathbb{R}^n$. Consider the above as a polynomial in λ. If $p \in \mathcal{P}(\Omega)$, then from the properties of $L(\Omega)$ it follows that for each fixed $\mathbf{a} \in \Omega$ we have $p(\lambda \mathbf{a}) = 0$ for all $\lambda \in \mathbb{R}$, and thus $p_r(\mathbf{a}) = 0$ for each $r = 0, \ldots, m$. That is, $p \in \mathcal{P}(\Omega)$ if and only if $p_r \in \mathcal{P}(\Omega)$ for each $r = 0, \ldots, m$, which is equivalent to demanding that each p_r vanish on Ω, $r = 0, \ldots, m$.

We recall, from (1.3), that for $q \in H_m^n$ we have

$$q(D)(\mathbf{a} \cdot \mathbf{x})^m = m! \, q(\mathbf{a}). \tag{5.1}$$

Furthermore, from (1.4), for $\mathbf{k}, \mathbf{j} \in \mathbb{Z}_+^n$, $|\mathbf{k}| = |\mathbf{j}|$, we also have

$$D^{\mathbf{k}} \mathbf{x}^{\mathbf{j}} = \delta_{\mathbf{k},\mathbf{j}} \mathbf{k}!, \tag{5.2}$$

where δ denotes the usual Dirac delta function.

Since $H_m^n = \text{span}\{\mathbf{x}^{\mathbf{j}} : |\mathbf{j}| = m\}$, it follows from (5.2) that every linear functional ℓ on the finite-dimensional linear space H_m^n may be represented by some $q \in H_m^n$ via

$$\ell(p) = q(D)p$$

for each $p \in H_m^n$. An element is in a closed linear subspace if and only if every continuous linear functional that vanishes on the subspace also annihilates the element. (We are repeating here an argument that was used in the proof of Proposition 3.5.) As such, the next few results are immediate consequences of equation (5.1).

Proposition 5.1 *Let $\Omega \subseteq \mathbb{R}^n$, and $p \in H_m^n$. Then*

$$p(\mathbf{x}) \in \text{span}\{(\mathbf{a} \cdot \mathbf{x})^m : \mathbf{a} \in \Omega\}$$

if and only if

$$q(D)p = 0$$

for every $q \in H_m^n$ that vanishes on Ω.

From Proposition 5.1 and equation (5.1), we have the following two results concerning the linear dependency of the ridge monomials $\{(\mathbf{a} \cdot \mathbf{x})^m : \mathbf{a} \in \Omega\}$.

Corollary 5.2 *Let $\Omega \subseteq \mathbb{R}^n$. Then for $\mathbf{b} \in \mathbb{R}^n \backslash \{\mathbf{0}\}$ we have*

$$(\mathbf{b} \cdot \mathbf{x})^m \in \operatorname{span}\{(\mathbf{a} \cdot \mathbf{x})^m : \mathbf{a} \in \Omega\}$$

if and only if

$$q(\mathbf{b}) = 0$$

for every $q \in H_m^n$ that vanishes on Ω.

If the set Ω is finite, then we can rewrite Corollary 5.2 as follows.

Corollary 5.3 *Let $\mathbf{a}^i$, $i = 1, \ldots, r$, be vectors in $\mathbb{R}^n$. Then the ridge monomials $\{(\mathbf{a}^i \cdot \mathbf{x})^m\}_{i=1}^r$ are linearly independent if and only if for each $j \in \{1, \ldots, r\}$ there exists a $q_j \in H_m^n$ satisfying*

$$q_j(\mathbf{a}^i) = \delta_{ij}, \qquad i, j = 1, \ldots, r.$$

Proof If the q_j exist, then from Corollary 5.2

$$(\mathbf{a}^j \cdot \mathbf{x})^m \notin \operatorname{span}\{(\mathbf{a}^i \cdot \mathbf{x})^m : i = 1, \ldots, r, i \neq j\}$$

for every $j \in \{1, \ldots, r\}$, and thus the r ridge monomials $\{(\mathbf{a}^i \cdot \mathbf{x})^m\}_{i=1}^r$ are linearly independent.

On the other hand, if q_j does not exist for some $j \in \{1, \ldots, r\}$, then for every $q \in H_m^n$ satisfying $q(\mathbf{a}^i) = 0$, $i = 1, \ldots, r$, $i \neq j$, we have $q(\mathbf{a}^j) = 0$. Thus, by Corollary 5.2,

$$(\mathbf{a}^j \cdot \mathbf{x})^m \in \operatorname{span}\{(\mathbf{a}^i \cdot \mathbf{x})^m : i = 1, \ldots, r, i \neq j\},$$

and the set of ridge monomials $\{(\mathbf{a}^i \cdot \mathbf{x})^m\}_{i=1}^r$ are linearly dependent. $\qquad\square$

In the literature Corollary 5.3 is sometimes referred to as Serret's Theorem, see Reznick [1992], p. 29. The polynomials q_i of Corollary 5.3 are termed a "dual basis" to the $(\mathbf{a}^i \cdot \mathbf{x})^m$, and are sometimes called "fundamental polynomials" with respect to the $\mathbf{a}^i$. Corollary 5.3 may also be rewritten in the following manner, highlighting the duality between linear independence and interpolation.

Corollary 5.4 *Let* $\mathbf{a}^i$, $i = 1, \ldots, r$, *be vectors in* $\mathbb{R}^n$. *The ridge monomials* $\{(\mathbf{a}^i \cdot \mathbf{x})^m\}_{i=1}^r$ *are linearly independent if and only if for every choice of real values* $\{\alpha_i\}_{i=1}^r$ *there exists a* $q \in H_m^n$ *satisfying* $q(\mathbf{a}^i) = \alpha_i$, $i = 1, \ldots, r$.

A matrix form of the above result is the statement that the linear independence of the $\{(\mathbf{a}^i \cdot \mathbf{x})^m\}_{i=1}^r$ is equivalent to the demand that the $r \times \dim H_m^n$ matrix

$$\left((\mathbf{a}^i)^{\mathbf{k}}\right)_{i=1}^r {}_{|\mathbf{k}|=m}$$

be of rank r.

The next few results concern the linear independence of the ridge monomials $\{(\mathbf{a}^i \cdot \mathbf{x})^m\}_{i=1}^r$. It follows from Corollary 5.4 that these results may be reworded as results on interpolation. In Chlebowicz and Wołowiec-Musial [2005] we find the following, which is a simple consequence of Corollary 5.3.

Proposition 5.5 *Let* $\mathbf{a}^i$, $i = 1, \ldots, r$, *be vectors in* $\mathbb{R}^n$. *If the ridge monomials* $\{(\mathbf{a}^i \cdot \mathbf{x})^m\}_{i=1}^r$ *are linearly independent in* H_m^n, *it then follows that the ridge monomials* $\{(\mathbf{a}^i \cdot \mathbf{x})^{m+1}\}_{i=1}^r$ *are linearly independent in* H_{m+1}^n.

Proof Since the ridge monomials $\{(\mathbf{a}^i \cdot \mathbf{x})^m\}_{i=1}^r$ are linearly independent there exist, by Corollary 5.3, $q_j \in H_m^n$, $j = 1, \ldots, r$, satisfying

$$q_j(\mathbf{a}^i) = \delta_{ij}, \qquad i, j = 1, \ldots, r.$$

Let $p \in H_1^n$ be such that $p(\mathbf{a}^i) \neq 0$, $i = 1, \ldots, r$. Then the

$$\widetilde{q}_j(\mathbf{x}) := \frac{p(\mathbf{x})}{p(\mathbf{a}^j)} q_j(\mathbf{x}), \qquad j = 1, \ldots, r,$$

are in H_{m+1}^n and satisfy $\widetilde{q}_j(\mathbf{a}^i) = \delta_{ij}$, $i, j = 1, \ldots, r$, and thus, by Corollary 5.3, the ridge monomials $\{(\mathbf{a}^i \cdot \mathbf{x})^{m+1}\}_{i=1}^r$ are linearly independent.

Alternatively, let p be as above. Given $\{\alpha_i\}_{i=1}^r$, let $q \in H_m^n$ satisfy

$$q(\mathbf{a}^i) = \frac{\alpha_i}{p(\mathbf{a}^i)}, \qquad i = 1, \ldots, r.$$

Then $qp \in H_{m+1}^n$, $(qp)(\mathbf{a}^i) = \alpha_i$, $i = 1, \ldots, r$, and we can apply Corollary 5.4. $\square$

Here is another simple and interesting consequence of Corollary 5.2. It may be found in Chlebowicz and Wołowiec-Musial [2005], see also Białynicki-Birula and Schinzel [2008].

Proposition 5.6 *Let* $r \leq m(n-1)+1$ *and assume that the vectors* $\mathbf{a}^i$, $i = 1, \ldots, r$, *in* $\mathbb{R}^n$ *have the property that every* $\min\{n, r\}$ *of them are linearly independent. Then the ridge monomials* $\{(\mathbf{a}^i \cdot \mathbf{x})^m\}_{i=1}^r$ *are linearly independent.*

Proof It suffices to prove the result for $r = m(n-1) + 1$. We will prove, without loss of generality, that

$$(\mathbf{a}^r \cdot \mathbf{x})^m \notin \mathrm{span}\{(\mathbf{a}^i \cdot \mathbf{x})^m : i = 1, \ldots, r-1\}.$$

Let $\mathbf{b}^j \in \mathbb{R}^n \backslash \{\mathbf{0}\}$, $j = 1, \ldots, m$, satisfy

$$(\mathbf{b}^j \cdot \mathbf{a}^i) = 0, \quad i = (j-1)(n-1) + 1, \ldots, j(n-1).$$

Such $\mathbf{b}^j$ exist. From our assumption concerning the linear independence of every n vectors of the $\mathbf{a}^i$ we have that

$$\mathbf{b}^j \cdot \mathbf{a}^r \neq 0, \quad j = 1, \ldots, m.$$

Set

$$q(\mathbf{x}) := \prod_{j=1}^m (\mathbf{b}^j \cdot \mathbf{x}).$$

Then $q \in H_m^n$, $q(\mathbf{a}^i) = 0$, $i = 1, \ldots, r-1$, but $q(\mathbf{a}^r) \neq 0$. Thus, by Corollary 5.2, we have that

$$(\mathbf{a}^r \cdot \mathbf{x})^m \notin \mathrm{span}\{(\mathbf{a}^i \cdot \mathbf{x})^m : i = 1, \ldots, r-1\}. \qquad \square$$

Is this limiting value $r = m(n-1) + 1$ optimal? The answer is yes, as has been shown by Białynicki-Birula and Schinzel [2008].

Proposition 5.7 *Let $r = m(n-1) + 2$. There exist $\{\mathbf{a}^i\}_{i=1}^r$ in $\mathbb{R}^n$ with the property that every n of them are linearly independent, while the ridge monomials $\{(\mathbf{a}^i \cdot \mathbf{x})^m\}_{i=1}^r$ are linearly dependent.*

Proof Let b_i, $i = 1, \ldots, r-1$, be any $r-1$ distinct points in $\mathbb{R}$. For $i = 1, \ldots, r-1$, set

$$\mathbf{a}^i := (1, b_i, b_i^2, \ldots, b_i^{n-1}),$$

and let $\mathbf{a}^r := \mathbf{e}^n = (0, \ldots, 0, 1)$. From simple properties of the Vandermonde matrix we see that every n of the vectors $\{\mathbf{a}^i\}_{i=1}^r$ are linearly independent.

Now for $i = 1, \ldots, r-1$ we have

$$(\mathbf{a}^i \cdot \mathbf{x})^m = \left(\sum_{j=1}^n b_i^{j-1} x_j \right)^m = \sum_{k=0}^{m(n-1)} b_i^k f_k(\mathbf{x}),$$

where

$$f_k(\mathbf{x}) := \sum_{\substack{|\mathbf{i}| = m \\ i_2 + 2i_3 + \cdots + (n-1)i_n = k}} \binom{m}{\mathbf{i}} \mathbf{x}^{\mathbf{i}}.$$

Furthermore,

$$(\mathbf{a}^r \cdot \mathbf{x})^m = x_n^m = f_{m(n-1)}(\mathbf{x}).$$

Thus each of the ridge monomials $(\mathbf{a}^i \cdot \mathbf{x})^m$ is a linear combination of the $r - 1 = m(n-1) + 1$ polynomials $f_k(\mathbf{x})$, $k = 0, 1, \ldots, m(n-1)$. As such these $\{(\mathbf{a}^i \cdot \mathbf{x})^m\}_{i=1}^r$ are linearly dependent. $\qquad\square$

Another technique for finding linearly independent ridge monomials goes back to Radon [1948], see also Stahl and de Boor [2011].

Proposition 5.8 *Let* $\mathbf{c} \in \mathbb{R}^n \backslash \{\mathbf{0}\}$. *Assume the* $\{\mathbf{b}^j\}_{j=1}^s$ *in* $\mathbb{R}^n$ *are such that* $\mathbf{b}^j \cdot \mathbf{c} \neq 0$, $j = 1, \ldots, s$, *and the ridge monomials* $\{(\mathbf{b}^j \cdot \mathbf{x})^{m-1}\}_{j=1}^s$ *are linearly independent. Assume the* $\{\mathbf{c}^i\}_{i=1}^t$ *in* $\mathbb{R}^n$ *are such that* $\mathbf{c}^i \cdot \mathbf{c} = 0$, $i = 1, \ldots, t$, *and the ridge monomials* $\{(\mathbf{c}^i \cdot \mathbf{x})^m\}_{i=1}^t$ *are linearly independent. Then the* $s + t$ *ridge monomials* $\{(\mathbf{b}^j \cdot \mathbf{x})^m\}_{j=1}^s$, $\{(\mathbf{c}^i \cdot \mathbf{x})^m\}_{i=1}^t$ *are linearly independent.*

Proof Assume we have

$$0 = \sum_{j=1}^s \beta_j (\mathbf{b}^j \cdot \mathbf{x})^m + \sum_{i=1}^t \alpha_i (\mathbf{c}^i \cdot \mathbf{x})^m. \tag{5.3}$$

From (1.5) we see that

$$D_\mathbf{c}(\mathbf{a} \cdot \mathbf{x})^m = m(\mathbf{a} \cdot \mathbf{c})(\mathbf{a} \cdot \mathbf{x})^{m-1}.$$

Applying $D_\mathbf{c}$ to (5.3) and since $\mathbf{c}^i \cdot \mathbf{c} = 0$, $i = 1, \ldots, t$, we obtain

$$0 = \sum_{j=1}^s m\beta_j (\mathbf{b}^j \cdot \mathbf{c})(\mathbf{b}^j \cdot \mathbf{x})^{m-1}.$$

By assumption, the $\mathbf{b}^j \cdot \mathbf{c} \neq 0$, $j = 1, \ldots, s$, and the $\{(\mathbf{b}^j \cdot \mathbf{x})^{m-1}\}_{j=1}^s$ are linearly independent ridge monomials. Thus $\beta_j = 0$, $j = 1, \ldots, s$. This reduces (5.3) to

$$0 = \sum_{i=1}^t \alpha_i (\mathbf{c}^i \cdot \mathbf{x})^m.$$

As the ridge monomials $\{(\mathbf{c}^i \cdot \mathbf{x})^m\}_{i=1}^t$ are linearly independent, we have $\alpha_i = 0$, $i = 1, \ldots, t$. $\qquad\square$

It should be noted that the assumptions of the proposition imply that $t \leq \dim H_m^{n-1}$ and $s \leq \dim H_{m-1}^n$.

For "generic" sets Ω of $\binom{n-1+m}{n-1} = \dim H_m^n$ distinct points in $\mathbb{R}^n$, no non-zero

$q \in H_m^n$ vanishes on Ω. But, of course, not every set has this property. Here is a particular set Ω of dim H_m^n points for which

$$\operatorname{span}\{(\mathbf{a} \cdot \mathbf{x})^m : \mathbf{a} \in \Omega\} = H_m^n.$$

It is called Biermann's Theorem in Reznick [1992], Proposition 2.11, because Biermann [1903] proved this result in the case $n = 3$.

Proposition 5.9 (Biermann's Theorem). *Let*

$$\Omega_m := \{\mathbf{k} : \mathbf{k} \in \mathbb{Z}_+^n, |\mathbf{k}| = m\}.$$

Then

$$H_m^n = \operatorname{span}\{(\mathbf{k} \cdot \mathbf{x})^m : \mathbf{k} \in \Omega_m\}.$$

Proof Set

$$q_{\mathbf{k}}(\mathbf{x}) := \prod_{\ell=1}^{n} \prod_{i=0}^{k_\ell - 1} (m x_l - i(x_1 + \cdots + x_n)).$$

Note that deg $q_{\mathbf{k}} = \sum_{\ell=1}^{n} k_l = |\mathbf{k}| = m$ and $q_{\mathbf{k}} \in H_m^n$. Furthermore, as is easily verified, $q_{\mathbf{k}}(\mathbf{k}) = m^m \mathbf{k}!$, while for $\mathbf{j} \in \Omega_m$, $\mathbf{j} \neq \mathbf{k}$, we have $q_{\mathbf{k}}(\mathbf{j}) = 0$ since for some $\ell \in \{1, \ldots, n\}$ we must have $k_\ell > j_\ell$. Thus, from Corollary 5.3, we have that the ridge monomials $\{(\mathbf{k} \cdot \mathbf{x})^m : \mathbf{k} \in \Omega_m\}$ are linearly independent. Since the cardinality of Ω_m is exactly dim H_m^n, we have that these ridge monomials $\{(\mathbf{k} \cdot \mathbf{x})^m : \mathbf{k} \in \Omega_m\}$ form a basis for H_m^n. $\qquad\square$

Remark 5.10 By a linear transformation this same result holds if we replace Ω_m by

$$\widetilde{\Omega}_m = \left\{ \sum_{i=1}^{n} k_i \mathbf{b}^i : \mathbf{k} \in \mathbb{Z}_+^n, |\mathbf{k}| = m \right\},$$

where the $\mathbf{b}^i$ are any n linearly independent vectors in $\mathbb{R}^n$. Proposition 5.9 may also be obtained from Proposition 5.8 by using induction and, for example, choosing $\mathbf{c} = \mathbf{e}^1$.

In the multivariate polynomial interpolation literature, see, for example, Chung and Yao [1977], the vectors $\{\mathbf{a}^i\}_{i=1}^r$ are said to satisfy a GC (Geometric Characterization) condition with respect to m if there exist hyperplanes $\{G_{j\ell}\}_{j=1}^r {}_{\ell=1}^m$ such that

$$\mathbf{a}^i \in \bigcup_{\ell=1}^{m} G_{j\ell}$$

if and only if $i \neq j$. If we let $G_{j\ell}(\mathbf{x})$ denote the linear polynomial that vanishes on $G_{j\ell}$, then the

$$q_j(\mathbf{x}) = \prod_{\ell=1}^{m} G_{j\ell}(\mathbf{x}), \qquad j = 1, \ldots, r,$$

are polynomials in Π_m^n that satisfy $q_j(\mathbf{a}^i) = \delta_{ij} c_j$, $i, j = 1, \ldots, r$, for some $c_j \neq 0$. Thus we can interpolate arbitrary data at the $\{\mathbf{a}^i\}_{i=1}^r$ by taking appropriate linear combinations of the $\{q_j\}_{j=1}^r$. In our case we are interested in H_m^n and hyperplanes that vanish at the origin, i.e., $G_{j\ell}(\mathbf{x}) = \mathbf{b}^{j\ell} \cdot \mathbf{x}$ for some $\mathbf{b}^{j\ell} \in \mathbb{R}^n \backslash \{\mathbf{0}\}$. Propositions 5.6 and 5.9 are examples of this approach.

A class of examples based on this principle is given by what Chung and Yao [1977] call a *natural lattice*. Translating from Π_m^n to H_m^n, we obtain the following. Let $\mathbf{b}^j$, $j = 1, \ldots, n-1+m$, be vectors in $\mathbb{R}^n$ such that every n of them are linearly independent. For each distinct $j_1, \ldots, j_{n-1}$ in $\{1, \ldots, n-1+m\}$, let $\mathbf{a} \in \mathbb{R}^n \backslash \{\mathbf{0}\}$ satisfy

$$\mathbf{b}^{j_\ell} \cdot \mathbf{a} = 0, \qquad \ell = 1, \ldots, n-1.$$

This defines $\mathbf{a}$ uniquely up to multiplication by a constant, and $\mathbf{a}$ cannot be orthogonal to $\mathbf{b}^k$, $k \notin \{j_1, \ldots, j_{n-1}\}$. There are $r = \binom{n-1+m}{n-1} = \dim H_m^n$ choices of $j_1, \ldots, j_{n-1}$, as above. Let $\mathbf{a}^i$, $i = 1, \ldots, r$, denote the associated vectors. It is easily proven that these $\mathbf{a}^i$ are pairwise linearly independent. Furthermore, for every choice of distinct $k_1, \ldots, k_m$ in $\{1, \ldots, n-1+m\}$,

$$\prod_{s=1}^{m} (\mathbf{b}^{k_s} \cdot \mathbf{x})$$

is a polynomial in H_m^n that vanishes at all the $\mathbf{a}^j$, except at the one $\mathbf{a}^i$ that is orthogonal to all the $\mathbf{b}^j$, with $j \notin \{k_1, \ldots, k_m\}$. Thus the associated ridge monomials $\{(\mathbf{a}^i \cdot \mathbf{x})^m\}_{i=1}^r$ are linearly independent, and in fact span H_m^n. Note that the examples of Propositions 5.6 and 5.9 are not natural lattices.

With regards to conditions for when the ridge monomials $\{(\mathbf{a} \cdot \mathbf{x})^m : \mathbf{a} \in \Omega\}$ span H_m^n we have the following consequences of Proposition 5.1.

Corollary 5.11 *Let $\Omega \subseteq \mathbb{R}^n$. Then*

$$H_m^n = \text{span}\{(\mathbf{a} \cdot \mathbf{x})^m : \mathbf{a} \in \Omega\}$$

if and only if no non-zero $q \in H_m^n$ vanishes on Ω.

Spanning H_m^n also implies spanning H_r^n for all $r < m$.

Corollary 5.12 *Let $\Omega \subseteq \mathbb{R}^n$. If*

$$H_m^n = \text{span}\{(\mathbf{a} \cdot \mathbf{x})^m : \mathbf{a} \in \Omega\},$$

then

$$H_r^n = \text{span}\{(\mathbf{a} \cdot \mathbf{x})^r : \mathbf{a} \in \Omega\}$$

for each $r = 0, \ldots, m - 1$.

Proof If

$$H_r^n \neq \text{span}\{(\mathbf{a} \cdot \mathbf{x})^r : \mathbf{a} \in \Omega\},$$

for some $r \in \{0, 1, \ldots, m-1\}$, then there exists a non-zero $q \in H_r^n$ that vanishes on Ω. Let p be any non-zero element in H_{m-r}^n. Then $pq \in H_m^n$ is non-zero and vanishes on Ω. This is a contradiction to Corollary 5.11. $\square$

Note that linear independence is preserved when going from m to $m+1$ (Proposition 5.5), while the spanning property is preserved when going from m to $m - 1$ (Corollary 5.12).

In the converse direction we have the following.

Corollary 5.13 *Let $\Omega_1, \Omega_2 \subseteq \mathbb{R}^n$. Assume*

$$H_{m_1}^n \neq \text{span}\{(\mathbf{a} \cdot \mathbf{x})^{m_1} : \mathbf{a} \in \Omega_1\}$$

and

$$H_{m_2}^n \neq \text{span}\{(\mathbf{b} \cdot \mathbf{x})^{m_2} : \mathbf{b} \in \Omega_2\}.$$

Then, for $m = m_1 + m_2$,

$$H_m^n \neq \text{span}\{(\mathbf{c} \cdot \mathbf{x})^m : \mathbf{c} \in \Omega_1 \cup \Omega_2\}.$$

Proof From Corollary 5.11 there exists a non-zero $q_1 \in H_{m_1}^n$ satisfying $q_1(\mathbf{a}) = 0$, $\mathbf{a} \in \Omega_1$, and a non-zero $q_2 \in H_{m_2}^n$ satisfying $q_2(\mathbf{b}) = 0$, $\mathbf{b} \in \Omega_2$. Set $q = q_1 q_2$. Then $q \in H_m^n$ is non-zero and vanishes on $\Omega_1 \cup \Omega_2$. The result follows from Corollary 5.11. $\square$

If we are given $\{\mathbf{a}^i\}_{i=1}^R$ in $\mathbb{R}^n$, where $R = \dim H_m^n$, then we have the following elegant criteria for determining if the ridge monomials $\{(\mathbf{a}^i \cdot \mathbf{x})^m\}_{i=1}^R$ form a basis for H_m^n.

Proposition 5.14 *Assume we are given $\mathbf{a}^i$, $i = 1, \ldots, R$, in $\mathbb{R}^n$, where $R = \dim H_m^n$. The following are equivalent.*

(a) *For every choice of real values $\{\alpha_j\}_{j=1}^{R}$ there exists a $q \in H_m^n$ satisfying*
   $q(\mathbf{a}^j) = \alpha_j, \ j = 1, \ldots, R.$
(b) *The $\{(\mathbf{a}^i \cdot \mathbf{x})^m\}_{i=1}^{R}$ are a basis for H_m^n.*
(c)

$$\det\left((\mathbf{a}^i \cdot \mathbf{a}^j)^m\right)_{i,j=1}^{R} \neq 0.$$

Proof From Corollary 5.4, and since $R = \dim H_m^n$, we have that (a) and (b) are equivalent. If (c) holds, then the ridge monomials $\{(\mathbf{a}^i \cdot \mathbf{x})^m\}_{i=1}^{R}$ are linearly independent and hence (b) holds.

If (b) holds, then every $q \in H_m^n$ is a linear combination of the $\{(\mathbf{a}^i \cdot \mathbf{x})^m\}_{i=1}^{R}$. From (a) we can arbitrarily interpolate at the $\{\mathbf{a}^j\}_{j=1}^{R}$. That is, for any $\{\alpha_j\}_{j=1}^{R}$ there exists $\{\beta_i\}_{i=1}^{R}$ such that

$$q(\mathbf{x}) = \sum_{i=1}^{R} \beta_i (\mathbf{a}^i \cdot \mathbf{x})^m$$

satisfies $q(\mathbf{a}^j) = \alpha_j, \ j = 1, \ldots, R$. In other words we can solve

$$\sum_{i=1}^{R} \beta_i (\mathbf{a}^i \cdot \mathbf{a}^j)^m = \alpha_j, \qquad j = 1, \ldots, R,$$

for any right-hand side. Thus

$$\det\left((\mathbf{a}^i \cdot \mathbf{a}^j)\right)_{i,j=1}^{R} \neq 0. \qquad \square$$

Remark 5.15 The matrix $((\mathbf{a}^i \cdot \mathbf{a}^j)^m)_{i,j=1}^{r}$ is positive semi-definite for any r. This follows from the fact that the matrix $((\mathbf{a}^i \cdot \mathbf{a}^j))_{i,j=1}^{r}$ is easily seen to be positive semi-definite and the Schur product theorem regarding Hadamard products. Additionally, assuming the $\mathbf{a}^i$ are non-zero, then the diagonal elements of the above matrices are positive, and it therefore follows that if $((\mathbf{a}^i \cdot \mathbf{a}^j)^m)_{i,j=1}^{r}$ is positive definite, then $((\mathbf{a}^i \cdot \mathbf{a}^j)^{m+1})_{i,j=1}^{r}$ is also positive definite, see, for example, Horn and Johnson [1991], Chapter 5.

Certain properties are much simpler in $\mathbb{R}^2$ than in $\mathbb{R}^n$ for $n > 2$. In particular, from Proposition 5.6 we obtain this next result.

Corollary 5.16 *Let $\{\mathbf{a}^i\}_{i=1}^{m+1}$ be any $m+1$ pairwise linearly independent vectors in $\mathbb{R}^2$. Then*

$$H_m^2 = \text{span}\{(\mathbf{a}^i \cdot \mathbf{x})^m : i = 1, \ldots, m+1\}.$$

Proof From Proposition 5.6 the ridge monomials $\{(\mathbf{a}^i \cdot \mathbf{x})^m\}_{i=1}^{m+1}$ are linearly independent. Since $\dim H_m^2 = m+1$, this proves the result. $\qquad \square$

Remark 5.17 Corollary 5.16 seems to have been repeatedly rediscovered, with different elementary proofs. It is also, for example, an immediate consequence of the fact that H_m^2 is a homogenization of Π_m^1, and that no non-zero $q \in \Pi_m^1$ has more than m distinct zeros.

For any given $\Omega \subseteq \mathbb{R}^n$ the set $\mathcal{P}(\Omega)$ of all polynomials that vanish on $L(\Omega)$ is a *polynomial ideal*. As such, assuming $\mathcal{P}(\Omega)$ is composed of more than the identically zero polynomial, it has, by the Hilbert Basis Theorem, a finite number of generators. When $n = 2$ these generators, and thus the set $\mathcal{P}(\Omega)$, is easily determined. There is only one generator, and it is given by the unique (up to multiplication by a constant) homogeneous polynomial of minimal degree that vanishes on Ω. From Proposition 5.1 and Corollary 5.16 we have the following.

Corollary 5.18 *Let* $\{\mathbf{a}^i = (a_1^i, a_2^i)\}_{i=1}^r$ *be any* r *pairwise linearly independent vectors in* $\mathbb{R}^2$, $r \leq m$. *Then for* $p \in H_m^2$ *we have*

$$p \in \mathrm{span}\{(\mathbf{a}^i \cdot \mathbf{x})^m : i = 1, \ldots, r\},$$

if and only if

$$q(D)p = 0$$

where

$$q(x_1, x_2) = \prod_{i=1}^r (a_2^i x_1 - a_1^i x_2).$$

This result, in a different but equivalent form over $\mathbb{C}$, is sometimes referred to as Sylvester's Theorem, see Sylvester [1886] and Brachat, Comon, Mourrain and Tsigaridas [2010].

The history of the results of this section is somewhat opaque. In addition to the references that were already given, and as they pertain to ridge functions, one can find some of these results in more or less this form in Vostrecov and Kreines [1961], [1962], and Lin and Pinkus [1993].

5.2 Algebraic Polynomials

In this section we translate some of the results of the previous section from H_m^n to Π_m^n. We start with the question of when ridge polynomials with fixed directions span Π_m^n. We have the exact same result as for H_m^n, namely the following.

Proposition 5.19 *Let* $\Omega \subseteq \mathbb{R}^n$. *Then*

$$\Pi_m^n = \mathrm{span}\{p(\mathbf{a} \cdot \mathbf{x}) : p \in \Pi_m^1, \mathbf{a} \in \Omega\}$$

if and only if no non-zero $q \in H_m^n$ vanishes on Ω.

Proof If

$$\Pi_m^n = \text{span}\{p(\mathbf{a} \cdot \mathbf{x}) \, : \, p \in \Pi_m^1, \, \mathbf{a} \in \Omega\},$$

then we must have

$$H_m^n = \text{span}\{(\mathbf{a} \cdot \mathbf{x})^m \, : \, \mathbf{a} \in \Omega\},$$

and thus, from Corollary 5.11, no non-zero $q \in H_m^n$ vanishes on Ω.

If no non-zero $q \in H_m^n$ vanishes on Ω, then from Corollaries 5.11 and 5.12 we have

$$H_r^n = \text{span}\{(\mathbf{a} \cdot \mathbf{x})^r \, : \, \mathbf{a} \in \Omega\},$$

for each $r = 0, \dots, m$. As each $p \in \Pi_m^n$ has a unique decomposition of the form

$$p = \sum_{r=0}^{m} p_r,$$

where $p_r \in H_r^n$, $r = 0, 1, \dots, m$, it therefore follows that

$$\Pi_m^n = \text{span}\{p(\mathbf{a} \cdot \mathbf{x}) \, : \, p \in \Pi_m^1, \, \mathbf{a} \in \Omega\}. \qquad \square$$

There is simple 1-1 correspondence between Π_m^n and H_m^{n+1} called *homogenization*. For each $p \in \Pi_m^n$ of the form

$$p(\mathbf{x}) = \sum_{|\mathbf{k}| \le m} b_{\mathbf{k}} \mathbf{x}^{\mathbf{k}}$$

set $\widetilde{\mathbf{x}} := (\mathbf{x}, x_{n+1}) \in \mathbb{R}^{n+1}$ and

$$\widetilde{p}(\widetilde{\mathbf{x}}) := \sum_{|\mathbf{k}| \le m} b_{\mathbf{k}} \mathbf{x}^{\mathbf{k}} x_{n+1}^{m-|\mathbf{k}|}.$$

Thus $\widetilde{p} \in H_m^{n+1}$. Similarly, if $\widetilde{p} \in H_m^{n+1}$, then $p(\mathbf{x}) := \widetilde{p}(\mathbf{x}, 1) \in \Pi_m^n$. As such, results on H_m^{n+1} can be translated to results on Π_m^n and vice versa.

Here are some results valid for Π_m^n obtained from the results of the previous section and homogenization. From Corollary 5.4 we obtain the following.

Corollary 5.20 *Let $\mathbf{a}^i$, $i = 1, \dots, r$, be vectors in $\mathbb{R}^n$. Then for every choice of real values $\{\alpha_i\}_{i=1}^r$ there exists a $p \in \Pi_m^n$ satisfying $p(\mathbf{a}^i) = \alpha_i$, $i = 1, \dots, r$, if and only if the ridge polynomials $\{((\mathbf{a}^i \cdot \mathbf{x}) + 1)^m\}_{i=1}^r$ are linearly independent.*

Corollary 5.20 allows us to state results in terms of interpolation or linear independence. In this section we choose the former. From Propositions 5.6 and 5.7 we obtain the following.

Corollary 5.21 *Let $r \leq mn+1$ and assume that the vectors $\{(\mathbf{a}^i, 1)\}_{i=1}^r$ in $\mathbb{R}^{n+1}$ have the property that every $\min\{n+1, r\}$ of them are linearly independent. Then for every choice of real values $\{\alpha_i\}_{i=1}^r$ there exists a $p \in \Pi_m^n$ satisfying $p(\mathbf{a}^i) = \alpha_i$, $i = 1, \ldots, r$. This result is not necessarily valid when $r = mn + 2$.*

The Radon result for homogeneous polynomials, Proposition 5.8, translates into the following.

Corollary 5.22 *Given $\mathbf{c} \in \mathbb{R}^n \backslash \{\mathbf{0}\}$ and $c^* \in \mathbb{R}$. Assume that the vectors $\{\mathbf{b}^i\}_{i=1}^s$ in $\mathbb{R}^n$ are such that $\mathbf{b}^i \cdot \mathbf{c} \neq c^*$, $i = 1, \ldots, s$, and for every choice of real values $\{\beta_i\}_{i=1}^s$ there exists a $q \in \Pi_{m-1}^n$ satisfying $q(\mathbf{b}^i) = \beta_i$, $i = 1, \ldots, s$. Assume that the vectors $\{\mathbf{c}^i\}_{i=1}^t$ in $\mathbb{R}^n$ are such that $\mathbf{c}^i \cdot \mathbf{c} = c^*$, $i = 1, \ldots, t$, and for every choice of real values $\{\gamma_i\}_{i=1}^t$ there exists a $p \in \Pi_m^n$ satisfying $p(\mathbf{c}^i) = \gamma_i$, $i = 1, \ldots, t$. Then for every choice of real values $\{\alpha_i\}_{i=1}^{s+t}$ there exists an $h \in \Pi_m^n$ satisfying $h(\mathbf{b}^i) = \alpha_i$, $i = 1, \ldots, s$, and $h(\mathbf{c}^i) = \alpha_{i+s}$, $i = 1, \ldots, t$.*

Proposition 5.9 can be restated in the following form.

Corollary 5.23 *We have*

$$\Pi_m^n = \operatorname{span}\{(\mathbf{k} \cdot \mathbf{x} + k_{n+1})^m : \mathbf{k} = (k_1, \ldots, k_n) \in \mathbb{Z}_+^n, k_{n+1} \in \mathbb{Z}_+, |\mathbf{k}| + k_{n+1} = m\}.$$

And from Proposition 5.14 we obtain the following result.

Proposition 5.24 *Assume we are given $\mathbf{a}^i$, $i = 1, \ldots, R$, in $\mathbb{R}^n$ with $R = \dim \Pi_m^n$. The following are equivalent.*

(a) *For every choice of real values $\{\alpha_j\}_{j=1}^R$ there exists a $p \in \Pi_m^n$ satisfying $p(\mathbf{a}^j) = \alpha_j$, $j = 1, \ldots, R$.*

(b) *The ridge polynomials $\{((\mathbf{a}^i \cdot \mathbf{x}) + 1)^m\}_{i=1}^R$ are a basis for Π_m^n.*

(c)

$$\det \left(((\mathbf{a}^i \cdot \mathbf{a}^j) + 1)^m \right)_{i,j=1}^R \neq 0.$$

5.3 Waring's Problem for Polynomials

Ridge functions and ridge polynomials appear in various guises. For example, *Waring's Problem* asks whether every positive integer can be expressed as a sum of at most $h(m)$ mth powers of positive integers, where $h(m)$ depends only upon m. This problem was solved in the affirmative by Hilbert [1909]. A key result in his proof was the following: for given m and n, and $N := \binom{n-1+2m}{n-1} =$

$\dim H_{2m}^n$, there exist $\mathbf{a}^i \in \mathbb{Z}^n$, $i = 1, \ldots, N+1$, and λ_i positive rational numbers, $i = 1, \ldots, N + 1$, such that

$$(x_1^2 + \cdots + x_n^2)^m = \sum_{i=1}^{N+1} \lambda_i(\mathbf{a}^i \cdot \mathbf{x})^{2m},$$

see also Stridsberg [1912]. A lucid exposition of Waring's Problem, and elementary proof of this result, can be found in Ellison [1971].

Waring's Problem has various generalizations. One of them is the following. Can each homogeneous polynomial of degree m in n variables, with coefficients in a field K, be written as a linear combination of r ridge monomials, i.e., of mth powers of linear homogeneous polynomials, where r depends only on n, m and K? And if it can, what is then the minimal number $r = h(m, n)$ such that every homogeneous polynomial of degree m in n variables, with coefficients in a field K, can be written as a linear combination of $h(m, n)$ ridge monomials? We are interested in the case $K = \mathbb{R}$. That is, we wish to find the minimal $h(n, m)$ such that each $p \in H_m^n$ can be written in the form

$$p(\mathbf{x}) = \sum_{i=1}^{h(m,n)} \alpha_i(\mathbf{a}^i \cdot \mathbf{x})^m,$$

for some choice of directions $\mathbf{a}^i$ in $\mathbb{R}^n$ and real values α_i, $i = 1, \ldots, h(m, n)$.

From the results of the previous sections we know that each $p \in H_m^n$ may be written as a linear combination of $\dim H_m^n = \binom{n-1+m}{n-1}$ ridge monomials $(\mathbf{a} \cdot \mathbf{x})^m$ with certain given distinct directions. Thus $h(m, n) \le \dim H_m^n$.

We can also ask this same question with respect to all polynomials of degree m in n variables. That is, what is the minimal number $g(m, n)$ such that each polynomial $p \in \Pi_m^n$ can be written as a linear combination of at most $g(m, n)$ ridge polynomials, i.e.,

$$p(\mathbf{x}) = \sum_{i=1}^{g(m,n)} p_i(\mathbf{a}^i \cdot \mathbf{x}),$$

for some $p_i \in \Pi_m^1$, and directions $\mathbf{a}^i$, $i = 1, \ldots, g(m, n)$?

From the proof of Proposition 5.19 it follows that $h(m, n) \le g(m, n) \le \dim H_m^n$. But this upper bound is not sharp. We will, in fact, prove that

$$h(m, n) \le g(m, n) \le \binom{n - 2 + m}{n - 1} (= \dim H_{m-1}^n).$$

The proof, as presented here, will use induction on both n and m. So we start with the cases $n \le 2$, and $m \le 2$, where we also prove that we have equality in the above. Note that it is easily verified that $h(m, 1) = g(m, 1) = h(1, n) =$

$g(1, n) = 1$ for all $m, n \in \mathbb{Z}_+$. Let us first consider the case $m = 2$, where $\dim H_2^n = n(n+1)/2$.

Proposition 5.25 *For all $n \in \mathbb{Z}_+$, $n \geq 2$, we have $h(2, n) = g(2, n) = n$.*

Proof We will prove that each $p \in H_2^n$ may be written in the form

$$p(\mathbf{x}) = \sum_{i=1}^{r} \alpha_i (\mathbf{a}^i \cdot \mathbf{x})^2,$$

where $r \leq n$ and the ridge monomials $\{(\mathbf{a}^i \cdot \mathbf{x})\}_{i=1}^{r}$ are linearly independent. It will also follow from the proof that there are $p \in H_2^n$ for which we must have $r = n$ terms in the above sum. Thus $h(2, n) = n$. Since any n linear ridge monomials with linearly independent directions span H_1^n, we also obtain $g(2, n) = n$.

The proof of the fact that $h(2, n) = n$ with n linear independent directions easily follows based on quadratic decomposition. Every $p \in H_2^n$ may be written in the form

$$p(\mathbf{x}) = \sum_{i,j=1}^{n} c_{ij} x_i x_j,$$

where, without loss of generality, we assume $c_{ji} = c_{ij}$ for all $i \neq j$. Let the symmetric matrix $C := (c_{ij})_{i,j=1}^{n}$ have the decomposition

$$C = A^T \Gamma A,$$

where A is an $n \times n$ matrix whose rows we denote by $\mathbf{a}^i \in \mathbb{R}^n$, $i = 1, \ldots, n$, while Γ is an $n \times n$ diagonal matrix with diagonal entries $\{\gamma_1, \ldots, \gamma_n\}$. Then

$$\mathbf{x}^T C \mathbf{x} = \mathbf{x}^T A^T \Gamma A \mathbf{x},$$

which translates into

$$p(\mathbf{x}) = \sum_{i,j=1}^{n} c_{ij} x_i x_j = \sum_{i=1}^{n} \gamma_i (\mathbf{a}^i \cdot \mathbf{x})^2.$$

There are many decompositions of this form for the matrix C (and not only the standard decomposition involving eigenvalues and eigenvectors that gives orthonormal $\{\mathbf{a}^i\}_{i=1}^{n}$.) If C is non-singular then A and Γ are non-singular, and we must therefore have n terms in the summand. Thus $h(2, n) = n$, and we may always choose linearly independent directions. $\square$

The next case we will consider is that of $n = 2$. Recall that $\dim H_m^2 = m + 1$ for all m. It transpires that we can always do one better but, in general, only one better. This result may be found in Oskolkov [2002] and in Schinzel [2002a]. There are various different proofs of this result. We choose to present a proof that is a simplification of the method of proof of the main Theorem 5.27. In both Oskolkov [2002] and Schinzel [2002a] are to be found examples of $p \in H_m^2$ that need m ridge monomials in their representation, whence the lower bound $h(m,2) \geq m$. In Boij, Carlini and Geramita [2011] it is shown that one needs m ridge monomials in the representation of each of the monomials $x_1^k x_2^{m-k}$, for $k = 1, \ldots, m - 1$. This is also proven below.

Proposition 5.26 *For all $m \in \mathbb{Z}_+$ we have $h(m,2) = g(m,2) = m$.*

Proof Since ridge monomials with m pairwise linearly independent directions span H_r^2, $r \leq m - 1$ (Corollary 5.16), then $h(m,2) = m$ implies $g(m,2) = m$. We prove the former.

Assume $p \in H_m^2$. If $\partial p / \partial x_1 = 0$, then

$$p(x_1, x_2) = \alpha x_2^m$$

and we are finished. If $\partial p / \partial x_1 \neq 0$, then

$$\frac{\partial p}{\partial x_1} \in H_{m-1}^2.$$

By an induction hypothesis we therefore obtain

$$\frac{\partial p}{\partial x_1}(\mathbf{x}) = \sum_{j=1}^{t} \alpha_j (\mathbf{a}^j \cdot \mathbf{x})^{m-1},$$

where $t \leq m - 1$, and the $\{\mathbf{a}^j\}_{j=1}^t$ are pairwise linearly independent vectors. By a linear change of variables we may assume, without loss of generality, that $\mathbf{a}^j = (a_{j1}, a_{j2})$ with $a_{j1} \neq 0$, $j = 1, \ldots, t$. Set

$$q(\mathbf{x}) := p(\mathbf{x}) - \sum_{j=1}^{t} \frac{\alpha_j}{m a_{j1}} (\mathbf{a}^j \cdot \mathbf{x})^m.$$

Then $q \in H_m^2$ and

$$\frac{\partial q}{\partial x_1} = 0,$$

whence

$$q(\mathbf{x}) = \alpha x_2^m.$$

This then implies that

$$p(\mathbf{x}) = \sum_{j=1}^{t} \frac{\alpha_j}{m a_{j1}} (\mathbf{a}^j \cdot \mathbf{x})^m + \alpha (\mathbf{a}^m \cdot \mathbf{x})^m,$$

where $\mathbf{a}^m = (0, 1)$. Thus $h(m, 2) \leq m$.

To prove that $h(m, 2) = m$ we must find $p \in H_m^2$ that cannot be represented as linear combinations of at most $m - 1$ ridge monomials of degree m. We will prove that this holds for each of $x_1^k x_2^{m-k}$, $k = 1, \ldots, m - 1$. In other words, we claim that there do not exist pairwise linearly independent vectors (a_j, b_j), $j = 1, \ldots, r$, with $r < m$, for which

$$\prod_{j=1}^{r} \left(a_j \frac{\partial}{\partial x_1} + b_j \frac{\partial}{\partial x_2} \right) x_1^k x_2^{m-k} = 0, \tag{5.4}$$

see Corollary 5.18.

Assume (5.4) does hold. We may assume that the a_j are all non-zero. If an $a_j = 0$ we then take $\frac{\partial}{\partial x_2}$ and consider the same problem with m replaced by $m - 1$. As the a_j are all non-zero, we can assume, with no loss of generality, that $a_j = 1$ for all $j = 1, \ldots, r$. Finally, if (5.4) holds for $r < m-1$, then it obviously holds for $r = m - 1$, and we therefore assume $r = m - 1$. Note that the vectors $\{(1, b_j)\}_{j=1}^{m-1}$ are pairwise linearly independent if and only if the b_j are distinct. With these assumptions, consider

$$\prod_{j=1}^{m-1} \left(\frac{\partial}{\partial x_1} + b_j \frac{\partial}{\partial x_2} \right) x_1^k x_2^{m-k}.$$

It is easily seen that this equals $C x_1 + D x_2$, where

$$C = k!(m - k)! \sum_{i_1, \ldots, i_{m-k} \text{ distinct}} b_{i_1} \cdots b_{i_{m-k}}$$

and

$$D = k!(m - k)! \sum_{i_1, \ldots, i_{m-k-1} \text{ distinct}} b_{i_1} \cdots b_{i_{m-k-1}}.$$

If $C = D = 0$ then we have that two consecutive symmetric functions of the $b_1, \ldots, b_{m-1}$ are zero. This is impossible since the b_j are distinct. To verify this fact, let $r(t) := \prod_{j=1}^{m-1}(t - b_j)$. If $C = D = 0$, then the coefficients of t^{k-1} and t^k in the expansion of r both vanish. But if two consecutive coefficients equal zero, i.e., $r^{(k-1)}(0) = r^{(k)}(0) = 0$, then from Rolle's Theorem we contradict the fact that the b_j are distinct. $\qquad\square$

In Schinzel [2002b] it is proven that $g(3,n) \le \binom{n+1}{2}$. In Białynicki-Birula and Schinzel [2008] it is proven that for all $m, n \in \mathbb{Z}_+$ we have

$$g(m,n) \le \binom{n-2+m}{n-1}.$$

We here prove this latter result using ideas from the Schinzel [2002b] paper. We will prove the following.

Theorem 5.27 *Every $p \in H_m^n$ can be written in the form*

$$p(\mathbf{x}) = \sum_{j=1}^{r} \alpha_j (\mathbf{a}^j \cdot \mathbf{x})^m,$$

where $r \le \binom{n-2+m}{n-1}$, and the ridge monomials $\{(\mathbf{a}^j \cdot \mathbf{x})^{m-1}\}_{j=1}^{r}$ are linearly independent.

For ease of notation, set

$$C_m^n = \binom{n-2+m}{n-1}.$$

Assume Theorem 5.27 is true. Then as $C_m^n = \dim H_{m-1}^n$, it follows that we can, if necessary, choose additional directions $\{\mathbf{a}^j\}_{j=r+1}^{C_m^n}$, so that the ridge monomials $\{(\mathbf{a}^j \cdot \mathbf{x})^{m-1}\}_{j=1}^{C_m^n}$ form a basis for H_{m-1}^n. Thus, as an immediate corollary to Theorem 5.27 and Corollary 5.12, we obtain the following.

Corollary 5.28 *For each $n, m \in \mathbb{Z}_+$,*

$$h(m,n) \le g(m,n) \le \binom{n-2+m}{n-1}.$$

Proof of Theorem 5.27 Our proof will be by induction on n and m. We have proven the result for $m = 2$, all n, and for $n = 2$, all m, in Propositions 5.25 and 5.26, respectively.

Assume $p \in H_m^n$. If $\partial p / \partial x_1 = 0$, then p is a homogeneous polynomial of degree m in the $n-1$ variables $x_2, \ldots, x_n$, i.e., $p \in H_m^{n-1}$. Thus by the induction hypothesis on n we have

$$p(\mathbf{x}) = \sum_{j=1}^{r} \alpha_j (\mathbf{a}^j \cdot \mathbf{x})^m,$$

where $r \le C_m^{n-1} \le C_m^n$ and the ridge monomials $\{(\mathbf{a}^j \cdot \mathbf{x})^{m-1}\}_{j=1}^{r}$ are linearly independent. The theorem therefore holds. (By this same argument we may assume that no directional derivative $\sum_{i=1}^{n} c_i \partial p / \partial x_i$ vanishes identically.)

As $\partial p / \partial x_1 \neq 0$, then

$$\frac{\partial p}{\partial x_1} \in H^n_{m-1}.$$

By the induction hypothesis on m

$$\frac{\partial p}{\partial x_1}(\mathbf{x}) = \sum_{j=1}^{t} \alpha_j (\mathbf{b}^j \cdot \mathbf{x})^{m-1},$$

where $t \leq C^n_{m-1}$ and the ridge monomials $\{(\mathbf{b}^j \cdot \mathbf{x})^{m-2}\}_{j=1}^t$ are linearly independent.

By a linear change of variable we may assume, without loss of generality, that $\mathbf{b}^j = (b_{j1}, \ldots, b_{jn})$, with $b_{j1} \neq 0$, $j = 1, \ldots, t$. Set

$$q(\mathbf{x}) = p(\mathbf{x}) - \sum_{j=1}^{t} \frac{\alpha_j}{m \, b_{j1}} (\mathbf{b}^j \cdot \mathbf{x})^m.$$

Thus

$$\frac{\partial q}{\partial x_1} = 0.$$

That is, $q \in H^{n-1}_m$ and by the induction hypothesis on n we have

$$q(\mathbf{x}) = \sum_{i=1}^{s} \beta_i (\mathbf{c}^i \cdot \mathbf{x})^m,$$

where $s \leq C^{n-1}_m$ and the $\{(\mathbf{c}^i \cdot \mathbf{x})^{m-1}\}_{i=1}^s$ are linearly independent. This implies that

$$p(\mathbf{x}) = \sum_{i=1}^{s} \beta_i (\mathbf{c}^i \cdot \mathbf{x})^m + \sum_{j=1}^{t} \frac{\alpha_j}{m \, b_{j1}} (\mathbf{b}^j \cdot \mathbf{x})^m.$$

Since

$$s + t \leq C^{n-1}_m + C^n_{m-1} = C^n_m$$

the theorem follows if we can prove that the $s + t$ ridge monomials

$$\{(\mathbf{c}^i \cdot \mathbf{x})^{m-1}, (\mathbf{b}^j \cdot \mathbf{x})^{m-1} : \quad i = 1, \ldots, s, \; j = 1, \ldots, t\},$$

are linearly independent. Note that as q is independent of x_1 we could have assumed that the $\mathbf{c}^i = (c_{i1}, \ldots, c_{in})$ satisfy $c_{i1} = 0$. In fact, since

$$0 = \frac{\partial q}{\partial x_1} = \sum_{i=1}^{s} \beta_i c_{i1} (\mathbf{c}^i \cdot \mathbf{x})^{m-1},$$

the ridge monomials $\{(\mathbf{c}^i \cdot \mathbf{x})^{m-1}\}_{i=1}^s$ are linearly independent, and the β_i can be assumed to be non-zero, it follows that $c_{i1} = 0$, $i = 1, \ldots, s$.

The result now follows from Proposition 5.8. But, for the convenience of the reader, we will repeat the proof here. Assume

$$0 = \sum_{i=1}^{s} \gamma_i (\mathbf{c}^i \cdot \mathbf{x})^{m-1} + \sum_{j=1}^{t} \delta_j (\mathbf{b}^j \cdot \mathbf{x})^{m-1}. \tag{5.5}$$

Taking derivatives with respect to x_1, and since

$$\frac{\partial}{\partial x_1} (\mathbf{c}^i \cdot \mathbf{x})^{m-1} = 0, \qquad i = 1, \dots, s,$$

we have

$$0 = \sum_{j=1}^{t} (m-1) b_{j1} \delta_j (\mathbf{b}^j \cdot \mathbf{x})^{m-2}.$$

Moreover $b_{j1} \neq 0$, $j = 1, \dots, t$, and the ridge monomials $\{(\mathbf{b}^j \cdot \mathbf{x})^{m-2}\}_{j=1}^{t}$ are linearly independent. Thus $\delta_j = 0$, $j = 1, \dots, t$. Returning to (5.5) we have

$$0 = \sum_{i=1}^{s} \gamma_i (\mathbf{c}^i \cdot \mathbf{x})^{m-1}.$$

The ridge monomials $\{(\mathbf{c}^i \cdot \mathbf{x})^{m-1}\}_{i=1}^{s}$ are linearly independent, and therefore $\gamma_i = 0$, $i = 1, \dots, s$. The desired linear independence holds. □

Question We have only proven the upper bound $g(m, n) \leq C_m^n$. Is it true that $h(m, n) = C_m^n$ for all n and m, as is the case for $n \leq 2$ and $m \leq 2$?

Question If we define $\mathcal{R}_r$ as the non-linear set given by linear combinations of r ridge monomials, then

$$h(m, n) = \min\{r : H_m^n \subseteq \mathcal{R}_r\}.$$

However, as may be easily shown, $\mathcal{R}_r \neq \overline{\mathcal{R}_r}$. What is not known, and is an interesting open question, is whether

$$\min\{r : H_m^n \subseteq \overline{\mathcal{R}_r}\}$$

also equals $h(m, n)$. In fact, from Corollary 5.18 it follows that for $n = 2$ we have that $p \in \overline{\mathcal{R}_r} \cap H_m^2$ if and only if

$$q(D)p = 0$$

for some $q(x_1, x_2) = \Pi_{i=1}^{r}(a_1^i x_1 - a_2^i x_2)$, where $(a_1^i, a_2^i) \neq (0, 0)$, but without the demand that the vectors $\{(a_1^i, a_2^i)\}_{i=1}^{r}$ be linearly independent. Thus, while for each $k \in \{1, \dots, m-1\}$, we have $x_1^k x_2^{m-k} \in \mathcal{R}_m \backslash \mathcal{R}_{m-1}$, we also have $x_1^k x_2^{m-k} \in \overline{\mathcal{R}_r}$, where $r = \min\{k+1, m-k+1\}$.

The question of which $p \in H_m^n$, for m even and $K = \mathbb{R}$, can be written as positive sums (and not simply linear combinations) of the ridge monomials $(\mathbf{a} \cdot \mathbf{x})^m$ is of significant interest. This problem has been extensively studied as have its interconnections with numerous different topics. An excellent survey of this subject is Reznick [1992].

The same questions, as above, have been asked when $K = \mathbb{C}$. While this is not within the purview of this work we note that from deep results of Alexander and Hirschowitz, see Iarrobino [1995], if $K = \mathbb{C}$, $h_{\mathbb{C}}(m,n)$ and $g_{\mathbb{C}}(m,n)$ are defined as previously, but with respect to $\mathbb{C}$, and $\lceil k \rceil$ is the smallest integer greater than or equal to k, then for $m > 2$ we have

$$h_{\mathbb{C}}(m,n) = \left\lceil \frac{1}{n} \binom{n+m-1}{n-1} \right\rceil,$$

except in the cases $(m,n) = (4,3), (4,4), (4,5)$ and $(3,5)$, where $h_{\mathbb{C}}(m,n)$ is 6, 10, 15 and 8, respectively. For $m = 2$ we have $h_{\mathbb{C}}(2,n) = n$. There is a vast literature on Waring's Problem over algebraic closed fields, and in particular over $\mathbb{C}$. The problem is sometimes also referred to as one of *symmetric tensor decomposition*. See, for example, Comon, Golub, Lim and Mourrain [2008], Brachat, Comon, Mourrain and Tsigaridas [2010], Usevich [2014], and references therein. One can also ask for estimates on the analogous $g_{\mathbb{C}}(m,n)$. Equality between $h_{\mathbb{C}}(m,n)$ and $g_{\mathbb{C}}(m,n)$ need not hold. It is proved in Schinzel [2002b] that $g_{\mathbb{C}}(3,3) = 5$, while from the above formula we have $h_{\mathbb{C}}(3,3) = 4$.

5.4 Generalized Ridge Polynomials

We consider in this section generalized ridge polynomials, by which we mean functions of the form $p(A\mathbf{x})$, where A is a fixed $d \times n$ real matrix, $1 \le d < n$, and $p \in \Pi^d$, i.e., p is a d-variate polynomial. When $d = 1$ this reduces to what we have been discussing in the previous sections.

Given a $d \times n$ matrix A, let $L(A)$ denote the span of the rows of A. We introduced the notation "L" at the beginning of this chapter for something seemingly different. As shall be proven, this is a slight, but justifiable, abuse of notation. We prove two fundamental results concerning generalized ridge polynomials. The first fundamental result reduces the analysis in this general setting to the previous analysis of the case $d = 1$.

Proposition 5.29 *Let A be any $d \times n$ matrix. Then*

$$\mathrm{span}\{p(A\mathbf{x}) : p \in H_m^d\} = \mathrm{span}\{(\mathbf{a} \cdot \mathbf{x})^m : \mathbf{a} \in L(A)\}.$$

Proof For $\mathbf{a} \in L(A)$ we have $\mathbf{a} = \mathbf{c}A$ for some $\mathbf{c} \in \mathbb{R}^d$, and thus $(\mathbf{a} \cdot \mathbf{x})^m =$

$(\mathbf{c} \cdot A\mathbf{x})^m$. Therefore

$$\text{span}\{(\mathbf{a} \cdot \mathbf{x})^m : \mathbf{a} \in L(A)\} \subseteq \text{span}\{p(A\mathbf{x}) : p \in H_m^d\}.$$

To prove the converse direction assume, with no loss of generality, that rank $A = d$. Let D denote the $n \times n$ non-singular matrix such that $AD = C = (c_{ij})$, where C is the $d \times n$ matrix of the simple form

$$c_{ij} = \delta_{ij}, \qquad i = 1, \ldots, d, \; j = 1, \ldots, n.$$

We apply the linear change of variable $\mathbf{y} = D^{-1}\mathbf{x}$. Thus

$$p(A\mathbf{x}) = p(AD\mathbf{y}) = p(C\mathbf{y}) = p(y_1, \ldots, y_d, 0, \ldots, 0),$$

and

$$(\mathbf{a} \cdot \mathbf{x})^m = (\mathbf{a} \cdot D\mathbf{y})^m = (\mathbf{a}D \cdot \mathbf{y})^m.$$

Since $AD = C$, as above, we have that

$$\{\mathbf{a}D : \mathbf{a} \in L(A)\}$$

is exactly the set

$$\{\mathbf{w} = (w_1, \ldots, w_n) : \; w_j = 0, j = d + 1, \ldots, n\}.$$

We have therefore reduced our problem to proving that the set of all ridge monomials, with arbitrary directions, in H_m^d spans H_m^d. This is certainly valid; see, for example, Corollary 5.11. $\qquad \square$

The second fundamental result is the following.

Proposition 5.30 *Let A and B be two $d \times n$ matrices. Then for $m \geq 1$*

$$\text{span}\{p(A\mathbf{x}) : p \in H_m^d\} = \text{span}\{q(B\mathbf{x}) : q \in H_m^d\}$$

if and only if $L(A) = L(B)$.

Proof This result is a direct consequence of Proposition 5.29. It can also be proven directly.

The set

$$\text{span}\{p(A\mathbf{x}) : p \in H_m^d\}$$

is the space of homogeneous polynomials in H_m^n that are constant on the hyperplanes parallel to the subspace

$$Z_A := \{\mathbf{x} : A\mathbf{x} = \mathbf{0}\}.$$

Note that $Z_A^\perp = L(A)$. Since $L(A) = L(B)$ if and only if $Z_A = Z_B$, the result therefore follows. $\qquad \square$

Note that in the case $d = 1$ Proposition 5.30 simply says that for $\mathbf{a}, \mathbf{b} \in \mathbb{R}^n \backslash \{\mathbf{0}\}$, and $m \geq 1$, we have $(\mathbf{a} \cdot \mathbf{x})^m = \lambda (\mathbf{b} \cdot \mathbf{x})^m$ for some $\lambda \in \mathbb{R}$ and all $\mathbf{x} \in \mathbb{R}^n$ if and only if $\mathbf{a} = \alpha \mathbf{b}$ for some $\alpha \in \mathbb{R}$.

Based on the results of the previous sections and Proposition 5.29 we obtain the following. Let Ω_d be a given set of $d \times n$ matrices. For each $A \in \Omega_d$, let $L(A)$, as above, denote the span of the rows of A, and set

$$L(\Omega_d) := \bigcup_{A \in \Omega_d} L(A).$$

From Proposition 5.29 it follows that there is no reason, other than convenience, to consider classes of matrices with the same numbers of rows. From Propositions 5.1 and 5.29 we have the following.

Proposition 5.31 *Let Ω_d and $L(\Omega_d)$ be as defined. Then $p \in H_m^n$ satisfies*

$$p \in \mathrm{span}\{h(A\mathbf{x}) : h \in H_m^d, A \in \Omega_d\}$$

if and only if

$$q(D)p = 0$$

for every $q \in H_n^m$ that vanishes on $L(\Omega_d)$.

Paralleling Corollary 5.2, we obtain the following.

Corollary 5.32 *Let Ω_d and $L(\Omega_d)$ be as defined. Then*

$$p(B\mathbf{x}) \in \mathrm{span}\{h(A\mathbf{x}) : h \in H_m^d, A \in \Omega_d\}$$

for some $k \times n$ matrix B and all $p \in H_m^k$ if and only if every $q \in H_m^n$ that vanishes on $L(\Omega_d)$ also vanishes on $L(B)$.

In addition, see Corollary 5.11 and Proposition 5.19, we have the following.

Corollary 5.33 *Let Ω_d and $L(\Omega_d)$ be as defined. Then the following are equivalent.*

(a)

$$H_m^n = \mathrm{span}\{h(A\mathbf{x}) : h \in H_m^d, A \in \Omega_d\}.$$

(b)

$$\Pi_m^n = \mathrm{span}\{p(A\mathbf{x}) : p \in \Pi_m^d, A \in \Omega_d\}.$$

(c) No non-zero $q \in H_m^n$ vanishes on $L(\Omega_d)$.

We end this chapter with the following direct generalization of Corollary 5.16.

Proposition 5.34 *Assume $d = n - 1$, and $A^1, \ldots, A^{m+1}$ are $(n-1) \times n$ matrices of rank $n - 1$ such that the associated $(n-1)$-dimensional subspaces $L(A^i)$ are all distinct, $i = 1, \ldots, m + 1$. Then*

$$H_m^n = \text{span}\{h_i(A^i \mathbf{x}) : h_i \in H_m^{n-1}, i = 1, \ldots, m + 1\},$$

and

$$\Pi_m^n = \text{span}\{p_i(A^i \mathbf{x}) : p_i \in \Pi_m^{n-1}, i = 1, \ldots, m + 1\}.$$

Proof It suffices, by Corollary 5.33, to prove that

$$H_m^n = \text{span}\{h_i(A^i \mathbf{x}) : h_i \in H_m^{n-1}, i = 1, \ldots, m + 1\}.$$

For each A^i there exists a $\mathbf{c}^i \in \mathbb{R}^n \backslash \{\mathbf{0}\}$, the normal to $L(A^i)$, unique up to multiplication by constants, such that $A^i \mathbf{c}^i = \mathbf{0}$. Let

$$q_i(\mathbf{x}) = \mathbf{c}^i \cdot \mathbf{x}, \quad i = 1, \ldots, m + 1.$$

q_i vanishes exactly on $L(A^i)$ and q_i is irreducible, $i = 1, \ldots, m + 1$.

Let $q \in H_m^n$ vanish on

$$\bigcup_{i=1}^{m+1} L(A^i).$$

For each $i \in \{1, \ldots, m + 1\}$, q vanishes on $L(A^i)$. As such, the linear polynomials q_i must be divisors of q. There are $m + 1$ $\mathbf{c}^i$ and they are pairwise linearly independent. Thus q must contain as divisors at least $m + 1$ irreducible distinct linear polynomials. But $q \in H_m^n$. This implies that q vanishes identically and thus, from (c) of Corollary 5.33, the result follows. $\qquad\square$

6

Density and Representation

In this chapter we consider the question of the density of linear combinations of ridge functions in the set of continuous functions on $\mathbb{R}^n$, in the topology of uniform convergence on compact subsets of $\mathbb{R}^n$. In Section 6.1 we consider a set of fixed directions and obtain necessary and sufficient conditions on the direction set for when we have density of linear combinations of all possible ridge functions with these directions. In Section 6.2 we discuss this same question with regard to generalized ridge functions. We discuss the question of density when permitting variable directions in Section 6.3. In Section 6.4 we ask for conditions on when a specific function in $C(\mathbb{R}^n)$ can be approximated by a linear combination of ridge function with given directions, without the density assumption. Much of the presentation of Sections 6.1, 6.2 and 6.4 is taken from Lin and Pinkus [1993]. In Section 6.5 we study a related but different question. Here we permit all possible directions, but restrict the set of permissible functions. We look at the class of ridge functions generated by shifts of a single function. This question is relevant in ridgelet analysis and in the MLP model in neural networks.

6.1 Density with Fixed Directions

In this section we consider the question of the density of linear combinations of ridge functions with a given set of directions. Let Ω denote any subset of vectors in $\mathbb{R}^n$, and set

$$\mathcal{M}(\Omega) := \operatorname{span}\{f(\mathbf{a} \cdot \mathbf{x}) : \mathbf{a} \in \Omega, \ f \in C(\mathbb{R})\}. \tag{6.1}$$

That is, in $\mathcal{M}(\Omega)$ we vary over all $\mathbf{a} \in \Omega$ and all $f \in C(\mathbb{R})$, and take arbitrary linear combinations of the elements of this set. This is our approximating set. The question we ask is one of density: when can elements of the above set approximate arbitrarily well any function in our class?

The class of functions that we will approximate are functions in $C(\mathbb{R}^n)$, in the topology of uniform convergence on compact subsets. That is, we wish to have the property that, for any given $G \in C(\mathbb{R}^n)$, any compact set $K \subset \mathbb{R}^n$, and any $\varepsilon > 0$, there exists an $F \in \mathcal{M}(\Omega)$ such that

$$\|G - F\|_K = \max_{\mathbf{x} \in K} |G(\mathbf{x}) - F(\mathbf{x})| < \varepsilon.$$

With regards to ridge function density, this is a very natural topology. If we can prove density in this topology, then we also obtain density for this same class of functions in many other topologies. For example, density will hold in $L^p(K, d\mu)$, where K is any compact subset of $\mathbb{R}^n$, $d\mu$ is some reasonable measure, and $p \in [1, \infty)$. Note that no ridge function (other than the identically zero function) is in any of the classical spaces $L^p(\mathbb{R}^n)$, for any $p \in [1, \infty)$. This is because if $|f(t)| \geq \varepsilon > 0$ for all $t \in [c, d]$, then for any $\mathbf{a} \in \mathbb{R}^n \backslash \{0\}$ we have that $|f(\mathbf{a} \cdot \mathbf{x})| \geq \varepsilon$ on the strip $\{\mathbf{x} : c \leq \mathbf{a} \cdot \mathbf{x} \leq d\}$ of infinite Lebesgue measure.

Linear combinations of ridge functions form a very rich class of functions, and when we consider all directions and all functions, or even some fixed "good" directions and "good" functions, then we always have the desired density result. Here is a simple example from Diaconis and Shahshahani [1984].

Proposition 6.1 *Linear combinations of the functions $e^{\mathbf{n} \cdot \mathbf{x}}$, where $\mathbf{n} \in \mathbb{Z}_+^n$, are dense in $C(\mathbb{R}^n)$, in the topology of uniform convergence on compact subsets.*

Proof This result is an immediate consequence of the Stone–Weierstrass Theorem since the approximating class contains the constant function, separates points and is a subalgebra. □

For $n = 2$ it is known that we have density of $\mathcal{M}(\Omega)$ in $C(\mathbb{R}^2)$, in the topology of uniform convergence on compact subsets, if and only if Ω contains an infinite number of pairwise linearly independent directions. Various proofs of this fact appear in the literature. It can be found, for example, in Logan and Shepp [1975]. From Corollary 5.16 and Proposition 5.19 it follows that if $\mathbf{a}^1, \ldots, \mathbf{a}^{m+1}$ are pairwise linearly independent directions in $\mathbb{R}^2$, then each polynomial of total degree at most m in $\mathbb{R}^2$ can be written as a sum of functions $p_i(\mathbf{a}^i \cdot \mathbf{x})$, $i = 1, \ldots, m+1$, where each p_i is a polynomial of degree at most m. Thus if Ω contains an infinite number of pairwise linearly independent directions, then $\mathcal{M}(\Omega)$ contains in its span all polynomials and density follows from the Weierstrass Approximation Theorem. The converse result also easily holds.

In fact, the definitive density result in the general $\mathbb{R}^n$ case may already be found in the earlier article of Vostrecov and Kreines [1961].

Theorem 6.2 *The space $\mathcal{M}(\Omega)$ is dense in $C(\mathbb{R}^n)$, in the topology of uniform* *convergence on compact subsets, if and only if no non-trivial homogeneous polynomial vanishes on* Ω.

This result seems to have gone unnoticed, as partial results were later reproved by others.

Proof ($\Leftarrow$). If there is no non-trivial $q \in H_m^n$ that vanishes on Ω, for any $m \in \mathbb{Z}_+$, then from Proposition 5.19 we have $\Pi_m^n \subset \mathcal{M}(\Omega)$ for all $m \in \mathbb{Z}_+$. Thus $\mathcal{M}(\Omega)$ contains all polynomials, and by the Weierstrass Approximation Theorem, $\overline{\mathcal{M}(\Omega)} = C(\mathbb{R}^n)$ in the topology of uniform convergence on compact sets.

($\Rightarrow$). Assume that for some $m \in \mathbb{Z}_+$ there exists a non-trivial $q \in H_m^n$ that vanishes on Ω. It follows from (1.2) that

$$q(D)(\mathbf{a} \cdot \mathbf{x})^\ell = 0$$

for all $\mathbf{a} \in \Omega$ and all $\ell \in \mathbb{Z}_+$. Thus, from the Weierstrass Approximation Theorem, we have that

$$q(D)f(\mathbf{a} \cdot \mathbf{x}) = 0$$

for all $f \in C^m(\mathbb{R})$ and all $\mathbf{a} \in \Omega$. In what follows we extend this non-trivial linear functional defined on $C^m(\mathbb{R}^n)$ to a non-trivial linear functional on $C(\mathbb{R}^n)$ that annihilates all of $\mathcal{M}(\Omega)$, thus proving that $\mathcal{M}(\Omega)$ is not dense in $C(\mathbb{R}^n)$.

Choose any $\phi \in C_0^\infty(\mathbb{R}^n)$, $\phi \neq 0$, i.e., ϕ is a non-trivial C^∞ function with compact support. Let

$$q(\boldsymbol{\xi}) = \sum_{|\mathbf{k}|=m} b_{\mathbf{k}} \boldsymbol{\xi}^{\mathbf{k}},$$

and define

$$\psi(\mathbf{x}) := q(D)\phi(\mathbf{x}) = \sum_{|\mathbf{k}|=m} b_{\mathbf{k}} D^{\mathbf{k}}\phi(\mathbf{x}).$$

Note that $\psi \in C_0^\infty(\mathbb{R}^n)$, $\psi \neq 0$, (supp$\psi \subseteq$ suppϕ), and

$$\widehat{\psi} = i^m \widehat{\phi} q,$$

where $\widehat{}$ denotes the Fourier transform.

We claim that

$$\int_{\mathbb{R}^n} f(\mathbf{a} \cdot \mathbf{x})\psi(\mathbf{x})dx = 0 \qquad (6.2)$$

for all $\mathbf{a} \in \Omega$ and $f \in C(\mathbb{R})$, i.e., the non-trivial linear functional defined by integrating against ψ annihilates $\mathcal{M}(\Omega)$. This implies the desired result.

We prove (6.2) as follows. Given $\mathbf{a} \in \Omega$. Write $\mathbf{x} =: (x', \mathbf{x}'')$, where $(x', 0)$

and $(0, \mathbf{x}'')$ are the orthogonal projections of $\mathbf{x}$ onto $L(\mathbf{a}) = \{\lambda \mathbf{a} : \lambda \in \mathbb{R}\}$ and its orthogonal complement, respectively. Then for any $\rho \in C_0^\infty(\mathbb{R}^n)$

$$\int_{\mathbb{R}^n} \rho(\mathbf{x}) d\mathbf{x} = \int_{\mathbb{R}} \left[\int_{\mathbb{R}^{n-1}} \rho(x', \mathbf{x}'') d\mathbf{x}'' \right] dx'.$$

Now, every $c' \in \mathbb{R}$ is such that $\mathbf{c} = (c', \mathbf{0})$ is a multiple of $\mathbf{a}$ and thus in $L(\mathbf{a})$. Therefore

$$0 = i^m \widehat{\phi}(\mathbf{c}) q(\mathbf{c}) = \widehat{\psi}(\mathbf{c}) = \frac{1}{(2\pi)^{n/2}} \int_{\mathbb{R}^n} \psi(\mathbf{x}) e^{-i\mathbf{c} \cdot \mathbf{x}} d\mathbf{x}$$

$$= \frac{1}{(2\pi)^{n/2}} \int_{\mathbb{R}} \left[\int_{\mathbb{R}^{n-1}} \psi(x', \mathbf{x}'') d\mathbf{x}'' \right] e^{-ic'x'} dx'.$$

Set

$$H(x') := \int_{\mathbb{R}^{n-1}} \psi(x', \mathbf{x}'') d\mathbf{x}''.$$

Then $H \in C_0^\infty(\mathbb{R})$, and the previous equation may be rewritten as

$$0 = \frac{1}{(2\pi)^{n/2}} \int_{\mathbb{R}} H(x') e^{-ic'x'} dx' = \widehat{H}(c')$$

for all $c' \in \mathbb{R}$. Thus $H = 0$.

Set $\widetilde{\mathbf{x}}' := (x', \mathbf{0})$. Since $(0, \mathbf{x}'')$ is orthogonal to $L(\mathbf{a})$, it is clear that

$$\mathbf{a} \cdot \mathbf{x} = \mathbf{a} \cdot \widetilde{\mathbf{x}}'$$

for all $\mathbf{x} = (x', \mathbf{x}'') \in \mathbb{R}^n$. Thus for any $f \in C(\mathbb{R})$,

$$\int_{\mathbb{R}^n} f(\mathbf{a} \cdot \mathbf{x}) \psi(\mathbf{x}) d\mathbf{x} = \int_{\mathbb{R}} \left[\int_{\mathbb{R}^{n-1}} \psi(x', \mathbf{x}'') d\mathbf{x}'' \right] f(\mathbf{a} \cdot \widetilde{\mathbf{x}}') dx'$$

$$= \int_{\mathbb{R}} H(x') f(\mathbf{a} \cdot \widetilde{\mathbf{x}}') dx' = 0.$$

This proves our result. $\qquad\qquad\qquad\qquad\qquad\qquad\qquad\qquad\qquad\qquad\square$

Note that Theorem 6.2 and Proposition 5.19 highlight a basic property of ridge functions. Namely, $\mathcal{M}(\Omega)$ is dense in $C(\mathbb{R}^n)$, in the topology of uniform convergence on compact subsets, if and only if $\mathcal{M}(\Omega)$ explicitly contains all polynomials. In addition, while our choice of the topology of uniform convergence on compact subsets is not arbitrary, the above shows that density will hold for other linear spaces defined on $\mathbb{R}^n$ or subsets thereof, if algebraic polynomials are dense therein, i.e., the Weierstrass Approximation Theorem holds.

Let us consider two simple consequences of Theorems 6.2 and our analysis.

Proposition 6.3 *Assume* $\Omega = \Omega_1 \cup \Omega_2$. *Then* $\mathcal{M}(\Omega)$ *is dense in* $C(\mathbb{R}^n)$, *in the topology of uniform convergence on compact subsets, if and only if* $\mathcal{M}(\Omega_j)$ *is dense in* $C(\mathbb{R}^n)$, *in the topology of uniform convergence on compact subsets, for* $j = 1$ *and/or* $j = 2$.

Proof The proof in one direction is trivial. To prove the other direction, assume $\overline{\mathcal{M}(\Omega_j)} \neq C(\mathbb{R}^n)$ for $j = 1$ and $j = 2$. From Theorem 6.2 there exist non-trivial homogeneous polynomials q_j that vanish on Ω_j, $j = 1, 2$. Thus $q = q_1 q_2$ is a non-trivial homogeneous polynomial that vanishes on Ω, and $\overline{\mathcal{M}(\Omega)} \neq C(\mathbb{R}^n)$. $\square$

We also have the following.

Proposition 6.4 *If* Ω *contains only a finite number of distinct directions, then* $\overline{\mathcal{M}(\Omega)} \neq C(\mathbb{R}^n)$.

This follows from the fact that it is easy to construct a non-trivial homogeneous polynomial that vanishes on Ω.

6.2 Generalized Ridge Function Density

The above results are for the case of our usual ridge functions. What happens when we deal with generalized ridge functions? In fact, the situation is little changed.

For a given d, $1 \leq d \leq n - 1$, let Ω_d denote any subset of $d \times n$ real matrices, and set

$$\mathcal{M}(\Omega_d) := \mathrm{span}\{f(A\mathbf{x}) : A \in \Omega_d, \, f \in C(\mathbb{R}^d)\}. \tag{6.3}$$

In the above we vary over all $A \in \Omega_d$ and all $f \in C(\mathbb{R}^d)$, and take arbitrary linear combinations of the elements of this set.

As in the previous chapter we let $L(A)$ denote the span of the d rows of A. Paralleling Proposition 5.30 we have this next result.

Proposition 6.5 *Let* A *and* B *be two* $d \times n$ *matrices. Then*

$$\mathrm{span}\{f(A\mathbf{x}) : f \in C(\mathbb{R}^d)\} = \mathrm{span}\{g(B\mathbf{x}) : g \in C(\mathbb{R}^d)\}$$

if and only if $L(A) = L(B)$.

Proof The set $\mathrm{span}\{f(A\mathbf{x}) : f \in C(\mathbb{R}^d)\}$ is, see Proposition 5.30, the space of continuous functions that are constant on the hyperplanes parallel to the subspace

$$Z_A = \{\mathbf{x} : A\mathbf{x} = 0\},$$

and $L(A) = L(B)$ if and only if $Z_A = Z_B$. $\qquad\square$

With regards to density, the case $d > 1$ is not much different from the case $d = 1$. This is because, for any $d \times n$ matrix A, the two sets

$$\mathcal{M}(A) = \text{span}\{g(A\mathbf{x}) : g \in C(\mathbb{R}^d)\}$$

and

$$\mathcal{M}(L(A)) = \text{span}\{f(\mathbf{a} \cdot \mathbf{x}) : \mathbf{a} \in L(A),\, f \in C(\mathbb{R})\},$$

while not exactly the same, do have the same closure in the topology of uniform convergence on compact subsets, i.e., $\overline{\mathcal{M}(L(A))} = \overline{\mathcal{M}(A)}$. Recall that in Proposition 5.29 we proved that these two spaces were identical when restricting f and g to polynomials of the appropriate degree. The proof in this case is the same, with a very minor modification.

Proposition 6.6 *Let A be any $d \times n$ matrix, and $L(A)$ denote the span of the d rows of A. Then $\overline{\mathcal{M}(L(A))} = \overline{\mathcal{M}(A)}$ in the topology of uniform convergence on compact subsets of $\mathbb{R}^n$.*

Proof On the one hand we have that $\mathcal{M}(A) \subseteq \mathcal{M}(L(A))$ since for $\mathbf{a} \in L(A)$ we have $f(\mathbf{a} \cdot \mathbf{x}) = f(\mathbf{c} \cdot A\mathbf{x})$ for some $\mathbf{c} \in \mathbb{R}^d$. To prove the converse direction assume, without loss of generality, that rank $A = d$. Let D denote the $n \times n$ non-singular matrix such that $AD = C = (c_{ij})$, where C is the $d \times n$ matrix satisfying

$$c_{ij} = \delta_{ij}, \quad i = 1, \ldots, d,\, j = 1, \ldots, n.$$

For each vector $\mathbf{w} := (w_1, \ldots, w_d, 0, \ldots, 0)$ there exists an easily found $\mathbf{a} \in L(A)$ such that $\mathbf{w} = \mathbf{a}D$. We apply the change of variable $\mathbf{x} = D\mathbf{y}$.

On the basis of Theorem 6.2 every continuous function that is of the form $g(y_1, \ldots, y_d, 0, \ldots, 0)$ can be approximated arbitrarily well in our topology by linear combinations of ridge functions of the form $f(w_1 y_1 + \cdots + w_d y_d)$, as we vary over all $f \in C(\mathbb{R})$ and $\mathbf{w} \in \mathbb{R}^d$. And every ridge function of the form $f(w_1 y_1 + \cdots + w_d y_d)$ is in the set $\{f(\mathbf{a}D\mathbf{y}) : \mathbf{a} \in L(A)\}$. $\qquad\square$

For $\mathcal{M}(\Omega_d)$ as in (6.3), let

$$L(\Omega_d) := \bigcup_{A \in \Omega} L(A).$$

As a consequence of Theorem 6.2 and Proposition 6.6 we can now state the following.

Theorem 6.7 $\mathcal{M}(\Omega_d)$ *is dense in* $C(\mathbb{R}^n)$, *in the topology of uniform convergence on compact subsets, if and only if no non-trivial polynomial vanishes on* $L(\Omega_d)$.

Analogs of Propositions 6.3 and 6.4 also hold in this setting.

6.3 Density with Variable Directions

In Section 6.1 we considered the question of the density of the class of ridge functions of the form

$$\mathcal{M}(\Omega) = \text{span}\{f(\mathbf{a} \cdot \mathbf{x}) : \mathbf{a} \in \Omega, \ f \in C(\mathbb{R})\},$$

where we fixed the "direction" set Ω. In Section 6.2 we considered an analogous multivariate version of this same question. However, we can also consider density from a somewhat different perspective. This we do in this section. We state the result in the generalized ridge function setting.

As an example of a different type of density result, fix a positive integer k, and consider the following question. Is it possible to approximate all functions in $C(\mathbb{R}^n)$, in the topology of uniform convergence on compact subsets, by linear combinations of k generalized ridge functions of the form $f(A\mathbf{x})$, where k is fixed but we are free the choose the "directions" A, as well as the functions f? That is, for any given $G \in C(\mathbb{R}^n)$, compact set $K \subset \mathbb{R}^n$, and $\varepsilon > 0$, do there exist k $d \times n$ matrices $A^1, \ldots, A^k$ and k functions $f_1, \ldots, f_k$ in $C(\mathbb{R}^d)$ for which

$$\max_{\mathbf{x} \in K} \left| G(\mathbf{x}) - \sum_{i=1}^{k} f_i(A^i \mathbf{x}) \right| < \varepsilon?$$

As we shall see, the answer to this question is no. Moreover we will prove a more general theorem which includes this result as a special case.

Rather than consider one set Ω of fixed directions let us consider sets Ω_j, of $d \times n$ real matrices, where j varies over an arbitrary index set J. We ask the following question. What are conditions on the collection of sets $\{\Omega_j\}_{j \in J}$ such that for any given $G \in C(\mathbb{R}^n)$, compact set $K \subset \mathbb{R}^n$, and $\varepsilon > 0$, there exists an $F \in \mathcal{M}(\Omega_j)$, for some $j \in J$, such that

$$\|G - F\|_K = \max_{\mathbf{x} \in K} |G(\mathbf{x}) - F(\mathbf{x})| < \varepsilon?$$

If $\Omega_j = \Omega$ for all $j \in J$, then this is exactly the problem considered in the previous sections. If the $\{\Omega_j\}_{j \in J}$ is the totality of all sets with at most k directions, then this is the problem considered in the previous paragraph.

To explain the next result we introduce the following quantity. To each set Ω of $d \times n$ matrices we let $r(\Omega)$ denote the minimal degree of the non-trivial (homogeneous) polynomials that vanish on $L(\Omega)$. If no non-trivial homogeneous polynomial vanishes on $L(\Omega)$ we then set $r(\Omega) = \infty$. In this latter case we know from Theorem 6.7 of the previous section that the associated $\mathcal{M}(\Omega)$ is dense in $C(\mathbb{R}^n)$. If Ω contains only k distinct directions, then as is easily shown, $r(\Omega) \leq k$.

Associated with each Ω_j we have $\mathcal{M}(\Omega_j)$ as defined by (6.3). We will say that $\bigcup_{j \in J} \mathcal{M}(\Omega_j)$ *is dense in* $C(\mathbb{R}^n)$ if to each $G \in C(\mathbb{R}^n)$, compact set $K \subset \mathbb{R}^n$, and $\varepsilon > 0$, there exists an $F \in \mathcal{M}(\Omega_j)$, for some $j \in J$, such that

$$\|G - F\|_K = \max_{\mathbf{x} \in K} |G(\mathbf{x}) - F(\mathbf{x})| < \varepsilon.$$

This next result, from Kroó [1997], is a generalization of Theorem 6.2.

Theorem 6.8 *The set* $\bigcup_{j \in J} \mathcal{M}(\Omega_j)$ *is dense in* $C(\mathbb{R}^n)$, *in the above sense, if and only if*

$$\sup_{j \in J} r(\Omega_j) = \infty.$$

Proof Based on Proposition 6.6, it suffices to prove the result for $d = 1$, i.e., replace each $d \times n$ matrix A in (6.3) by $L(A)$. We use elements from the proof of Theorem 6.2 to prove this theorem.

One direction is elementary based on our previous results. We have from Proposition 5.19 that if $r(\Omega_j) = m$, then it follows that $\Pi_{m-1}^n \subset \mathcal{M}(\Omega_j)$. Thus, if $\sup_{j \in J} r(\Omega_j) = \infty$, then we have, as a consequence of the Weierstrass Approximation Theorem, that $\bigcup_{j \in J} \mathcal{M}(\Omega_j)$ is dense in $C(\mathbb{R}^n)$.

The converse direction is more detailed. Assume that

$$\sup_{j \in J} r(\Omega_j) \leq m,$$

for some finite m. Given any compact set $K \subset \mathbb{R}^n$ with non-empty interior we will prove the existence of an entire function G defined on $\mathbb{R}^n$ for which

$$\inf_{j \in J} \inf_{F \in \mathcal{M}(\Omega_j)} \|G - F\|_K > 0.$$

This proves the converse direction.

To this end, let B_m be any finite point set in $\mathbb{R}^n$ such that for every $h \in H_{2m}^n$, $h \neq 0$, we have

$$\max_{\mathbf{b} \in B_m} |h(\mathbf{b})| > 0,$$

i.e., maximizing over this point set B_m is a norm on H_{2m}^n. Since H_{2m}^n is a finite-dimensional subspace, such B_m abound. For any $h \in H_{2m}^n$, written as

$$h(\mathbf{x}) =: \sum_{|\mathbf{r}| = 2m} c_{\mathbf{r}} \mathbf{x}^{\mathbf{r}},$$

we have, by the equivalence of norms on finite-dimensional subspaces,

$$\sum_{|\mathbf{r}|=2m} |c_{\mathbf{r}}| \le b_1 \max_{\mathbf{b}\in B_m} |h(\mathbf{b})|$$

for some $b_1 > 0$.

Let K be any compact subset of $\mathbb{R}^n$, with non-empty interior, and let ϕ be any non-trivial non-negative $C^\infty(\mathbb{R}^n)$ function with $\operatorname{supp}\phi \subset \operatorname{int} K$. Given Ω, with $r(\Omega) \le m$, let $h \in H_m^n$ be any non-trivial homogeneous polynomial vanishing on $L(\Omega)$. Thus $h^2 \in H_{2m}^n$, h^2 is non-negative, and h^2 also vanishes on $L(\Omega)$. Normalize h so that

$$\max_{\mathbf{b}\in B_m} |h(\mathbf{b})| = 1,$$

and let

$$h^2(\mathbf{x}) =: \sum_{|\mathbf{r}|=2m} d_{\mathbf{r}}\mathbf{x}^{\mathbf{r}}.$$

As in the proof of Theorem 6.2 we define

$$\psi(\mathbf{x}) := h^2(D)\phi(\mathbf{x}) = \sum_{|\mathbf{r}|=2m} d_{\mathbf{r}} D^{\mathbf{r}}\phi(\mathbf{x}).$$

Note that $\psi \in C^\infty(\mathbb{R}^n)$, $\psi \ne 0$, $\operatorname{supp}\psi \subseteq \operatorname{supp}\phi \subset \operatorname{int} K$, and

$$\widehat{\psi} = i^{2m}\widehat{\phi}\, h^2,$$

where $\widehat{}$ denotes the Fourier transform. Furthermore, as verified in the proof of Theorem 6.2 we have

$$\int_{\mathbb{R}^n} \psi(\mathbf{x}) F(\mathbf{x}) d\mathbf{x} = 0 \tag{6.4}$$

for all $F \in \mathcal{M}(\Omega)$, i.e., the non-trivial linear functional defined by integrating against ψ annihilates $\mathcal{M}(\Omega)$.

Set

$$G(\mathbf{x}) := \sum_{\mathbf{b}\in B_m} e^{\mathbf{b}\cdot\mathbf{x}}.$$

Since $h^2 \in H_{2m}^n$ and $\phi, h^2 \ge 0$ we have

$$
\begin{aligned}
&\left| \int_{\mathbb{R}^n} \psi(\mathbf{x}) G(\mathbf{x}) d\mathbf{x} \right| = \left| \sum_{\mathbf{b}\in B_m} \int_{\mathbb{R}^n} \psi(\mathbf{x}) e^{\mathbf{b}\cdot\mathbf{x}} d\mathbf{x} \right| \\
=\ & (2\pi)^{n/2} \left| \sum_{\mathbf{b}\in B_m} \widehat{\psi}(i\mathbf{b}) \right| = (2\pi)^{n/2} \left| \sum_{\mathbf{b}\in B_m} h^2(\mathbf{b})\widehat{\phi}(i\mathbf{b}) \right| \\
=\ & \sum_{\mathbf{b}\in B_m} h^2(\mathbf{b}) \int_{\mathbb{R}^n} \phi(\mathbf{x}) e^{\mathbf{b}\cdot\mathbf{x}} d\mathbf{x} \ge b_2 \max_{\mathbf{b}\in B_m} |h^2(\mathbf{b})| = b_2,
\end{aligned}
$$

where

$$b_2 := \min_{\mathbf{b} \in B_m} \int_K \phi(\mathbf{x}) e^{\mathbf{b} \cdot \mathbf{x}} d\mathbf{x} > 0.$$

Note that this is a minimum since B_m is a finite point set, and it is strictly positive since ϕ is a non-trivial non-negative function. Thus,

$$\left| \int_{\mathbb{R}^n} \psi(\mathbf{x}) G(\mathbf{x}) d\mathbf{x} \right| \geq b_2.$$

On the other hand,

$$\|\psi\|_{L^1(\mathbb{R}^n)} = \int_{\mathbb{R}^n} |\psi(\mathbf{x})| d\mathbf{x} \leq b_3 \sum_{|\mathbf{r}|=2m} |d_\mathbf{r}| \leq b_3 b_1,$$

where

$$b_3 = \max_{|\mathbf{r}|=2m} \int_{\mathbb{R}^n} |D^\mathbf{r} \phi(\mathbf{x})| d\mathbf{x}.$$

Using (6.4) we have that for every $F \in \mathcal{M}(\Omega)$

$$b_2 \leq \left| \int_{\mathbb{R}^n} \psi(\mathbf{x}) G(\mathbf{x}) d\mathbf{x} \right| = \left| \int_{\mathbb{R}^n} \psi(\mathbf{x})(G(\mathbf{x}) - F(\mathbf{x})) d\mathbf{x} \right|$$

$$\leq \|G - F\|_K \|\psi\|_{L^1(\mathbb{R}^n)} \leq \|G - F\|_K b_3 b_1,$$

i.e.,

$$\|G - F\|_K \geq \frac{b_2}{b_3 b_1} > 0$$

for every $F \in \mathcal{M}(\Omega)$, where the b_1, b_2, and b_3 depend only upon m, n, ϕ and K, and are independent of Ω (and ψ). Thus

$$\inf_{j \in J} \inf_{F \in \mathcal{M}(\Omega_j)} \|G - F\|_K > 0,$$

which proves our result. □

6.4 Representation

In this section we consider the question of which functions $F \in C(\mathbb{R}^n)$ can be approximated by linear combinations of ridge function with given directions, without our necessarily having density. For ease of exposition we will present the results in the case $d = 1$ (the usual ridge functions). We know, from Proposition 6.6, how to generalize these results to the case $d > 1$.

As in Chapter 5, set

$$\mathcal{P}(\Omega) := \{p : p|_{L(\Omega)}, \ p \in \Pi^n = 0\},$$

and let

$$\mathcal{C}(\Omega) := \operatorname{span}\{p : q(D)p = 0 \text{ for all } q \in \mathcal{P}(\Omega), p \in \Pi^n\}.$$

Then we have the following generalization of Theorem 6.2.

Theorem 6.9 *In the topology of uniform convergence on compact subsets we have*
$$\overline{\mathcal{M}(\Omega)} = \overline{\mathcal{C}(\Omega)}.$$

Proof We first claim that $\overline{\mathcal{M}(\Omega)} \subseteq \overline{\mathcal{C}(\Omega)}$. From (1.2) it follows that if $\mathbf{a} \in \Omega$, then for all $q_k \in \mathcal{P}(\Omega) \cap H_k^n$ we have

$$q_k(D)(\mathbf{a} \cdot \mathbf{x})^\ell = 0$$

for all $\ell \in \mathbb{Z}_+$, and thus for all $q \in \mathcal{P}(\Omega)$ we have that

$$q(D)(\mathbf{a} \cdot \mathbf{x})^\ell = 0$$

for all $\ell \in \mathbb{Z}_+$. That is,

$$(\mathbf{a} \cdot \mathbf{x})^\ell \in \mathcal{C}(\Omega)$$

for all $\ell \in \mathbb{Z}_+$ and $\mathbf{a} \in \Omega$. From the Weierstrass Approximation Theorem it therefore follows that $f(\mathbf{a} \cdot \mathbf{x}) \in \overline{\mathcal{C}(\Omega)}$ for all $f \in C(\mathbb{R})$ and all $\mathbf{a} \in \Omega$, implying that $\overline{\mathcal{M}(\Omega)} \subseteq \overline{\mathcal{C}(\Omega)}$.

It remains to prove that $\overline{\mathcal{C}(\Omega)} \subseteq \overline{\mathcal{M}(\Omega)}$. Since $\overline{\mathcal{M}(\Omega)}$ and $\overline{\mathcal{C}(\Omega)}$ are closed linear subspaces of $C(\mathbb{R}^n)$ it suffices to prove that every continuous linear functional on $C(\mathbb{R}^n)$ that annihilates $\mathcal{M}(\Omega)$ also annihilates $\mathcal{C}(\Omega)$.

Each continuous linear functional ℓ on $C(\mathbb{R}^n)$ (in the topology of uniform convergence on compact subsets) has the representation

$$\ell(h) = \int_{\mathbb{R}^n} h(\mathbf{x}) d\mu(\mathbf{x}),$$

where μ is a Borel measure of finite total variation and compact support; see, for example, Edwards [1965], p. 203. Let $\widehat{\mu}$ denote the Fourier transform of μ, i.e.,

$$\widehat{\mu}(\boldsymbol{\xi}) := \frac{1}{(2\pi)^{n/2}} \int_{\mathbb{R}^n} e^{-i\boldsymbol{\xi} \cdot \mathbf{x}} d\mu(\mathbf{x}).$$

As is well-known, see, for example, Edwards [1965], p. 389, $\widehat{\mu}$ is an entire analytic function on $\mathbb{C}^n$. Furthermore, assuming ℓ annihilates $\mathcal{M}(\Omega)$, i.e.,

$$\int_{\mathbb{R}^n} f(\mathbf{a} \cdot \mathbf{x}) d\mu(\mathbf{x}) = 0$$

for all $\mathbf{a} \in \Omega$ and $f \in C(\mathbb{R})$, we have that $\widehat{\mu}$ vanishes on $L(\Omega)$. Set

$$\widehat{\mu}(\boldsymbol{\xi}) = \sum_{k=0}^{\infty} \widehat{\mu}_k(\boldsymbol{\xi})$$

where $\widehat{\mu}_k$ is the homogeneous polynomial of total degree k in the power series expansion of $\widehat{\mu}$. From the form of $L(\Omega)$ it follows that each $\widehat{\mu}_k$ vanishes on $L(\Omega)$. That is, $\widehat{\mu}_k \in \mathcal{P}(\Omega)$ for each $k \in \mathbb{Z}_+$.

Write

$$\widehat{\mu}_k(\boldsymbol{\xi}) = \sum_{|\mathbf{m}|=k} b_{\mathbf{m}} \boldsymbol{\xi}^{\mathbf{m}} ,$$

and note that for $\mathbf{m}$ satisfying $|\mathbf{m}| = k$ we have

$$\mathbf{m}! \, b_{\mathbf{m}} = D^{\mathbf{m}} \widehat{\mu}(\boldsymbol{\xi})\big|_{\boldsymbol{\xi}=0} = \frac{(-i)^k}{(2\pi)^{n/2}} \int_{\mathbb{R}^n} \mathbf{x}^{\mathbf{m}} d\mu(\mathbf{x}) .$$

For any $p_k \in H_k^n$ of the form

$$p_k(\mathbf{x}) := \sum_{|\mathbf{m}|=k} c_{\mathbf{m}} \mathbf{x}^{\mathbf{m}} ,$$

we therefore have from (1.4) that

$$\int_{\mathbb{R}^n} p_k(\mathbf{x}) \, d\mu(\mathbf{x}) = (2\pi)^{n/2} (-i)^{-k} \sum_{|\mathbf{m}|=k} \mathbf{m}! \, b_{\mathbf{m}} c_{\mathbf{m}} = (2\pi)^{n/2} (-i)^{-k} \widehat{\mu}_k(D) p_k .$$

Furthermore, as is easily verified,

$$\widehat{\mu}_k(D) p_\ell(\mathbf{x})\big|_{\mathbf{x}=0} = 0$$

if $\ell \neq k$. Thus if $p \in \Pi^n$, and

$$p := \sum_{\ell=0}^{N} p_\ell ,$$

where each p_ℓ is a homogeneous polynomial of total degree ℓ, then

$$\int_{\mathbb{R}^n} p(\mathbf{x}) \, d\mu(\mathbf{x}) = (2\pi)^{n/2} \sum_{k=0}^{N} (-i)^{-k} \widehat{\mu}_k(D) p(\mathbf{x})\big|_{\mathbf{x}=0} .$$

This formula together with the fact that $\widehat{\mu}_k \in \mathcal{P}(\Omega)$ for all k implies that for each $p \in \mathcal{C}(\Omega)$, i.e., $p \in \Pi^n$ satisfying $q(D)p = 0$ for all $q \in \mathcal{P}(\Omega)$, we have

$$\ell(p) = \int_{\mathbb{R}^n} p(\mathbf{x}) d\mu(\mathbf{x}) = 0 .$$

This proves that $\overline{\mathcal{C}(\Omega)} \subseteq \overline{\mathcal{M}(\Omega)}$. $\qquad \square$

This result, when Ω is a finite point set, and under some additional constraints, can be found in Vostrecov [1963]. We also recall from Chapter 5 (just after Remark 5.17) that the polynomials in the set $\mathcal{P}(\Omega)$ vanish on $L(\Omega)$ and form a *polynomial ideal*. As such, assuming $\mathcal{P}(\Omega)$ is composed of more than the identically zero polynomial, it has, by the Hilbert Basis Theorem, a finite number of generators. When $n = 2$ the situation is very much simpler. If Ω contains an infinite number of directions, then from Corollary 5.16 $\mathcal{P}(\Omega)$ is composed of only the zero polynomial, thus $\mathcal{M}(\Omega)$ contains all polynomials and $\overline{\mathcal{M}(\Omega)} = C(\mathbb{R}^2)$. When Ω contains a finite number of directions, then the generators of the polynomial ideal are easily determined. There is only one generator, and it is given by the unique (up to multiplication by a constant) homogeneous polynomial of minimal degree that vanishes on Ω. Thus we obtain the following.

Proposition 6.10 *If $n = 2$ and Ω contains an infinite number of pairwise linearly independent directions, then $\overline{\mathcal{M}(\Omega)} = C(\mathbb{R}^2)$. If Ω contains a finite number of pairwise linearly independent directions $\{\mathbf{a}^i := (a_1^i, a_2^i)\}_{i=1}^r$, then $F \in \overline{\mathcal{M}(\Omega)}$ if and only if*

$$\prod_{i=1}^{r} \left(a_2^i \frac{\partial}{\partial x_1} - a_1^i \frac{\partial}{\partial x_2} \right) F = 0,$$

where the derivatives are understood in the sense of distributions.

An additional consequence of the above Theorem 6.9 is the following result first proved in Vostrecov and Kreines [1962] by other methods.

Proposition 6.11 *For given $\mathbf{b} \in \mathbb{R}^n \setminus \{\mathbf{0}\}$, we have*

$$\text{span}\{g(\mathbf{b} \cdot \mathbf{x}) : g \in C(\mathbb{R})\} \subseteq \text{span}\{f(\mathbf{a} \cdot \mathbf{x}) : \mathbf{a} \in \Omega, \, f \in C(\mathbb{R})\}$$

if and only if all polynomials that vanish on $L(\Omega)$ also vanish at $\mathbf{b}$.

Proposition 6.10 has the following generalization. Consider a set Ω_{n-1} of $(n-1) \times n$ matrices of rank $n - 1$. Associated with each $A \in \Omega_{n-1}$ we have the $(n-1)$-dimensional subspace $L(A)$. As in Proposition 5.34 and its proof, to each such A there exists a $\mathbf{c}_A \in \mathbb{R}^n \setminus \{\mathbf{0}\}$, the normal to $L(A)$, such that $A\mathbf{c}_A = \mathbf{0}$. Set $q_A(\mathbf{x}) = \mathbf{c}_A \cdot \mathbf{x}$. Then q_A vanishes on $L(A)$ and is irreducible. If Ω_{n-1} contains an infinite number of distinct A, i.e., the $L(A)$ are distinct, then from Proposition 5.34 $\mathcal{M}(\Omega_{n-1})$ contains all polynomials and thus $\overline{\mathcal{M}(\Omega_{n-1})} = C(\mathbb{R}^n)$. When $\Omega_{n-1} = \{A^1, \ldots, A^r\}$, r finite, with the $L(A^i)$, $i = 1, \ldots, r$, distinct, the the generator of the polynomial ideal $\mathcal{P}(\Omega_{n-1})$ is given by

$$\prod_{i=1}^{r} q_{A^i}(\mathbf{x}).$$

Thus we obtain the following.

Proposition 6.12 *Let Ω_{n-1} be a set of $(n-1) \times n$ matrices of rank $n-1$. If there are an infinite number of distinct matrices, i.e., the associated $L(A)$ are distinct, then $\overline{\mathcal{M}(\Omega_{n-1})} = C(\mathbb{R}^n)$. If $\Omega_{n-1} = \{A^1, \ldots, A^r\}$ with associated distinct $L(A^i)$, $i = 1, \ldots, r$, then $F \in \overline{\mathcal{M}(\Omega_{n-1})}$ if and only if*

$$\prod_{i=1}^{r} q_{A^i}(D)F = 0,$$

where the derivatives are understood in the sense of distributions.

6.5 Ridgelet Density

In the first four sections of this chapter we considered various questions concerning the density of linear combinations of ridge functions as we varied over all possible functions f (see (6.1) and (6.3)), but restricted the direction set. What about the converse question? That is, can we in some way restrict the set of permissible functions?

Let σ be any fixed function defined on all of $\mathbb{R}$. Set

$$\Gamma := \mathbb{R}^n \times \mathbb{R} = \{\gamma := (\mathbf{a}, b) : \mathbf{a} \in \mathbb{R}^n, b \in \mathbb{R}\},$$

and for each $\gamma \in \Gamma$ let

$$\sigma_\gamma(\mathbf{x}) := \sigma(\mathbf{a} \cdot \mathbf{x} + b).$$

For a given σ, these $\{\sigma_\gamma\}_{\gamma \in \Gamma}$ are called the *ridgelets* generated by σ. Ridgelets generated by any σ are a subset of ridge functions.

In this section we ask how restrictive it is, from a density point of view, to consider linear combinations of ridgelets generated by a given σ, rather than linear combinations of all ridge functions.

Ridgelets were introduced in the late 1990s by Candès and Donoho in an attempt to provide for a constructive and stable method of ridge function approximation; see, for example, Candès [1998], [1999] and Candès and Donoho [1999]. We will discuss ridgelets again in Chapter 10. However, they already appeared prominently in the neural network literature in the 1980s and early 1990s in the *multilayer feedforward perceptron* (MLP) model. In that theory σ is termed an *activation function*.

To state the basic result, set

$$\mathcal{N}(\sigma) := \text{span}\{\sigma(\mathbf{a} \cdot \mathbf{x} + b) : \mathbf{a} \in \mathbb{R}^n, b \in \mathbb{R}\}.$$

From Leshno, Lin, Pinkus and Schoken [1993] we have the following. See also

Pinkus [1999], pp. 151–153, for a history of this result. It in fact transpires that the main ingredient in the proof can be essentially found in Schwartz [1944].

Theorem 6.13 *Let $\sigma \in C(\mathbb{R})$. Then $\mathcal{N}(\sigma)$ is dense in $C(\mathbb{R}^n)$, in the topology of uniform convergence on compact subsets, if and only if σ is not a polynomial.*

Proof If σ is a polynomial of degree m, then $\sigma(\mathbf{a} \cdot \mathbf{x} + b)$ is a polynomial of total degree at most m for every $\mathbf{a} \in \mathbb{R}^n$ and $b \in \mathbb{R}$. Thus $\mathcal{N}(\sigma) \subseteq \Pi_m^n$ and hence it is not dense in $C(\mathbb{R}^n)$.

Let

$$\mathcal{N}_1(\sigma) := \operatorname{span}\{\sigma(\lambda t + b) \; : \; \lambda, b \in \mathbb{R}\}.$$

If $\mathcal{N}_1(\sigma)$ is dense in $C(\mathbb{R})$, in the topology of uniform convergence on compact subsets of $\mathbb{R}$, then $\mathcal{N}(\sigma)$ is dense in $C(\mathbb{R}^n)$, in the topology of uniform convergence on compact subsets of $\mathbb{R}^n$. This is a simple consequence of the fact that ridge functions are dense in $C(\mathbb{R}^n)$, in the topology of uniform convergence on compact subsets.

That is, assume $\mathcal{N}_1(\sigma)$ is dense in $C(\mathbb{R})$. Consider any ridge function $f(\mathbf{a} \cdot \mathbf{x})$, where $f \in C(\mathbb{R})$ and $\mathbf{a} \in \mathbb{R}^n \backslash \{\mathbf{0}\}$. As f is in the closure of $\mathcal{N}_1(\sigma)$ it follows that $f(\mathbf{a} \cdot \mathbf{x})$ is in the closure of

$$\operatorname{span}\{\sigma(\lambda \, \mathbf{a} \cdot \mathbf{x} + b) \; : \; \lambda, b \in \mathbb{R}\},$$

which, in turn, is a subset of the closure of $\mathcal{N}(\sigma)$. As all ridge functions are in the closure of the linear space $\mathcal{N}(\sigma)$, it now follows from Theorem 6.2 that $\mathcal{N}(\sigma)$ is dense in $C(\mathbb{R}^n)$, in the topology of uniform convergence on compact subsets of $\mathbb{R}^n$.

Assume $\mathcal{N}_1(\sigma)$ is not dense in $C(\mathbb{R})$, in the topology of uniform convergence on compact subsets of $\mathbb{R}$. There then exists a non-trivial linear functional on $C(\mathbb{R})$ that annihilates $\mathcal{N}_1(\sigma)$. Each linear functional ℓ on $C(\mathbb{R})$ (in the above topology) has the representation

$$\ell(h) = \int_{\mathbb{R}} h(t) \, d\mu(t),$$

where μ is a Borel measure of finite total variation and compact support, see, for example, Edwards [1965], p. 203. Thus

$$\int_{\mathbb{R}} \sigma(\lambda t + b) \, d\mu(t) = 0,$$

for all $\lambda, b \in \mathbb{R}$. Let $\phi \in C_0^\infty(\mathbb{R})$, i.e., ϕ is in C^∞ and has compact support. Set

$$F_\phi(t) := \int_{\mathbb{R}} \sigma(t + s) \phi(s) \, ds.$$

The function F_ϕ is well-defined and is in $C^\infty(\mathbb{R})$. Furthermore

$$\int_\mathbb{R} F_\phi(\lambda t + b)\, d\mu(t) = \int_\mathbb{R} \left[\int_\mathbb{R} \sigma(\lambda t + b + s)\phi(s)\, ds \right] d\mu(t)$$

$$= \int_\mathbb{R} \left[\int_\mathbb{R} \sigma(\lambda t + b + s)\, d\mu(t) \right] \phi(s)\, ds = 0.$$

As this is true for every linear functional that annihilates $\mathcal{N}_1(\sigma)$, it therefore follows that $F_\phi(\lambda t + b)$ is in the closure of $\mathcal{N}_1(\sigma)$ for each $\lambda, b \in \mathbb{R}$ and all $\phi \in C_0^\infty(\mathbb{R})$. But this then implies, by taking differences and limits, that

$$\left. \frac{d^m}{d\lambda^m} F_\phi(\lambda t + b) \right|_{\lambda=0} = t^m F_\phi^{(m)}(b)$$

is in the closure of $\mathcal{N}_1(\sigma)$ for each $m \in \mathbb{Z}_+$ and $b \in \mathbb{R}$. If $\mathcal{N}_1(\sigma)$ is not dense in $C(\mathbb{R})$, then by the Weierstrass Approximation Theorem t^m is not in the closure of $\mathcal{N}_1(\sigma)$ for some m. By the above it therefore follows that we must have $F_\phi^{(m)}(b) = 0$ for all $b \in \mathbb{R}$ and all $\phi \in C_0^\infty(\mathbb{R})$. That is, F_ϕ is a polynomial of degree at most $m - 1$ for each $\phi \in C_0^\infty(\mathbb{R})$.

As is well-known, there exist sequences of $\phi_n \in C_0^\infty(\mathbb{R})$ for which the associated F_{ϕ_n} converge uniformly to σ as $n \to \infty$ on any compact subset of $\mathbb{R}$. We can, for example, take what are called *mollifiers*, see, for example, Adams [1975], p. 29. As each F_{ϕ_n} is a polynomial of degree at most $m - 1$ it therefore follows that σ is a polynomial of degree at most $m - 1$. $\square$

Based on the above proof and Theorem 6.2 we immediately obtain the following result.

Proposition 6.14 *Let* $\sigma \in C(\mathbb{R})$, *and* Ω *be any subset of* $\mathbb{R}^n$ *such that no nontrivial homogeneous polynomial vanishes thereon. Then*

$$\text{span}\{\sigma(\lambda \, \mathbf{a} \cdot \mathbf{x} + b) : \mathbf{a} \in \Omega, \ \lambda, b \in \mathbb{R}\}$$

is dense in $C(\mathbb{R}^n)$, *in the topology of uniform convergence on compact subsets, if and only if* σ *is not a polynomial.*

Numerous other refinements of these results may be found in Pinkus [1999], §3. For example, we have the following where the parameter λ is absent.

Proposition 6.15 *Let* $\sigma \in C(\mathbb{R}) \cap L^p(\mathbb{R})$ *for some* $p \in [1, \infty)$, *and let* S^{n-1} *denote the unit sphere in* $\mathbb{R}^n$. *Then*

$$\text{span}\{\sigma(\mathbf{a} \cdot \mathbf{x} + b) : \mathbf{a} \in S^{n-1}, \ b \in \mathbb{R}\}$$

is dense in $C(\mathbb{R}^n)$.

Even the continuity of the σ is not critical. The above three results also hold when σ is bounded and Riemann integrable on each finite interval of $\mathbb{R}$.

7

Closure

Let K be a bounded set in $\mathbb{R}^n$. For a given $d \times n$ matrix A, set

$$\mathcal{M}(A; K) := \{f(A\mathbf{x}) : \mathbf{x} \in K, \text{all possible } f : \mathbb{R}^d \to \mathbb{R}\},$$

and for each $p \in [1, \infty]$, let

$$L^p(A; K) := \mathcal{M}(A; K) \cap L^p(K).$$

That is, $L^p(A; K)$ is the set of functions in $L^p(K)$ of the form $f(A\mathbf{x})$. In this chapter we consider the question of the closure of

$$\sum_{i=1}^{r} L^p(A^i; K) \tag{7.1}$$

in $L^p(K)$. This question has been studied with an eye to computerized tomography. It is relevant to the problem of the existence of best approximations, see Chapter 8, and also to the rate of convergence of some best approximation algorithms, see Chapter 9. It is also an interesting question in and of itself. In Section 7.1 we present various theorems providing conditions for when closure holds, and in Section 7.2 some examples of when closure is lacking. Some additional results are given in Section 7.3. In Section 7.4 we consider the case of $C(K)$. For two directions closure in $C(K)$ is equivalent to certain geometric properties of the set K and the directions. However, nothing seems to be known in the case of more than two directions. This chapter is more of a survey as the theorems are presented without proofs. The inclusion of their proofs would lead us too far afield.

7.1 General Closure Results in L^p

The space $L^p(K)$, $p \in [1, \infty)$, is the standard linear space of functions G defined on $K \subseteq \mathbb{R}^n$ for which $|G|^p$ is Lebesgue integrable, and with norm given by

$$\|G\|_{L^p(K)} := \left(\int_K |G(\mathbf{x})|^p d\mathbf{x} \right)^{1/p}.$$

$L^\infty(K)$ is the space of Lebesgue measurable, essentially bounded functions G, with norm

$$\|G\|_{L^\infty(K)} := \operatorname*{ess\,sup}_{\mathbf{x} \in K} |G(\mathbf{x})|.$$

The first general results on closure seem to be due to Hamaker and Solmon [1978] who considered the case where $p = 2$, K is a disk with center at the origin in $\mathbb{R}^2$, and $\{\mathbf{a}^i\}_{i=1}^r$ is a set of pairwise linearly independent vectors in $\mathbb{R}^2$. They proved closure in this setting. These results were then generalized by Falconer [1979]. He provided conditions on K under which we have closure of the sum (7.1) in L^p, for $p \in [2, \infty]$, where $\{\mathbf{a}^i\}_{i=1}^r$ is a set of pairwise linearly independent vectors in $\mathbb{R}^n$.

Falconer considers ridge functions of the standard form $f(\mathbf{a} \cdot \mathbf{x})$, i.e., $d = 1$. He assumes that K is a non-empty compact convex subset of $\mathbb{R}^n$ and ∂K, i.e., the boundary of K, has a certain smoothness with respect to the pairwise linearly independent directions $\{\mathbf{a}^i\}_{i=1}^r$. Namely, set

$$\pi_i := \{\mathbf{x} : \mathbf{a}^i \cdot \mathbf{x} = 0\}, \qquad i = 1, \ldots, r.$$

Falconer defines K to be *normal* (with respect to the $\{\mathbf{a}^i\}_{i=1}^r$) if for each $\mathbf{x} \in \partial K$ we have that for at most one $i \in \{1, \ldots, r\}$ the $(n-1)$-dimensional Lebesgue measure of $(\mathbf{x} + \pi_i) \cap \overline{K}$ is zero. If ∂K is smooth, i.e., C^1, then this is not a restriction. His result is the following.

Theorem 7.1 *Assume that K is a normal compact convex subset of $\mathbb{R}^n$, and $\{\mathbf{a}^i\}_{i=1}^r$ is a set pairwise linearly independent vectors. Then for all $p \in [2, \infty]$ we have that*

$$\sum_{i=1}^r L^p(\mathbf{a}^i; K)$$

is closed in $L^p(K)$.

The result of Petersen, Smith and Solmon [1979] is somewhat more general, although it does not contain the previous result in its entirety. Their result makes use of what are called Lipschitz graph domains. These are defined as follows.

Definition 7.2 A *Lipschitz graph domain* in $\mathbb{R}^n$ is a bounded open set K such that for each point $\mathbf{x}^* \in \partial K$ there is a number $s > 0$ such that in some coordinate system

$$K \cap B(\mathbf{x}^*, s) = \{\mathbf{x} : x_n > h(\mathbf{x}')\} \cap B(\mathbf{x}^*, s),$$

where $B(\mathbf{x}^*, s)$ is the ball centered at $\mathbf{x}^*$ with radius s, $\mathbf{x} := (\mathbf{x}', x_n)$, and h is a Lipschitz function on $\mathbb{R}^{n-1}$.

Alternatively, a Lipschitz graph domain is a bounded open set satisfying a suitable cone condition.

Their result applies to generalized ridge functions. Let A^i be $d \times n$ matrices that we assume are of rank d. Recall, from Chapters 2 and 3, that when discussing the smoothness of each component inherited from the sum, and uniqueness of the representation, we imposed the condition that the $2d$ rows of A^i and A^j be linearly independent for all $i \neq j$. Under this assumption Petersen, Smith and Solmon [1979] obtain the following result.

Theorem 7.3 *Let K be a bounded open set of $\mathbb{R}^n$ satisfying $K_0 \subset K \subset \overline{K}_0$, where K_0 is a finite union of Lipschitz graph domains. Assume the A^i are $d \times n$ matrices of rank d, and the $2d$ rows of A^i and A^j are linearly independent for all $i \neq j$. Then for all $p \in (1, \infty)$ we have that*

$$\sum_{i=1}^{r} L^p(A^i; K)$$

is closed in $L^p(K)$.

Remark 7.4 In Petersen, Smith and Solmon [1979] these conditions on the matrices $\{A^i\}_{i=1}^r$ are stated differently. They demand that each A^i be of rank d, and $\ker A^i + \ker A^j = \mathbb{R}^n$ for all $i \neq j$. These are equivalent conditions. If A^i has rank d for each i, then from the formula for the dimension of the sum of subspaces we have for all $i \neq j$

$$\dim(\ker A^i + \ker A^j) = \dim(\ker A^i) + \dim(\ker A^j) - \dim(\ker A^i \cap \ker A^j)$$

$$= 2n - 2d - \dim(\ker A^i \cap \ker A^j).$$

Furthermore, the $2d$ rows of A^i and A^j are linearly independent if and only if

$$\dim(\ker A^i \cap \ker A^j) = n - 2d.$$

From these two formulae the equivalence easily follows.

Boman [1984] considered the cases $n = 2$ and $n = 3$ in greater detail. For $n = 2$ he proved the following result.

Theorem 7.5 *Assume K is an open bounded connected subset of $\mathbb{R}^2$, the boundary of K is of class C^1, and the $\{\mathbf{a}^i\}_{i=1}^r$ are pairwise linearly independent vectors. Let $1 \le p \le \infty$. Then*

$$\sum_{i=1}^r L^p(\mathbf{a}^i; K)$$

is closed in $L^p(K)$.

The smoothness of the boundary is not strictly necessary. This result can be generalized as follows. An open *wedge* in $\mathbb{R}^2$ is an open connected set bounded by two intersecting straight lines. The open set K in $\mathbb{R}^2$ is said to satisfy an *interior wedge condition* at $\mathbf{y} \in \partial K$ if there exists a neighbourhood V of $\mathbf{y}$ and an open wedge Γ with vertex at $\mathbf{y}$ such that $V \cap \Gamma \subseteq K$.

Theorem 7.6 *Assume K is an open bounded connected subset of $\mathbb{R}^2$ which satisfies the interior wedge condition at every point of ∂K, and the $\{\mathbf{a}^i\}_{i=1}^r$ are pairwise linearly independent vectors. Then, for every $p \in [1, \infty)$,*

$$\sum_{i=1}^r L^p(\mathbf{a}^i; K)$$

is closed in $L^p(K)$.

Note that this result is stated only for $n = 2$ and, contrary to Theorem 7.5, is not claimed to hold for $p = \infty$.

7.2 Counterexamples

Further insights into these results are provided by examples where closure does not hold. The following three examples are from Boman [1984].

Example 7.1 In this example we have $n = 2$, $p = \infty$, and K is an open bounded, convex subset of $\mathbb{R}^2$. However the boundary of K, while it is both Lipschitz and satisfies the interior wedge condition, is neither C^1 nor is it normal with respect to $\mathbf{a}^1$ and $\mathbf{a}^2$. We show that

$$L^\infty(\mathbf{a}^1; K) + L^\infty(\mathbf{a}^2; K)$$

need **not** be closed (see Theorems 7.1, 7.5 and 7.6). This same example is valid when replacing L^∞ by C.

Let $\mathbf{a}^1 = (1,0)$, $\mathbf{a}^2 = (0,1)$, and

$$K := \{\mathbf{x} = (x_1, x_2) : x_2 < x_1 < 2x_2, \; 0 < x_2 < 1/4\}.$$

Set

$$G(\mathbf{x}) := \ln|\ln x_1| - \ln|\ln x_2|.$$

Note that $G \in L^\infty(K)$ since $G(\mathbf{x})$ tends to 0 as $\mathbf{x}$ tends to $\mathbf{0}$ from within K. In fact, G is also continuous on K and can be extended to be continuous on $\overline{K}$.

We first show that G is not in $L^\infty(\mathbf{a}^1; K) + L^\infty(\mathbf{a}^2; K)$. Recall that representations of a sum of two ridge functions are unique up to constants, see Chapter 3. Moreover $f(x_i) := \ln|\ln x_i| + c$ is not in $L^\infty(\mathbf{a}^i; K)$ for any constant c. Thus $G \notin L^\infty(\mathbf{a}^1; K) + L^\infty(\mathbf{a}^2; K)$.

We claim, however, that G is in the closure of this set. That is,

$$G \in \overline{L^\infty(\mathbf{a}^1; K) + L^\infty(\mathbf{a}^2; K)}.$$

To verify this fact we construct a sequence of functions that uniformly approximate G from $L^\infty(\mathbf{a}^1; K) + L^\infty(\mathbf{a}^2; K)$. To this end, for $\varepsilon > 0$, set

$$f_\varepsilon(t) := \ln|\ln(\max\{t, \varepsilon\})|.$$

We claim that

$$f_\varepsilon(x_1) - f_\varepsilon(x_2)$$

converges uniformly to G as $\varepsilon \to 0$.

To see this, set

$$G_\varepsilon(\mathbf{x}) := \begin{cases} G(\mathbf{x}), & \varepsilon \le x_2 \\ 0, & x_2 < \varepsilon, \end{cases}$$

in K. Note that G_ε converges uniformly to G on K as $\varepsilon \to 0$. However $G_\varepsilon(\mathbf{x})$ is not quite equal to $f_\varepsilon(x_1) - f_\varepsilon(x_2)$. Define

$$h_\varepsilon(\mathbf{x}) := \begin{cases} \ln|\ln x_1| - \ln|\ln \varepsilon|, & x_2 < \varepsilon < x_1 \\ 0, & \text{otherwise,} \end{cases}$$

in K. It is easily seen that $h_\varepsilon(\mathbf{x})$ converges uniformly to 0 on K as $\varepsilon \to 0$, and

$$G_\varepsilon(\mathbf{x}) + h_\varepsilon(\mathbf{x}) = f_\varepsilon(x_1) - f_\varepsilon(x_2).$$

Thus it follows that $f_\varepsilon(x_1) - f_\varepsilon(x_2)$ converges uniformly to G on K as $\varepsilon \to 0$.

Example 7.2 In this example we consider the case where $p \in [1, \infty)$ and K is a domain with a cusp. Thus K is neither convex nor a finite union of Lipschitz graph domains. We again show, by example, that we do not have closure of

$$L^p(\mathbf{a}^1; K) + L^p(\mathbf{a}^2; K).$$

Let $\mathbf{a}^1 = (1,0)$, $\mathbf{a}^2 = (0,1)$, and

$$K := \{\mathbf{x} = (x_1, x_2) : x_1 < x_2 < x_1 + x_1^\beta, \ 0 < x_1 < 1\},$$

with any fixed $\beta > 1$. Set

$$G(\mathbf{x}) := \frac{1}{x_1^\alpha} - \frac{1}{x_2^\alpha},$$

where $\alpha := (1 + 3\beta)/2p$. We will prove that $G \notin L^p(\mathbf{a}^1; K) + L^p(\mathbf{a}^2; K)$, $G \in L^p(K)$, and

$$G \in \overline{L^p(\mathbf{a}^1; K) + L^p(\mathbf{a}^2; K)}.$$

To prove that G is not in $L^p(\mathbf{a}^1; K) + L^p(\mathbf{a}^2; K)$ we again recall that representations of a sum of two ridge functions are unique up to constants. Moreover $f(x_1) = x_1^{-\alpha} + c$ is not in $L^p(K)$ for any constant c since

$$\int_0^1 \left(\int_{x_1}^{x_1 + x_1^\beta} \frac{1}{x_1^{\alpha p}} \, dx_2 \right) dx_1 = \int_0^1 x_1^{\beta - \alpha p} \, dx_1$$

and this integral does not converge as by our choice of α,

$$\beta - \alpha p + 1 = \beta - \frac{1 + 3\beta}{2} + 1 = \frac{1 - \beta}{2} < 0.$$

However, we do have $G \in L^p(K)$. To see this, note that

$$\int_K |G(\mathbf{x})|^p \, d\mathbf{x} = \int_0^1 \int_{x_1}^{x_1 + x_1^\beta} \left(\frac{1}{x_1^\alpha} - \frac{1}{x_2^\alpha} \right)^p dx_2 \, dx_1$$

$$= \int_0^1 x_1^{-\alpha p} \int_{x_1}^{x_1 + x_1^\beta} \left(1 - \left(\frac{x_1}{x_2} \right)^\alpha \right)^p dx_2 \, dx_1.$$

Substituting $t := (x_2/x_1) - 1$ we get

$$= \int_0^1 x_1^{1 - \alpha p} \int_0^{x_1^{\beta - 1}} \left(1 - (1 + t)^{-\alpha} \right)^p dt \, dx_1.$$

The inner integral is of order $(x_1^{\beta - 1})^{p+1}$ as $x_1 \to 0$. Thus the condition for the convergence of the double integral is

$$1 - \alpha p + (\beta - 1)(p + 1) + 1 > 0$$

which, since $\alpha = (1 + 3\beta)/2p$, simplifies to

$$(\beta - 1)(p - (1/2)) > 0.$$

As $\beta > 1$ and $p \geq 1$, we have $G \in L^p(K)$.

We claim that

$$G \in \overline{L^p(\mathbf{a}^1; K) + L^p(\mathbf{a}^2; K)}.$$

For $\varepsilon > 0$, small, set

$$f_\varepsilon(t) := \begin{cases} \frac{1}{t^\alpha}, & \varepsilon \le t \\ 0, & 0 < t < \varepsilon. \end{cases}$$

We claim that

$$f_\varepsilon(x_1) - f_\varepsilon(x_2)$$

converges in $L^p(K)$ to G as $\varepsilon \to 0$. To see this, let

$$G_\varepsilon(\mathbf{x}) := \begin{cases} G(\mathbf{x}), & \varepsilon \le x_1 \\ 0, & 0 < x_1 < \varepsilon. \end{cases}$$

Thus G_ε converges in $L^p(K)$ to G as $\varepsilon \to 0$. Set

$$h_\varepsilon(\mathbf{x}) := G_\varepsilon(\mathbf{x}) - f_\varepsilon(x_1) + f_\varepsilon(x_2).$$

It suffices to show that h_ε converges in $L^p(K)$ to 0 as $\varepsilon \to 0$. Now $h_\varepsilon(\mathbf{x})$ identically vanishes for $\varepsilon \le x_1 < x_2$ and $x_1 < x_2 < \varepsilon$. For $x_1 < \varepsilon \le x_2$ we have

$$h_\varepsilon(\mathbf{x}) := \frac{1}{x_2^\alpha}.$$

Set

$$D_\varepsilon := \{\mathbf{x} \in K : x_1 < \varepsilon \le x_2\}.$$

D_ε is bounded by a right-angle triangle of height ε^β and base less than ε^β. Thus the area of D_ε is less than $\varepsilon^{2\beta}$. Moreover, since $\varepsilon \le x_2$ on D_ε we have

$$h_\varepsilon(\mathbf{x}) = \frac{1}{x_2^\alpha} \le \varepsilon^{-\alpha}$$

on D_ε. We therefore obtain

$$\|h_\varepsilon\|_{L^p(K)} \le \varepsilon^{-\alpha} \varepsilon^{2\beta/p} = \varepsilon^{(-\alpha p + 2\beta)/p}.$$

As $\alpha = (1 + 3\beta)/2p$, we have

$$-\alpha p + 2\beta = -\frac{1 + 3\beta}{2} + 2\beta = \frac{\beta - 1}{2} > 0,$$

and thus $\|h_\varepsilon\|_{L^p(K)} \to 0$ as $\varepsilon \to 0$.

Example 7.3 In this example we construct a bounded strictly convex set $K \subset \mathbb{R}^3$, with C^∞ boundary, and two 2×3 matrices A^1 and A^2. We show that for each $p \in [1, \infty]$, the set

$$L^p(A^1; K) + L^p(A^2; K)$$

is not closed in $L^p(K)$. Here the rows of A^1 and A^2 are linearly dependent, see Theorem 7.3.

Set

$$A^1 = \begin{pmatrix} 0 & 1 & 0 \\ 0 & 0 & 1 \end{pmatrix}, \qquad A^2 = \begin{pmatrix} 1 & 0 & 0 \\ 0 & 0 & 1 \end{pmatrix}.$$

Thus we are dealing with functions of the form

$$f_1(x_2, x_3) + f_2(x_1, x_3).$$

Set $\psi(x_1, x_2) := (x_1 - x_2)^2 + (x_1 + x_2)^4$, and let K be any bounded and strictly convex domain with C^∞ boundary such that $\mathbf{0} \in \partial K$. Assume, in addition, that ∂K, near the origin, has the form $x_3 = \psi(x_1, x_2)$ and K lies in the region $x_3 > \psi(x_1, x_2)$. For $\lambda > 0$, set

$$K_\lambda := K \cap \{x_3 = \lambda\}.$$

It may be verified that for $\lambda > 0$ small, K_λ is an ellipse-like domain with length and width of order $\lambda^{1/4}$ and $\lambda^{1/2}$, respectively.

Assume $p \in [1, \infty)$, $\alpha = (3 + 14/p)/8$, and set

$$G(\mathbf{x}) := \frac{x_2 - x_1}{x_3^\alpha}.$$

We claim that $G \in L^p(K)$ and $G \in \overline{L^p(A^1; K) + L^p(A^2; K)}$. However, we also show that $G \notin L^p(A^1; K) + L^p(A^2; K)$.

To prove that $G \in L^p(K)$ note that, up to a constant C,

$$
\begin{aligned}
\|G\|^p_{L^p(K)} &= \int_{K_\lambda} \int_\lambda |G|^p \\
&\leq C \int_0^1 \lambda^{-\alpha p} \lambda^{1/4} \int_0^{\sqrt{\lambda}} t^p \, dt \, d\lambda \\
&\leq \frac{C}{p+1} \int_0^1 \lambda^{-\alpha p + 1/4 + (p+1)/2} \, d\lambda \\
&= \int_0^1 \lambda^{-1 + p/8} \, d\lambda < \infty,
\end{aligned}
$$

since $-\alpha p + 1/4 + (p+1)/2 = -(3p + 14)/8 + 1/4 + (p+1)/2 = -1 + p/8$.

To see that $G \in \overline{L^p(A^1; K) + L^p(A^2; K)}$ set, for $\varepsilon > 0$,

$$G_\varepsilon(\mathbf{x}) := \begin{cases} G(\mathbf{x}), & \varepsilon < x_3 \\ 0, & x_3 \leq \varepsilon. \end{cases}$$

Then G_ε tends to G in $L^p(K)$ as $\varepsilon \to 0$. Furthermore, set

$$f_\varepsilon(y, z) := \begin{cases} y/z^\alpha, & \varepsilon < z \\ 0, & z \leq \varepsilon. \end{cases}$$

Then

$$G_\varepsilon(\mathbf{x}) = f_\varepsilon(x_2, x_3) - f_\varepsilon(x_1, x_3)$$

on K, and $f_\varepsilon(x_j, x_3) \in L^p(A^j; K)$, $j = 1, 2$. That is, for each $\varepsilon > 0$, $G_\varepsilon \in L^p(A^1; K) + L^p(A^2; K)$.

It remains to prove that $G \notin L^p(A^1; K) + L^p(A^2; K)$. It may be shown that any function in $L^p(A^1; K) + L^p(A^2; K)$ is unique, up to functions in x_3. That is, if G is in $L^p(A^1; K) + L^p(A^2; K)$, then it is of the form

$$\left(\frac{x_2}{x_3^\alpha} + g(x_3) \right) - \left(\frac{x_1}{x_3^\alpha} + g(x_3) \right)$$

for some $g \in L^p(K)$ that depends upon x_3, and is independent of x_2 and x_1. Thus, it suffices to prove that $f(x_2, x_3) = x_2/x_3^\alpha$ is not in $L^p(K)$. For some constants $C, \delta > 0$,

$$\begin{aligned} \int_K |f(x_2, x_3)|^p \, d\mathbf{x} & \geq C \int_0^\delta \lambda^{-\alpha p} \lambda^{1/2} \int_0^{\lambda^{1/4}} t^p \, dt \, d\lambda \\ & = \frac{C}{p+1} \int_0^\delta \lambda^{-\alpha p + 1/2 + (p+1)/4} \, d\lambda \\ & = \frac{C}{p+1} \int_0^\delta \lambda^{-1 - p/8} \, d\lambda = \infty, \end{aligned}$$

since $-\alpha p + 1/2 + (p+1)/4 = -(3p+14)/8 + 1/2 + (p+1)/4 = -1 - p/8$. In the case $p = \infty$ we set $\alpha = 3/8$ and define G as above.

7.3 More General Closure Results

In the above Example 7.3 one of the principal curvatures of ∂K vanishes near the origin. This is critical as from Boman [1984], Theorem 1.8, we have the following.

Theorem 7.7 *Let K be an open bounded convex subset of $\mathbb{R}^3$ whose boundary is of class C^2, and assume that both principal curvatures of ∂K are non-zero at* *every point. Let A^i be 2×3 matrices of rank 2, $i = 1, \ldots, r$, and $p \in [1, \infty]$. Then*

$$\sum_{i=1}^{r} L^p(A^i; K)$$

is closed in $L^p(K)$.

A different proof of this theorem also appears in Svensson [1989].

A totally different approach to this closure problem is via properties of continuous projection maps from $L^p(K)$ onto $L^p(\mathbf{a}; K)$. The following is a specific case of what may be found in Lang [1984].

Theorem 7.8 *Let K be an open, bounded subset of $\mathbb{R}^n$. Let P_i be a continuous projection map from $L^p(K)$ onto $L^p(\mathbf{a}^i; K)$, $i = 1, \ldots, r$. If $P_i P_j$ is compact for all $i \neq j$, then*

$$\sum_{i=1}^{r} L^p(\mathbf{a}^i; K)$$

is closed in $L^p(K)$.

There are other closure results for ridge functions to be found in the literature. See, for example, the paper by Vostrecov and Ignat'eva [1967].

Why do we care about closure? As mathematicians we always want to understand what properties hold, what properties do not hold, and why. But there is a more prosaic reason. Namely, closure of a subspace is necessary, and sometimes also sufficient, for the existence of a best approximation to each element of the space from the subspace. For subspaces of $L^p(K)$, $p \in (1, \infty)$, it is both necessary and sufficient, see Chapter 8. There is also another reason why closure is a desirable property. It has to do with the rate of convergence of an algorithm for calculating the best approximation. We will discuss this in Chapter 9.

Remark 7.9 An additional example of the lack of closure is something we have already noted in Chapter 5. Consider $\mathbb{R}^2$ and

$$\mathcal{M}(\mathbf{a}^1, \mathbf{a}^2) := \{ f_1(\mathbf{a}^1 \cdot \mathbf{x}) + f_2(\mathbf{a}^2 \cdot \mathbf{x}) : f_1, f_2 : \mathbb{R} \to \mathbb{R} \},$$

for any directions $\mathbf{a}^1$ and $\mathbf{a}^2$. We claim that the set

$$\mathcal{M}_2 := \bigcup_{\mathbf{a}^1, \mathbf{a}^2} \mathcal{M}(\mathbf{a}^1, \mathbf{a}^2),$$

is not closed. We have $x_1 x_2^2 \in \overline{\mathcal{M}_2}$ because

$$\lim_{\varepsilon \to 0} \frac{(\varepsilon x_1 + x_2)^3 - x_2^3}{3\varepsilon} = x_1 x_2^2,$$

and $(\varepsilon x_1 + x_2)^3$ and x_2^3 are ridge functions. On the other hand $x_1 x_2^2 \notin \mathcal{M}(\mathbf{a}^1, \mathbf{a}^2)$ for any linearly independent $\mathbf{a}^1$ and $\mathbf{a}^2$. This follows from the results of Section 2.1 for only two directions and Proposition 5.26. In fact, it may be deduced, see Proposition 6.10, that the closure of $\mathcal{M}_2$ will include all functions F satisfying

$$\left(b \frac{\partial}{\partial x_1} - a \frac{\partial}{\partial x_2} \right) \left(d \frac{\partial}{\partial x_1} - c \frac{\partial}{\partial x_2} \right) F(x, y) = 0,$$

where the derivatives are understood in the sense of distributions, and where (a, b) and (c, d) are non-zero vectors, that need not be linearly independent. The function $x_1 x_2^2$ satisfies

$$\frac{\partial^2}{\partial x_1^2} \left(x_1 x_2^2 \right) = 0.$$

7.4 Closure in $C(K)$

Let K be a compact subset of $\mathbb{R}^n$. We consider the space $C(K)$ of real-valued continuous functions defined on K, equipped with the uniform norm. For any $d \times n$ matrix A, set

$$C(A; K) := \{ f(A\mathbf{x}) : \mathbf{x} \in K, f \in C(\mathbb{R}^d) \},$$

(f need only be continuous on $\{A\mathbf{x} : \mathbf{x} \in K\}$). Equivalently

$$C(A; K) = \mathcal{M}(A; K) \cap C(K).$$

Conditions for the closure of the sum

$$\sum_{i=1}^{r} C(A^i; K)$$

in $C(K)$ seem rather complicated. For each A the space $C(A; K)$ is closed. But this does not imply that the sum of such spaces is also closed. In what follows we present criteria for when

$$C(A; K) + C(B; K)$$

is closed in $C(K)$. In fact these results are not limited to ridge functions. They apply to any two subalgebras of $C(K)$. Note that each $C(A; K)$ is an algebra. There are, to the best of our knowledge, no known results in the case of more than two summands.

There are two known characterizations for when the sum of two subalgebras of $C(K)$ are closed. The first is due to Marshall and O'Farrell [1979]. The second characterization, both easier to state and slightly more general, and built upon the first, is due to Medvedev [1991]. We state, but do not prove, this latter result as it pertains to generalized ridge functions. These results may also be found in Khavinson [1997].

We start with the definition of a path. In Chapters 8, 11 and 12 we will return to a consideration of paths as they are relevant to questions of characterization of best approximations and interpolation by ridge functions.

Definition 7.10 The sequence of points $\{\mathbf{v}^i\}_{i=1}^p$ is a *path* with respect to the $d \times n$ matrices A and B if either

$$A\mathbf{v}^{2i-1} = A\mathbf{v}^{2i}, \qquad i = 1, \ldots, \lfloor p/2 \rfloor \tag{7.2}$$

and

$$B\mathbf{v}^{2i} = B\mathbf{v}^{2i+1}, \qquad i = 1, \ldots, \lfloor (p-1)/2 \rfloor, \tag{7.3}$$

or (7.2) and (7.3) hold with A and B interchanged.

That is, we have $A\mathbf{v}^1 = A\mathbf{v}^2$, $B\mathbf{v}^2 = B\mathbf{v}^3$, $A\mathbf{v}^3 = A\mathbf{v}^4$, etc., or the same with A and B interchanged. The number p, $p \geq 2$, is said to be the *length* of the path. A path with respect to A and B is said to be *irreducible* if there is no path of smaller length with the same starting and ending point.

From Medvedev [1991], we have the following.

Theorem 7.11 *The sum*

$$C(A; K) + C(B; K)$$

is closed in $C(K)$ if and only if the lengths of all irreducible paths with respect to A and B in K are uniformly bounded.

Example 7.4 In Example 7.1 we considered the directions $\mathbf{a}^1 = (1, 0)$, $\mathbf{a}^2 = (0, 1)$, where the closure of the set therein is

$$K := \{\mathbf{x} = (x_1, x_2) : x_2 \leq x_1 \leq 2x_2, \, 0 \leq x_2 \leq 1/4\}.$$

It is very easily seen that the lengths of the irreducible paths in K cannot be uniformly bounded, as paths have edges parallel to the axes. For example, the length of the path from $(c, c) \in K$ to $(1/4, 1/4) \in K$ tends to infinity as $c \downarrow 0$. The same result holds in Example 7.2. Thus $C(\mathbf{a}^1; K) + C(\mathbf{a}^2; K)$ is not closed in $C(K)$.

The same idea as that in Example 7.4 can be used to deduce the following example that may be found in Ismailov [2009].

Example 7.5 Let $\mathbf{a} = (1,1)$, $\mathbf{b} = (2,1)$, and $K := [0,1]^2$. The following, for each p, is an irreducible path of length $2p + 2$.

$$\{(1,0), (0,1), (1/2,0), (0,1/2), (1/4,0), (0,1/4), \ldots, (1/2^p, 0), (0, 1/2^p)\}.$$

Thus $C(\mathbf{a}; K) + C(\mathbf{b}; K)$ is not closed in $C(K)$.

Some geometries imply that the lengths of all irreducible paths are uniformly bounded. For example, we have the following.

Example 7.6 Given $d \times n$ matrices A and B, we will say that K has a *cross-section* with respect to A if there exists some $c \in \mathbb{R}$ such that to each $\mathbf{x} \in K$ there exists a vector

$$\mathbf{y} \in K \cap \{\mathbf{w} : A\mathbf{w} = c\}$$

such that $B\mathbf{x} = B\mathbf{y}$. Note that the cross-section depends upon A, B and K. For example, if we are given two perpendicular directions $\mathbf{a}$ and $\mathbf{b}$, then any ball in $\mathbb{R}^n$ has a cross-section with respect to either direction. If K has a cross-section then there are no irreducible paths in K of length greater than 4, and thus we have closure of $C(A; K) + C(B; K)$.

Another example of non-closure with K denumerable may be found in Example 12.1 of Chapter 12. (The K therein is not compact. It is the union of two straight lines. However, just truncate the lines with the intersection point within K.) Additional examples of when we have closure in this setting may be found in Ismailov [2009].

Remark 7.12 Note that $\sum_{i=1}^{r} C(A^i; K)$ is not necessarily the same as

$$\mathcal{M}(A^1, \ldots, A^r) \cap C(K),$$

i.e., the set of functions in $\mathcal{M}(A^1, \ldots, A^r)$ that are continuous on K. This latter set may be significantly larger than $\sum_{i=1}^{r} C(A^i; K)$. This same comment holds with respect to the $L^p(A^i; K)$.

Question: Can you find some (any) general conditions implying that the space $\sum_{i=1}^{r} C(A^i; K)$ is closed when $r > 2$?

8

Existence and Characterization of Best Approximations

In this chapter we study the question of the existence and characterization of best approximations from the space of linear combinations of ridge functions with a finite number of directions. That is, from the space given by the restriction of

$$\mathcal{M}(A^1, \ldots, A^r) := \left\{ \sum_{i=1}^{r} f_i(A^i \mathbf{x}) : f_i : \mathbb{R}^d \to \mathbb{R}, \ i = l, \ldots, r \right\} \quad (8.1)$$

to a domain $K \subseteq \mathbb{R}^n$, and to where all the $f_i(A^i \mathbf{x})$ lie in an appropriate normed linear space. These normed linear spaces will be $X = L^p(K)$, $p \in (1, \infty)$, and $X = C(K)$.

Section 8.1 contains some general results regarding existence and characterization of a best approximation from a linear subspace. In Section 8.2 we consider the space $L^p(K)$ for $p \in (1, \infty)$, and highlight the case $p = 2$, while Section 8.3 contains a few simple examples of that theory. In Section 8.4 we look at $C(K)$ where, unfortunately, we only have results when approximating from linear combination of ridge functions with two directions. Very little seems to be known about these questions in other normed linear spaces.

8.1 General Results

In approximation theory, a set M in a normed linear space X is said to be an *existence* set (sometimes called a proximinal set) if to each $G \in X$ there exists at least one best approximation to G from M. That is, to each $G \in X$ there exists an $F^* \in M$ satisfying

$$\|G - F^*\| = \inf_{F \in M} \|G - F\|.$$

A necessary condition for M to be an existence set is that it be closed. But closure, in general, is insufficient to guarantee existence.

Closed convex subsets of finite-dimensional subspaces are existence sets. But linear combinations of ridge functions of the form (8.1) are not finite-dimensional, unless K is very restricted. However, closed convex sets of a uniformly convex Banach space are existence sets. We recall that a normed linear space X is said to be *uniformly convex* if to each $\varepsilon > 0$ there exists a $\delta > 0$ such that whenever $f, g \in X$ satisfy $\|f\| = \|g\| = 1$ and $\|(f + g)/2\| > 1 - \delta$, then $\|f - g\| < \varepsilon$. In addition, if M is a convex set in a uniformly convex normed linear space X, then there is at most one best approximation from M to any $G \in X$. That is, a best approximation, if it exists, is unique. (For a proof of these facts see, for example, Cheney [1966], p. 22.) We will consider the spaces $X = L^p(K), p \in (1, \infty)$, and $X = C(K)$. The spaces $L^p(K)$, for $p \in (1, \infty)$, are uniformly convex. Thus, for such spaces, and if M is a linear subspace, then closure is equivalent to existence, and a best approximation, if it exists, is unique.

We are interested in characterizing best approximations, if they exist. One general characterization result is the following. If X is a normed linear space and M is a linear subspace of X, then as a consequence of the Hahn–Banach Theorem we have that $F^* \in M$ is a best approximation to $G \in X \backslash \overline{M}$ from M if and only if there exists a linear functional $\ell \in X^*$ (X^* is the continuous dual to X) with the following properties.

(a) $\|\ell\|_{X^*} = 1$.
(b) $\ell(G - F^*) = \|G - F^*\|$.
(c) $\ell(F) = 0$ for all $F \in M$.

Translating the above to the spaces $L^p(K), p \in (1, \infty)$, and $C(K)$, K compact, we obtain these next classic results.

Theorem 8.1 *Let M be a linear subspace of $L^p(K), p \in (1, \infty)$. Let $G \in L^p(K)$. Then $F^* \in M$ is the best approximation to G from M if and only if*

$$\int_K |G(\mathbf{x}) - F^*(\mathbf{x})|^{p-1} \operatorname{sgn}(G(\mathbf{x}) - F^*(\mathbf{x})) F(\mathbf{x})\, d\mathbf{x} = 0$$

for all $F \in M$, where

$$\operatorname{sgn}(G(\mathbf{x}) - F^*(\mathbf{x})) := \begin{cases} 1, & G(\mathbf{x}) - F^*(\mathbf{x}) > 0 \\ 0, & G(\mathbf{x}) - F^*(\mathbf{x}) = 0 \\ -1, & G(\mathbf{x}) - F^*(\mathbf{x}) < 0. \end{cases}$$

Theorem 8.2 *Let M be a linear subspace of $C(K)$, K compact. Let $G \in C(K)$. Then $F^* \in M$ is a best approximation to G from M if and only if*

$$\inf_{\mathbf{x} \in J(G - F^*)} [G(\mathbf{x}) - F^*(\mathbf{x})] F(\mathbf{x}) \le 0$$

for all $F \in M$, where

$$J(G - F^*) := \{\mathbf{x} : |G(\mathbf{x}) - F^*(\mathbf{x})| = \|G - F^*\|\}.$$

8.2 $L^p(K)$, $p \in (1, \infty)$

As in Chapter 7, let

$$L^p(A; K) := \mathcal{M}(A; K) \cap L^p(K).$$

We also assume that K has finite Lebesgue measure. We are interested in approximating from the linear subspace

$$\sum_{i=1}^{r} L^p(A^i; K),$$

where we assume that the A^i are $d \times n$ matrices. From the results of Section 8.1, if this subspace is closed then it is an existence set. Furthermore a best approximation from this subspace, if it exists, is unique. With regards to characterization, the specific ridge function form of this subspace implies the following.

Theorem 8.3 *Assume $p \in (1, \infty)$, and $G \in L^p(K)$. Then*

$$F^*(\mathbf{x}) = \sum_{i=1}^{r} f_i^*(A^i \mathbf{x})$$

is the best approximation to $G \in L^p(K)$ from $\sum_{i=1}^{r} L^p(A^i; K)$ if and only if

$$\int_{K \cap \{A^j \mathbf{x} = \mathbf{c}\}} |G(\mathbf{x}) - F^*(\mathbf{x})|^{p-1} \operatorname{sgn}(G(\mathbf{x}) - F^*(\mathbf{x})) \, d\sigma(\mathbf{x}) = 0, \qquad (8.2)$$

a.e. $\mathbf{c} \in \mathbb{R}^d$, $j = 1, \ldots, r$, where $d\sigma(\mathbf{x})$ is the natural hyperplane measure.

Proof From Theorem 8.1 we have the characterization of the best approximation F^* from $\sum_{i=1}^{r} L^p(A^i; K)$ to G. That is, $F^*(\mathbf{x}) = \sum_{i=1}^{r} f_i^*(A^i \mathbf{x})$ is the best approximation to $G \in L^p(K)$ from $\sum_{i=1}^{r} L^p(A^i; K)$ if and only if

$$\int_{K} |G(\mathbf{x}) - F^*(\mathbf{x})|^{p-1} \operatorname{sgn}(G(\mathbf{x}) - F^*(\mathbf{x})) \sum_{j=1}^{r} f_j(A^j \mathbf{x}) \, d\mathbf{x} = 0$$

for all f_j such that $f_j(A^j \mathbf{x}) \in L^p(A^j; K)$. By linearity this is the same as demanding that

$$\int_{K} |G(\mathbf{x}) - F^*(\mathbf{x})|^{p-1} \operatorname{sgn}(G(\mathbf{x}) - F^*(\mathbf{x})) f(A^j \mathbf{x}) \, d\mathbf{x} = 0$$

for all f such that $f(A^j\mathbf{x}) \in L^p(A^j; K)$ and all $j = 1, \ldots, r$. Since this must hold for all such f, it follows that this, in turn, is equivalent to (8.2). $\qquad\square$

Recall that while (8.2) uniquely determines $F^*(\mathbf{x}) = \sum_{i=1}^r f_i^*(A^i\mathbf{x})$ on K a.e., it does not uniquely define the f_i^*, $i = 1, \ldots, r$.

The case $p = 2$ is especially interesting and also æsthetically pleasing. As $|f|\operatorname{sgn} f = f$, (8.2) reduces to the fact that $F^*(\mathbf{x})$ is the unique best $L^2(K)$ approximation to G from $\sum_{i=1}^r L^2(A^i; K)$ if and only if

$$\int_{K \cap \{A^j\mathbf{x}=\mathbf{c}\}} G(\mathbf{x}) - F^*(\mathbf{x}) \, d\sigma(\mathbf{x}) = 0, \tag{8.3}$$

a.e. $\mathbf{c} \in \mathbb{R}^d$, $j = 1, \ldots, r$. What exactly does this tell us about F^*? What we now explain is essentially to be found in Section 2 of Logan and Shepp [1975], although they only consider the case where K is the unit ball in $\mathbb{R}^2$, and the $\{\mathbf{a}^j\}_{j=1}^r$ are equally spaced directions. (In this case they are also able to "calculate" F^*.)

The function F^* has three important properties that we state in a formal theorem.

Theorem 8.4 *Assume that F^* is the unique best $L^2(K)$ approximation to G from the space $\sum_{i=1}^r L^2(A^i; K)$. Then*

(i)

$$\int_{K \cap \{A^j\mathbf{x}=\mathbf{c}\}} G(\mathbf{x}) \, d\sigma(\mathbf{x}) = \int_{K \cap \{A^j\mathbf{x}=\mathbf{c}\}} F^*(\mathbf{x}) \, d\sigma(\mathbf{x}), \tag{8.4}$$

a.e. $\mathbf{c} \in \mathbb{R}^d$, $j = 1, \ldots, r$. Furthermore, F^* is the unique function in $\sum_{i=1}^r L^2(A^i; K)$ satisfying (8.4).

(ii) For all $H \in L^2(K)$ satisfying (8.4) we have

$$\|H\|_{L^2(K)} \geq \|F^*\|_{L^2(K)}$$

with equality if and only if $H = F^*$.

(iii) For all $H \in L^2(K)$ satisfying (8.4) we have

$$\|H - \overline{H}\|_{L^2(K)} \geq \|F^* - \overline{F^*}\|_{L^2(K)},$$

where $\overline{H}$ ($= \overline{F^*}$) is the average of H over K, and equality holds if and only if $H = F^*$.

Proof Equation (8.4) is simply a rewrite of (8.3). We have that F^* has the same "projections" as G along the hyperplanes $K \cap \{A^j\mathbf{x} = \mathbf{c}\}$, a.e. $\mathbf{c} \in \mathbb{R}^d$, $j = 1, \ldots, r$. In fact, from the above analysis, a function from $\sum_{i=1}^r L^2(A^i; K)$ has the same "projections" as G along the hyperplanes $K \cap \{A^j\mathbf{x} = \mathbf{c}\}$, a.e. $\mathbf{c} \in \mathbb{R}^d$, $j = 1, \ldots, r$, i.e., satisfies (8.4), if and only if it is the unique best $L^2(K)$

approximation to G from $\sum_{i=1}^{r} L^2(A^i; K)$. From the uniqueness of the best approximation it follows that there is at most one function in $\sum_{i=1}^{r} L^2(A^i; K)$ with these "projections".

The second property states that among the functions in $L^2(K)$ with the same "projections" as G along the hyperplanes $K \cap \{A^j \mathbf{x} = \mathbf{c}\}$, a.e. $\mathbf{c} \in \mathbb{R}^d$, $j = 1, \ldots, r$, our F^* is the unique one of minimal $L^2(K)$ norm. This is an immediate consequence of the fact that the norm of a best approximant from a linear subspace of a Hilbert space always has norm less than or equal to the element being approximated. For if F^* is the best approximation from a linear subspace to G in a Hilbert space, then the orthogonality conditions characterizing best approximations imply

$$\|G - F^*\|_{L^2(K)}^2 = \|G\|_{L^2(K)}^2 - \|F^*\|_{L^2(K)}^2$$

so that $\|G\|_{L^2(K)} \geq \|F^*\|_{L^2(K)}$, with equality if and only if $G = F^*$. As such, if $H \in L^2(K)$ is a function that satisfies (8.4), then (from (8.3) or (8.4)) F^* is also the unique best $L^2(K)$ approximation to H from $\sum_{i=1}^{r} L^2(A^i; K)$, and therefore $\|H\|_{L^2(K)} \geq \|F^*\|_{L^2(K)}$ with equality if and only if $H = F^*$.

The third property is that from the set of all functions H in $L^2(K)$ with the same "projections" as G along the hyperplanes $K \cap \{A^j \mathbf{x} = \mathbf{c}\}$, a.e. $\mathbf{c} \in \mathbb{R}^d$, $j = 1, \ldots, r$, the function F^* also attains the unique minimum in

$$\min \|H - \overline{H}\|_{L^2(K)},$$

with $\overline{H}$ being the average of H over K, i.e.,

$$\overline{H} := \frac{1}{\nu(K)} \int_K H(\mathbf{x}) \, d\mathbf{x},$$

where $\nu(K)$ is the Lebesgue measure of K. To prove this inequality we first note that $\overline{H}$ is identical for all functions in $L^2(K)$ with the same "projections" as G along the hyperplanes $K \cap \{A^j \mathbf{x} = \mathbf{c}\}$, a.e. $\mathbf{c} \in \mathbb{R}^d$, $j = 1, \ldots, r$. This follows from the fact that, for any $j \in \{1, \ldots, r\}$,

$$
\begin{aligned}
\overline{H} &= \frac{1}{\nu(K)} \int_K H \, d\mathbf{x} = \frac{1}{\nu(K)} \int_{\mathbb{R}^d} \left(\int_{K \cap \{A^j \mathbf{x} = \mathbf{c}\}} H(\mathbf{x}) \, d\sigma(\mathbf{x}) \right) d\mathbf{c} \\
&= \frac{1}{\nu(K)} \int_{\mathbb{R}^d} \left(\int_{K \cap \{A^j \mathbf{x} = \mathbf{c}\}} G(\mathbf{x}) \, d\sigma(\mathbf{x}) \right) d\mathbf{c} = \overline{G}.
\end{aligned}
$$

In addition,

$$
\begin{aligned}
\|H - \overline{H}\|_{L^2(K)}^2 &= \|H\|_{L^2(K)}^2 - 2\overline{H} \int_K H(\mathbf{x}) \, d\mathbf{x} + \nu(K)\overline{H}^2 \\
&= \|H\|_{L^2(K)}^2 - \nu(K)\overline{H}^2.
\end{aligned}
$$

Thus from (ii), and since $\overline{H} = \overline{G} = \overline{F^*}$, we have

$$\|H - \overline{H}\|^2_{L^2(K)} = \|H\|^2_{L^2(K)} - \nu(K)\overline{H}^2$$

$$\geq \|F^*\|^2_{L^2(K)} - \nu(K)\overline{F^*}^2 = \|F^* - \overline{F^*}\|_{L^2(K)},$$

with equality if and only if $H = F^*$. $\qquad\qquad\qquad\qquad\qquad\qquad\qquad$ $\square$

Theorem 8.4 is a basic result in the theory of computerized tomography as it was developed in the late 1970s and in the 1980s.

8.3 Examples

Let us consider some simple examples where we apply Theorems 8.3 and 8.4.

Example 8.1 Let $p \in (1, \infty)$ and $r = 1$. This example is of importance as certain approximation algorithms will be based on repeated iterations of this case. The characterization (8.2) in the case $r = 1$ reduces to the fact that $f^*(A\mathbf{x})$ is the best approximation to $G \in L^p(K)$ from $L^p(A; K)$ if and only if

$$\int_{K \cap \{A\mathbf{x}=\mathbf{c}\}} |G(\mathbf{x}) - f^*(A\mathbf{x})|^{p-1} \, \text{sgn} \, (G(\mathbf{x}) - f^*(A\mathbf{x})) \, d\sigma(\mathbf{x}) = 0,$$

a.e. $\mathbf{c} \in \mathbb{R}^d$, i.e.,

$$\int_{K \cap \{A\mathbf{x}=\mathbf{c}\}} |G(\mathbf{x}) - f^*(\mathbf{c})|^{p-1} \, \text{sgn} \, (G(\mathbf{x}) - f^*(\mathbf{c})) \, d\sigma(\mathbf{x}) = 0, \qquad (8.5)$$

a.e. $\mathbf{c} \in \mathbb{R}^d$. In other words, $f^*(\mathbf{c})$ is the unique constant that best approximates G on the set $K \cap \{A\mathbf{x} = \mathbf{c}\}$ in the associated norm. Note that for each $p \in (1, \infty)$

$$\|G - a\|_{L^p(K \cap \{A\mathbf{x}=\mathbf{c}\})}$$

is a strictly convex function of the constant a and, as such, its unique minimum (the value $f^*(\mathbf{c})$) is "relatively" easily calculated. In the case $p = 2$ we simply have

$$\int_{K \cap \{A\mathbf{x}=\mathbf{c}\}} G(\mathbf{x}) \, d\sigma(\mathbf{x}) = \mu(\mathbf{c})f^*(\mathbf{c}),$$

a.e. $\mathbf{c} \in \mathbb{R}^d$, where

$$\mu(\mathbf{c}) := \int_{K \cap \{A\mathbf{x}=\mathbf{c}\}} d\sigma(\mathbf{x}).$$

This uniquely defines f^* for all $\mathbf{c}$ with $\mu(\mathbf{c}) > 0$.

Example 8.2 Let $p = 2$, and $I = [0, 1]$, $I^n = [0, 1]^n$, denote the unit interval and n-dimensional unit cube, respectively. Consider the problem of explicitly finding the best $L^2(I^n)$ approximation to $G \in L^2(I^n)$ from

$$\left\{ \sum_{i=1}^{r} f_i(x_i) : f_i \in L^2(I), 1 \leq r \leq n \right\},$$

i.e., we are considering ridge functions with directions $\mathbf{a}^i = \mathbf{e}^i$, $i = 1, \ldots, r$, where $\mathbf{e}^i$ is the ith unit vector. Let $I^{n-1}(j; \lambda)$ denote the restriction of the cube to $x_j = \lambda$, i.e., $I^n \cap \{x_j = \lambda\}$. The characterization (8.4) then reduces to

$$\int_{I^{n-1}(j;\lambda)} G(\mathbf{x}) \, d\mathbf{x} = \int_{I^{n-1}(j;\lambda)} \sum_{i=1}^{r} f_i^*(x_i) \, d\mathbf{x},$$

a.e. $\lambda \in [0, 1]$ and $j = 1, \ldots, r$. Set

$$\overline{G} := \int_{I^n} G(\mathbf{x}) \, d\mathbf{x}$$

and

$$g_j(\lambda) := \int_{I^{n-1}(j;\lambda)} G(x_1, \ldots, x_{j-1}, \lambda, x_{j+1}, \ldots, x_n) \, d\mathbf{x},$$

for $\lambda \in [0, 1]$, $j = 1, \ldots, r$. Then a best $L^2(I^n)$ approximation to $G \in L^2(I^n)$ from

$$\left\{ \sum_{i=1}^{r} f_i(x_i) : f_i \in L^2(I), 1 \leq r \leq n \right\}$$

is given by setting

$$f_i^*(x_i) := g_i(x_i) + c_i,$$

where the c_i are arbitrary constants satisfying

$$\sum_{i=1}^{r} c_i = -(r - 1)\overline{G}.$$

That is,

$$\sum_{i=1}^{r} f_i^*(x_i) = \sum_{i=1}^{r} g_i(x_i) - (r - 1)\overline{G}.$$

To verify this claim, first note that

$$\int_0^1 f_i^*(x_i) \, dx_i = \overline{G} + c_i.$$

Thus

$$
\int_{I^{n-1}(j;\lambda)} G(\mathbf{x}) - \sum_{i=1}^{r} f_i^*(x_i) \, d\mathbf{x} \;=\; g_j(\lambda) - \sum_{\substack{i=1 \\ i\neq j}}^{r} \int_0^1 f_i^*(x_i) \, dx_i - f_j^*(\lambda)
$$

$$
=\; f_j^*(\lambda) - c_j - \sum_{\substack{i=1 \\ i\neq j}}^{r} (\overline{G} + c_i) - f_j^*(\lambda)
$$

$$
=\; 0,
$$

which is (8.4). In fact, since the $\{e^i\}_{i=1}^r$ are linearly independent, it follows that the f_i^*, $i = 1, \ldots, r$, are necessarily explicitly of the above form.

Example 8.2 may be easily generalized to considering best approximations in $L^2(I^n)$ from

$$
\left\{ \sum_{i=1}^{r} f_i(x_{j_1^i}, \ldots, x_{j_k^i}) : f_i \in L^2(I^k), i = 1, \ldots, r \right\},
$$

where the $\{j_1^i, \ldots, j_k^i\}$, $i = 1, \ldots, r$, are disjoint subsets of $\{1, \ldots, n\}$. That is, each $\ell \in \{1, \ldots, n\}$ appears in at most one of the sets $\{j_1^i, \ldots, j_k^i\}$, $i = 1, \ldots, r$.

Example 8.3 The previous example can also be generalized as follows. Fix $r \in \{1, \ldots, n\}$, and let $I_i \subseteq \mathbb{R}$ be bounded sets of positive Lebesgue measure γ_i, $i = 1, \ldots, r$. For $r > n$ let K_{n-r} be a bounded set of positive Lebesgue measure γ_K in $\mathbb{R}^{n-r}$. (If $r = n$ we have no K_{n-r}.)

Consider the set

$$
K := I_1 \times \cdots I_r \times K_{n-r} \subset \mathbb{R}^n,
$$

which is of Lebesgue measure $\gamma = \gamma_1 \cdots \gamma_r \gamma_K$. We are interested in the problem of finding the best $L^2(K)$ approximation to $G \in L^2(K)$ from

$$
\left\{ \sum_{i=1}^{r} f_i(x_i) : f_i \in L^2(I_i), i = 1, \ldots, r \right\}.
$$

The characterization (8.4) in this case may be written as

$$
\int_{K(j;\lambda)} G(\mathbf{x}) \, d\mathbf{x} = \int_{K(j;\lambda)} \sum_{i=1}^{r} f_i^*(x_i) \, d\mathbf{x},
$$

$\lambda \in I_j$, $j = 1, \ldots, r$, where $K(j; \lambda) = K \cap \{x_j = \lambda\}$. Set

$$
\overline{G} := \int_K G(\mathbf{x}) \, d\mathbf{x}
$$

and

$$f_i^*(\lambda) := \frac{\gamma_i}{\gamma} \int_{K(i;\lambda)} G(x_1, \ldots, x_{i-1}, \lambda, x_{i+1}, \ldots, x_n) \, d\mathbf{x} + c_i,$$

for $\lambda \in I_i$, where the c_i are arbitrary constants satisfying

$$\sum_{i=1}^{r} c_i = \frac{-(r-1)\overline{G}}{\gamma}.$$

Note that

$$\int_{I_i} f_i^*(x_i) \, dx_i = \frac{\gamma_i}{\gamma} \overline{G} + \gamma_i c_i.$$

Thus for each $\lambda \in I_j$, $j = 1, \ldots, r$,

$$\int_{K(j;\lambda)} \left(G(\mathbf{x}) - \sum_{i=1}^{r} f_i^*(x_i) \right) d\mathbf{x}$$

$$= \left(\frac{\gamma}{\gamma_j} f_j^*(\lambda) - \frac{\gamma}{\gamma_j} c_j \right) - \sum_{i=1}^{r} \int_{K(j;\lambda)} f_i^*(x_i) \, d\mathbf{x}$$

$$= \left(\frac{\gamma}{\gamma_j} f_j^*(\lambda) - \frac{\gamma}{\gamma_j} c_j \right) - \frac{\gamma}{\gamma_j} f_j^*(\lambda) - \sum_{\substack{i=1 \\ i \neq j}}^{r} \frac{\gamma}{\gamma_j \gamma_i} \int_{I_i} f_i^*(x_i) \, dx_i$$

$$= -\frac{\gamma}{\gamma_j} c_j - \sum_{\substack{i=1 \\ i \neq j}}^{r} \frac{\gamma}{\gamma_j \gamma_i} \left(\frac{\gamma_i}{\gamma} \overline{G} + \gamma_i c_i \right)$$

$$= -\frac{\gamma}{\gamma_j} \left(\sum_{i=1}^{r} c_i + \frac{(r-1)\overline{G}}{\gamma} \right) = 0,$$

which is (8.4).

Example 8.3 can be further generalized, by a non-singular linear transformation, to ridge functions with directions $\mathbf{a}^i$, $i = 1, \ldots, r$, where the domain is such that each $\mathbf{a}^i \cdot \mathbf{x}$ varies over a fixed set in $\mathbb{R}$, $i = 1, \ldots, r$. Note, however, that the domains for which the above hold are very restrictive and depend on the directions. This example and its elementary generalizations may be found in Mordashev [1969], see Khavinson [1997], pp. 163–164, and Ismailov [2007a].

8.4 $C(K)$

We recall that $C(K)$ denotes the space of real-valued continuous functions on a compact set K in $\mathbb{R}^n$, equipped with the uniform norm. We also recall from

Chapter 7 that, for any $d \times n$ matrix A,

$$C(A; K) := \{f(A\mathbf{x}) : \mathbf{x} \in K, f \in C(\mathbb{R}^d)\}.$$

Since the closure of

$$\sum_{i=1}^{r} C(A^i; K)$$

in $C(K)$ is only understood in the case $r = 2$, it is hardly surprising that nothing is known about when $\sum_{i=1}^{r} C(A^i; K)$ is an existence set for $r > 2$. In the case $r = 2$ some sufficient results may be found in Ismailov [2009]. It is conjectured therein that the conditions for closure and existence are equivalent in the case $r = 2$.

Regarding the characterization of a best approximation in this setting, we only have results for $r = 2$, and even these do not cover all cases. The following is taken from Ismailov [2007b] and Ismailov [2014].

In Definition 7.10 we defined a path. We will here need the concept of a closed path, also to be used in Chapters 11 and 12.

Definition 8.5 The sequence of points $\{\mathbf{v}^i\}_{i=1}^{p}$ is a *closed path* with respect to the distinct directions A and B if $p = 2q$, and for some permutation of the $\{\mathbf{v}^i\}_{i=1}^{2q}$ (which we assume to be as given) we have

$$A\mathbf{v}^{2j-1} = A\mathbf{v}^{2j}, \qquad j = 1, \ldots, q,$$

and

$$B\mathbf{v}^{2j} = B\mathbf{v}^{2j+1}, \qquad j = 1, \ldots, q,$$

where we set $\mathbf{v}^{2q+1} := \mathbf{v}^1$.

That is, a closed path is a path that circles back upon itself. We also use the following terminology.

Definition 8.6 A sequence of distinct points $\{\mathbf{v}^i\}_{i=1}^{p}$ in K, p may be finite or infinite, is said to be *extremal* for $G \in C(K)$ if $G(\mathbf{v}^i) = \varepsilon(-1)^i \|G\|$, $i = 1, \ldots, p$, for some $\varepsilon \in \{-1, 1\}$.

These two concepts are used in the following result, which is based on Ismailov [2007b] and Ismailov [2014].

Theorem 8.7 *Let K be any convex, compact set in $\mathbb{R}^n$, and A and B be $d \times n$ matrices. Then F^* is a best approximation to $G \in C(K)$ from $C(A; K) + C(B; K)$ if and only if there exists a finite closed path, or an infinite path, with respect to the directions A and B that is extremal for $G - F^*$.*

Proof The sufficiency is proven as follows. Let us first assume that we are given an $F^* \in C(A; K) + C(B; K)$ with the property that there exists a sequence of points $\{\mathbf{v}^i\}_{i=1}^p$ that is a finite closed path with respect to the directions A and B and that is extremal for $G - F^*$. We define the linear functional ℓ on $C(K)$ by

$$\ell(H) := \frac{1}{p} \sum_{i=1}^{p} \varepsilon (-1)^i H(\mathbf{v}^i),$$

where $(G - F^*)(\mathbf{v}^i) = \varepsilon (-1)^i \|G - F^*\|$ for $i = 1, \dots, p$.

Then ℓ, as is easily verified, satisfies $\|\ell\| = 1$ and $\ell(G - F^*) = \|G - F^*\|$. From the closed path property we have

$$A\mathbf{v}^{2j-1} = A\mathbf{v}^{2j}, \qquad j = 1, \dots, q$$

and

$$B\mathbf{v}^{2j} = B\mathbf{v}^{2j+1}, \qquad j = 1, \dots, q,$$

where $\mathbf{v}^{2q+1} = \mathbf{v}^1$. The first set of equalities implies that $\ell(f_1(A\mathbf{x})) = 0$ for all f_1, while from the second set of equalities we obtain $\ell(f_2(B\mathbf{x})) = 0$ for all f_2. Thus $\ell(F) = 0$ for all $F \in C(A; K) + C(B; K)$. This implies that F^* is a best approximation to G from $C(A; K) + C(B; K)$, since

$$\|G - F^*\| = \ell(G - F^*) = \ell(G - F) \leq \|G - F\|$$

for all $F \in C(A; K) + C(B; K)$.

The other option is the existence of an infinite path $\{\mathbf{v}^i\}_{i=1}^\infty$, with respect to the directions A and B, extremal for $G - F^*$. We define the linear functionals $\{\ell_p\}_{p=1}^\infty$ on $C(K)$ by

$$\ell_p(H) := \frac{1}{p} \sum_{i=1}^{p} \varepsilon (-1)^i H(\mathbf{v}^i),$$

where $(G - F^*)(\mathbf{v}^i) = \varepsilon (-1)^i \|G - F^*\|$ for $i = 1, 2, \dots$. Note that $\|\ell_p\| = 1$ and $\ell_p(G - F^*) = \|G - F^*\|$, for all p. Furthermore, it is readily verified from the path property that

$$|\ell_p(f_1(A\mathbf{x}))| \leq \frac{2}{p}\|f_1\|$$

$$|\ell_p(f_2(B\mathbf{x}))| \leq \frac{2}{p}\|f_2\|,$$

where the (uniform) norms of f_1 and f_2 are taken over $\{A\mathbf{x} : \mathbf{x} \in K\}$ and

$\{B\mathbf{x} : \mathbf{x} \in K\}$, respectively. Thus, for any $F \in C(A;K) + C(B;K)$ we have that

$$\lim_{p \to \infty} \ell_p(F) = 0.$$

The unit ball in the weak*-topology of $C(K)$ is weak*-compact by the Banach–Alaoglu Theorem, see, for example, Rudin [1973], p. 66. Thus there exists a weak*-cluster point $\ell \in (C(K))^*$ of the sequence $\{\ell_p\}_{p=1}^{\infty}$. From the previous properties we have that $\|\ell\| \leq 1$, $\ell(G - F^*) = \|G - F^*\|$ (thus $\|\ell\| = 1$), and

$$\ell(F) = 0$$

for all $F \in C(A;K) + C(B;K)$. As previously, this ℓ then implies that F^* is a best approximation to G from $C(A;K) + C(B;K)$.

The proof of necessity is a bit lengthier. Assume F^* is a best approximation to $G \in C(K)$ from $C(A;K) + C(B;K)$, but $G - F^*$ has no finite closed path or infinite path, with respect to A and B, that is extremal for $G - F^*$. This implies that there exists a positive integer N such that each extremal finite path for $G - F^*$ is not closed and is of length at most N.

In Section 9.4 we will discuss the Diliberto–Straus Algorithm. We are going to apply essentially the same algorithm here, but for a different purpose. For a given $G \in C(K)$ and $d \times n$ matrix A we define, for $\mathbf{y} \in K$,

$$P_A G(\mathbf{y}) := \frac{1}{2} \left[\max_{\{\mathbf{x}:A\mathbf{x}=A\mathbf{y}\}\cap K} G(\mathbf{x}) + \min_{\{\mathbf{x}:A\mathbf{x}=A\mathbf{y}\}\cap K} G(\mathbf{x}) \right].$$

Note that $P_A G(\mathbf{y})$ is constant on the intersection of the hyperplane $\{\mathbf{x} : A\mathbf{x} = A\mathbf{y}\}$ with K. Furthermore, since K is convex, both

$$\max_{\{\mathbf{x}:A\mathbf{x}=A\mathbf{y}\}\cap K} G(\mathbf{x})$$

and

$$\min_{\{\mathbf{x}:A\mathbf{x}=A\mathbf{y}\}\cap K} G(\mathbf{x})$$

are continuous functions on K. Thus $P_A G \in C(A;K)$. The operator $P_A G$ simply looks for the constant that best approximates, in the uniform norm, the function G on $\{\mathbf{x} : A\mathbf{x} = A\mathbf{y}\} \cap K$. As such we also have

$$\|G - P_A G\| \leq \|G\|. \tag{8.6}$$

Let $G^{(1)} := G - F^*$ and $M := \|G - F^*\|$. For each $n = 2, 3, \ldots$, we define

$$H^{(n-1)} := G^{(n-1)} - P_A G^{(n-1)}$$

and

$$G^{(n)} := H^{(n-1)} - P_B H^{(n-1)}.$$

By construction,

$$G^{(n)}(\mathbf{x}) = G^{(n-1)}(\mathbf{x}) - f^1_{n-1}(A\mathbf{x}) - f^2_{n-1}(B\mathbf{x}) = G(\mathbf{x}) - F_n(\mathbf{x})$$

for some $F_n \in C(A; K) + C(B; K)$. Since F^* is a best approximation to G from $C(A; K) + C(B; K)$, it follows from (8.6) that

$$\|G^{(n)}\| = \|H^{(n)}\| = M$$

for all n.

For any given $\mathbf{y} \in K$ we have

$$
\begin{aligned}
H^{(n-1)}(\mathbf{y}) &= G^{(n-1)}(\mathbf{y}) - \frac{1}{2} \Big[\max_{\{\mathbf{x}:A\mathbf{x}=A\mathbf{y}\} \cap K} G^{(n-1)}(\mathbf{x}) \\
&\qquad\qquad + \min_{\{\mathbf{x}:A\mathbf{x}=A\mathbf{y}\} \cap K} G^{(n-1)}(\mathbf{x}) \Big] \\
&\le \max_{\{\mathbf{x}:A\mathbf{x}=A\mathbf{y}\} \cap K} G^{(n-1)}(\mathbf{x}) - \frac{1}{2} \Big[\max_{\{\mathbf{x}:A\mathbf{x}=A\mathbf{y}\} \cap K} G^{(n-1)}(\mathbf{x}) \\
&\qquad\qquad + \min_{\{\mathbf{x}:A\mathbf{x}=A\mathbf{y}\} \cap K} G^{(n-1)}(\mathbf{x}) \Big] \\
&= \frac{1}{2} \Big[\max_{\{\mathbf{x}:A\mathbf{x}=A\mathbf{y}\} \cap K} G^{(n-1)}(\mathbf{x}) - \min_{\{\mathbf{x}:A\mathbf{x}=A\mathbf{y}\} \cap K} G^{(n-1)}(\mathbf{x}) \Big] \\
&\le M,
\end{aligned}
$$

since $\|G^{(n-1)}\| = M$. For equality to hold throughout it is both necessary and sufficient that

$$G^{(n-1)}(\mathbf{y}) = M,$$

and

$$\min_{\{\mathbf{x}:A\mathbf{x}=A\mathbf{y}\} \cap K} G^{(n-1)}(\mathbf{x}) = -M. \tag{8.7}$$

Similarly, $G^{(n)}(\mathbf{y}) = M$ if and only if

$$H^{(n-1)}(\mathbf{y}) = M,$$

and

$$\min_{\{\mathbf{x}:B\mathbf{x}=B\mathbf{y}\} \cap K} H^{(n-1)}(\mathbf{x}) = -M. \tag{8.8}$$

The parallel conditions to the above are that $H^{(n-1)}(\mathbf{y}) = -M$ if and only if

$$G^{(n-1)}(\mathbf{y}) = -M,$$

and

$$\max_{\{\mathbf{x}:A\mathbf{x}=A\mathbf{y}\}\cap K} G^{(n-1)}(\mathbf{x}) = M, \tag{8.9}$$

while $G^{(n)}(\mathbf{y}) = -M$ if and only if

$$H^{(n-1)}(\mathbf{y}) = -M,$$

and

$$\max_{\{\mathbf{x}:B\mathbf{x}=B\mathbf{y}\}\cap K} H^{(n-1)}(\mathbf{x}) = M. \tag{8.10}$$

Thus, in particular, it follows from the above that if $G^{(n)}(\mathbf{y}) = M$, then $H^{(n-1)}(\mathbf{y}) = M$ and $G^{(n-1)}(\mathbf{y}) = M$. Similarly, if $G^{(n)}(\mathbf{y}) = -M$, then $H^{(n-1)}(\mathbf{y}) = -M$ and $G^{(n-1)}(\mathbf{y}) = -M$. We therefore have that every extremal path for $G^{(n)}$ is a subpath of an extremal path for $H^{(n-1)}$ with the same signs, and every extremal path for $H^{(n-1)}$ is a subpath of an extremal path for $G^{(n-1)}$ with the same signs. Thus every extremal path for $G^{(n)}$ is a subpath of an extremal path for $G^{(1)} = G - F^*$. By assumption, every extremal finite path for $G^{(1)}$ is not closed and is of length at most N. This implies that every extremal finite path for $G^{(n)}$ is not closed and of length at most N.

We will now show that each extremal path of $G^{(n)}$ of length r can be embedded in an extremal path for $G^{(n-1)}$ of length at least $r + 2$. That is, assume $\{\mathbf{v}^i\}_{i=1}^r$ is an extremal path for $G^{(n)}$. We will show the existence of $\mathbf{v}^0$ and $\mathbf{v}^{r+1}$ such that $\{\mathbf{v}^i\}_{i=0}^{r+1}$ is an extremal path for $G^{(n-1)}$. This leads us to a contradiction since if $n > N/2$ we will either have that $G^{(1)} = G - F^*$ has an extremal path of length greater than N or we have a $G^{(n)} \in C(K)$ that does not attain its norm. Neither conclusion is viable.

Assume $G^{(n)}(\mathbf{v}^i) = \varepsilon(-1)^i M$, $i = 1, \ldots, r$, where $\varepsilon \in \{-1, 1\}$. From the previous analysis, this immediately implies that $H^{(n-1)}(\mathbf{v}^i) = G^{(n-1)}(\mathbf{v}^i) = \varepsilon(-1)^i M$, $i = 1, \ldots, r$. We will prove the existence of a $\mathbf{v}^0 \in K$ such that $G^{(n-1)}(\mathbf{v}^0) = \varepsilon M$ and $\{\mathbf{v}^i\}_{i=0}^r$ is an extremal path for $G^{(n-1)}$. The similar analysis is used to obtain a $\mathbf{v}^{r+1} \in K$, as desired. Note that if $\mathbf{v}^0 = \mathbf{v}^i$ for any $i \in \{1, \ldots, r\}$, then we will have constructed a closed extremal path for $G^{(n-1)}$, which in turn implies a closed extremal path for $G^{(1)}$, in contradiction to our assumption. There are four cases to consider depending on whether $A\mathbf{v}^1 = A\mathbf{v}^2$ or $B\mathbf{v}^1 = B\mathbf{v}^2$, and depending on if the ε at the beginning of this paragraph is -1 or 1. We consider two of these cases.

(1) Assume

$$B\mathbf{v}^1 = B\mathbf{v}^2$$

and $\varepsilon = -1$, i.e., $G^{(n)}(\mathbf{v}^1) = H^{(n-1)}(\mathbf{v}^1) = G^{(n-1)}(\mathbf{v}^1) = M$. From (8.7)

$$\min_{\{\mathbf{x}: A\mathbf{x} = A\mathbf{v}^1\} \cap K} G^{(n-1)}(\mathbf{x}) = -M.$$

Thus there exists a $\mathbf{v}^0 \in K$ satisfying $A\mathbf{v}^0 = A\mathbf{v}^1$ and $G^{(n-1)}(\mathbf{v}^0) = -M$. The $\{\mathbf{v}^i\}_{i=0}^r$ is therefore an extremal path for $G^{(n-1)}$.

(2) Assume

$$A\mathbf{v}^1 = A\mathbf{v}^2$$

and $\varepsilon = -1$, i.e., $G^{(n)}(\mathbf{v}^1) = H^{(n-1)}(\mathbf{v}^1) = G^{(n-1)}(\mathbf{v}^1) = M$. From (8.8)

$$\min_{\{\mathbf{x}: B\mathbf{x} = B\mathbf{v}^1\} \cap K} H^{(n-1)}(\mathbf{x}) = -M.$$

Thus there exists a $\mathbf{v}^0 \in K$ satisfying $B\mathbf{v}^0 = B\mathbf{v}^1$ and $H^{(n-1)}(\mathbf{v}^0) = -M$. This, in turn, implies that $G^{(n-1)}(\mathbf{v}^0) = -M$, and therefore $\{\mathbf{v}^i\}_{i=0}^r$ is an extremal path for $G^{(n-1)}$.

The other two cases are proven in a similar fashion using (8.9) and (8.10). □

For more on the existence of best approximations, in the $L^\infty(K)$ norm, to bounded functions by linear combinations of (bounded) ridge function with two directions, see Garkavi, Medvedev and Khavinson [1995].

9

Approximation Algorithms

We are interested in algorithmic methods for finding best approximations from spaces of linear combinations of ridge functions. The main problem we will consider is that of approximating from the linear space

$$\mathcal{M}(A^1, \ldots, A^r) := \left\{ \sum_{i=1}^{r} f_i(A^i \mathbf{x}) : f_i : \mathbb{R}^d \to \mathbb{R}, \, i = l, \ldots, r \right\}$$

over some domain in $\mathbb{R}^n$, where r is finite and each $f_i(A^i \mathbf{x})$ is in an appropriate normed linear space X. Recall that the A^i are fixed $d \times n$ matrices and the d-variate functions f_i are the variables. That is, we are looking at the question of approximating by generalized ridge functions with fixed directions. We are also interested in the problem of approximating from the set of ridge functions with variable directions. This problem is significantly different.

We predicate these algorithmic approximation methods on the following basic assumption. For each $i \in \{1, \ldots, r\}$, set

$$\mathcal{M}(A^i) := \{f(A^i \mathbf{x}) : f : \mathbb{R}^d \to \mathbb{R}\},$$

where A^i is a fixed $d \times n$ matrix and $f(A^i \mathbf{x})$ lies in the appropriate space. Let P_i be a best approximation operator to $\mathcal{M}(A^i)$, i.e., to each G the element $P_i G$ is a best approximation to G from $\mathcal{M}(A^i)$. The major assumption underlying the methods discussed in this chapter is that each P_i is computable (see Example 8.1). Based on this assumption we outline various approximation approaches.

In Section 9.1 we discuss approximation algorithms in a Hilbert space setting. The theory is the most detailed when $\mathcal{M}(A^1, \ldots, A^r)$ is closed. However, some convergence results are also known without the closure property. In Section 9.2 we generalize the above to consider a "greedy-type algorithm". This permits us to deal with the possibility of an infinite number of directions. In Section 9.3 we consider the same problem as in Section 9.1, but in a uniformly convex and uniformly smooth Banach space. We are able to prove results only for the alternating algorithm. Finally, Section 9.4 contains a discussion of the Diliberto–Straus algorithm (an alternating algorithm) in the uniform norm, where it converges as desired with respect to any two directions, again assuming the closedness of the sum of the subspaces. Examples are given to show that we need not have convergence in the uniform norm when we have more than two directions, or when considering the L^1 norm and two directions.

The results of the first three sections are not in the least confined to ridge functions. We can and will simply assume that we are given subspaces $\mathcal{M}^i$, in place of our specific $\mathcal{M}(A^i)$, $i = 1, \ldots, r$, that are fixed, closed, and generally infinite-dimensional.

9.1 Fixed Directions in Hilbert Space

Assume that P_i is the best approximation operator to the linear subspace $\mathcal{M}(A^i)$ in a Hilbert space H. The question we consider is how and when we can find a best approximation to $G \in H$ from

$$\mathcal{M}(A^1, \ldots, A^r) = \mathcal{M}(A^1) + \cdots + \mathcal{M}(A^r)$$

based on the knowledge of these P_i.

The fact that we are dealing with ridge functions is not truly relevant in this problem. So let us consider a slightly more general setting. Assume that the $\mathcal{M}^1, \ldots, \mathcal{M}^r$ are fixed, closed, infinite (or finite)-dimensional linear subspaces of a Hilbert space H with norm $\| \cdot \|$, r is finite, and P_i is the best approximation operator from $\mathcal{M}^i$, $i = 1, \ldots, r$. That is, to each $G \in H$ the element $P_i G$ is the best approximation to G from $\mathcal{M}^i$. Recall that in a Hilbert space the operator of best approximation to a linear subspace is the orthogonal projection thereon and vice versa. That is, $P_i G \in \mathcal{M}^i$ is defined via

$$(G - P_i G, m_i) = 0$$

for all $m_i \in \mathcal{M}^i$. Our goal is to construct and analyze methods, using these P_i, for finding the best approximation to G from $\overline{\mathcal{M}}$, where

$$\mathcal{M} := \mathcal{M}^1 + \cdots + \mathcal{M}^r.$$

To this end, we will consider iterations of operators of the form

$$L_n := I - \sum_{i=1}^{r} \mu_i^{(n)} P_i, \qquad (9.1)$$

where $\mu_i^{(n)} \in [0, 2]$, $i = 1, \ldots, r$, and $\sum_{i=1}^{r} \mu_i^{(n)} \leq 2$.

Historically, these L_n were generally written in the form

$$L_n = I - \sum_{i=1}^{r} \lambda_i^{(n)} \alpha_i^{(n)} P_i,$$

where the $\alpha_i^{(n)}$, called *relaxation parameters*, are chosen from $[0, 2]$. They, in some way, demonstrate the "robustness" or stability of these algorithms. The $\lambda_i^{(n)}$ satisfy $\lambda_i^{(n)} \geq 0$ and $\sum_{i=1}^{r} \lambda_i^{(n)} = 1$. That is, we take convex combinations of the $\alpha_i^{(n)} P_i$ (or $I - \alpha_i^{(n)} P_i$). For every choice of $\mu_i^{(n)}$, as above, there exist associated $\alpha_i^{(n)}$ and $\lambda_i^{(n)}$, and vice versa.

We shall iterate using the L_n, i.e., we consider

$$E_n := L_n \cdots L_1,$$

and ask what happens to

$$\lim_{n \to \infty} E_n G$$

for any element $G \in H$. From the form of the L_n it follows that for each n we have $E_n G = G - F_n$ for some $F_n \in \mathcal{M}$. The question we ask is whether $E_n G$ necessarily converges in norm to $G - F^*$, where F^* is the best approximation to G from $\overline{\mathcal{M}}$? Or, more exactly, what are conditions implying that it converges as desired, and if it does converge, can we also say something about the rate of convergence?

The following two lemmas will be used in this chapter. They also illustrate why considering operators like L_n makes sense.

Lemma 9.1 *Assume that the $\mathcal{M}^i$, $i = 1, \ldots, r$, are closed linear subspaces of a Hilbert space H. Let P_i denote the best approximation operator from $\mathcal{M}^i$, $i = 1, \ldots, r$. Let*

$$L := I - \sum_{i=1}^{r} \mu_i P_i,$$

where $\mu_i \in [0, 2)$, $i = 1, \ldots, r$, and $\sum_{i=1}^{r} \mu_i < 2$. Then

$$\|LG\| \leq \|G\|.$$

Furthermore $\|LG\| = \|G\|$ if and only if $LG = G$ and if and only if $P_i G = 0$ for those i satisfying $\mu_i > 0$.

Proof The inequality $\|LG\| \leq \|G\|$ is a consequence of convexity and the following important fact. For any $c \in (0, 2)$ we have

$$\|(I - cP_i)G\|^2 = \|G\|^2 - c(2 - c)\|P_i G\|^2 \leq \|G\|^2,$$

with equality if and only if $P_i G = 0$.

Let $\sum_{i=1}^{r} \mu_i = c$. If $c = 0$, there is nothing to prove. Assume $c \in (0, 2)$, and set $\lambda_i := \mu_i / c$. Thus $\lambda_i \geq 0$ and $\sum_{i=1}^{r} \lambda_i = 1$. Now

$$
\begin{aligned}
\|LG\| &= \|(I - \sum_{i=1}^{r} \mu_i P_i)G\| = \|\sum_{i=1}^{r} \lambda_i (I - cP_i)G\| \\
&\leq \sum_{i=1}^{r} \lambda_i \|(I - cP_i)G\| \leq \sum_{i=1}^{r} \lambda_i \|G\| = \|G\|.
\end{aligned}
$$

If $P_i G = 0$ for those i satisfying $\mu_i > 0$, then $LG = G$. Assume $\|LG\| = \|G\|$. Then, as previously,

$$
\|G\| = \|LG\| \leq \sum_{i=1}^{r} \lambda_i \|(I - cP_i)G\| \leq \sum_{i=1}^{r} \lambda_i \|G\| = \|G\|.
$$

This implies that we must have equality in all the above inequalities. As $\lambda_i \geq 0$, $\sum_{i=1}^{r} \lambda_i = 1$, it follows that $\|(I - cP_i)G\| = \|G\|$ for those i for which $\mu_i > 0$ ($\lambda_i > 0$). This proves that $P_i G = 0$ for these same i, and thus $LG = G$. $\qquad \square$

Lemma 9.2 F^* *is a best approximation to G from $\overline{\mathcal{M}}$ if and only if $P_i(G - F^*) = 0$ for $i = 1, \ldots, r$.*

Proof This is a consequence of the linearity of the best approximation operator in a Hilbert space. $\qquad \square$

In what follows we first discuss two prototypes of the above-mentioned schemes. These are the alternating algorithm, and iterates of a fixed convex combination of the P_i, with or without "relaxation parameters". We then present and prove in Theorem 9.5 the convergence of a more general scheme containing both these prototypes, independent of whether $\mathcal{M}$ is closed or not. Unfortunately, in the more general arbitrary case, we are able to show convergence only when $\mathcal{M}$ is closed. This is where the theory is still lacking. Convergence should also hold, with perhaps some assumptions, in this more general case. In almost all cases where $\mathcal{M}$ is closed we also get results on the rate of convergence of the algorithm to its limit.

In Hilbert space the algorithms discussed herein have been studied in detail by many authors in the optimization literature. Some of their results are more general, as they are interested in projections onto convex subsets that are not necessarily closed linear subspaces. On the other hand, some of their results do not apply as none of our $\mathcal{M}^i$ is a finite-dimensional linear subspace or has interior. The problem, as presented here, is also in a slightly different form from that found in the optimization literature. It is, however, equivalent to solving a convex feasibility problem. The interested reader should consult the review article by Bauschke and Borwein [1996], the many references therein, and the many, many references to that paper. Surprisingly there are still unresolved problems, as mentioned in the previous paragraph.

The Alternating and Fixed Convex Combination Algorithms Historically the first method of the above form that was studied seems to have been the alternating algorithm. This algorithm goes under various names in different settings. Particular variants have been called, among other things, the von Neumann Alternating Algorithm, the Cyclic Coordinate Algorithm, the Cyclic Projection Algorithm, the Schwarz Domain Decomposition method, and the Diliberto–Straus Algorithm.

The basic idea is the following. We start with $G^{(1)} := G \in H$. We then find the best approximation $m_1 := P_1 G^{(1)}$ to $G^{(1)}$ from $\mathcal{M}^1$, and set $G^{(2)} := G^{(1)} - m_1$. We then find the best approximation $m_2 := P_2 G^{(2)}$ to $G^{(2)}$ from $\mathcal{M}^2$, and set $G^{(3)} := G^{(2)} - m_2$, then find the best approximation $m_3 := P_3 G^{(3)}$ to $G^{(3)}$ from $\mathcal{M}^3$, etc..., and after cycling through all the subspaces $\mathcal{M}^j$, $j = 1, \ldots, r$, we then start again, i.e., after finding the best approximation from $\mathcal{M}^r$ we then go to $\mathcal{M}^1$.

More precisely, set

$$E := (I - P_r)(I - P_{r-1}) \cdots (I - P_1).$$

Thus, for each $G \in H$,

$$EG = G - m_1 - \cdots - m_r,$$

where m_i is the best approximation to $G - m_1 - \cdots - m_{i-1}$ from $\mathcal{M}^i$, $i = 1, \ldots, r$, i.e., $m_i = P_i(G - m_1 - \cdots - m_{i-1})$. Now consider

$$\lim_{s \to \infty} E^s G.$$

Note that for every s we have that $E^s G = G - F_s$ for some $F_s \in \mathcal{M}$. The hope is that this scheme will converge, and converge to $G - F^*$, where F^* is a best approximation to G from $\mathcal{M}$.

In the Hilbert space setting, von Neumann already in 1933 (see von Neumann [1950]) showed the desired convergence of the above-mentioned alternating algorithm in the case of two subspaces. This was extended to more than two subspaces in Halperin [1962]. See Deutsch [1979] for a discussion of this method. There are, by now, numerous different proofs of this result. In fact this algorithm also converges as desired if we introduce fixed relaxation parameters $\alpha_i \in (0, 2)$,

$i = 1, \ldots, r$, i.e., set

$$E := (I - \alpha_r P_r)(I - \alpha_{r-1} P_{r-1}) \cdots (I - \alpha_1 P_1).$$

We state the result in this latter form. We will prove the more general Theorem 9.5 which subsumes this result.

Theorem 9.3 *Assume that the* $\mathcal{M}^i$, $i = 1, \ldots, r$, *are closed linear subspaces of a Hilbert space* H. *Let* P_i *denote the best approximation operator from* $\mathcal{M}^i$, $i = 1, \ldots, r$, *and* $\mathcal{M} := \mathcal{M}^1 + \cdots + \mathcal{M}^r$. *Let* $\alpha_i \in (0, 2)$, $i = 1, \ldots, r$, *and set*

$$E := (I - \alpha_r P_r)(I - \alpha_{r-1} P_{r-1}) \cdots (I - \alpha_1 P_1).$$

Then, for each $G \in H$,

$$\lim_{s \to \infty} E^s G = G - F^*,$$

where F^* *is the best approximation to* G *from* $\overline{\mathcal{M}}$.

Another approach is to take a fixed strictly convex combination of the $I - P_i$ and then iterate this fixed linear operator. It will also converge to $G - F^*$, where F^* is the best approximation to G from $\mathcal{M}$. That is, we define the operator

$$E := I - \sum_{i=1}^{r} \lambda_i P_i,$$

where $\lambda_i > 0$ and $\sum_{i=1}^{r} \lambda_i = 1$, and consider $E^n G$. Again in this case we can add relaxation parameters $\alpha_i \in (0, 2)$, $i = 1, \ldots, r$, i.e., set

$$E := I - \sum_{i=1}^{r} \lambda_i \alpha_i P_i.$$

We state the result in this latter form. Its proof is also a consequence of Theorem 9.5.

Theorem 9.4 *Assume that the* $\mathcal{M}^i$, $i = 1, \ldots, r$, *are closed linear subspaces of a Hilbert space* H. *Let* P_i *denote the best approximation operator from* $\mathcal{M}^i$, $i = 1, \ldots, r$, *and* $\mathcal{M} := \mathcal{M}^1 + \cdots + \mathcal{M}^r$. *Let* $\lambda_i > 0$, $\sum_{i=1}^{r} \lambda_i = 1$, *and* $\alpha_i \in (0, 2)$, $i = 1, \ldots, r$. *Set*

$$E := I - \sum_{i=1}^{r} \lambda_i \alpha_i P_i.$$

Then, for each $G \in H$,

$$\lim_{n \to \infty} E^n G = G - F^*,$$

where F^* is the best approximation to G from $\overline{\mathcal{M}}$.

We now present the more general result that contains both Theorems 9.3 and 9.4. The framework is that we take a product of a fixed finite number of operators of the form (9.1), and then iterate that operator. Under reasonable assumptions we obtain the desired convergence result.

Theorem 9.5 *Assume that the $\mathcal{M}^i$, $i = 1, \ldots, r$, are closed linear subspaces of a Hilbert space H. Let P_i denote the best approximation operator from $\mathcal{M}^i$, $i = 1, \ldots, r$, and $\mathcal{M} := \mathcal{M}^1 + \cdots + \mathcal{M}^r$. Set*

$$L_k := I - \sum_{i=1}^{r} \mu_i^{(k)} P_i, \qquad k = 1, \ldots, N,$$

where $\mu_i^{(k)} \in [0, 2)$, $i = 1, \ldots, r$, $k = 1, \ldots, N$, and $\sum_{i=1}^{r} \mu_i^{(k)} < 2$, $k = 1, \ldots, N$. Define

$$T := L_N \cdots L_1.$$

Assume that for each $i \in \{1, \ldots, r\}$ there exists a $k \in \{1, \ldots, N\}$ for which $\mu_i^{(k)} > 0$. Then, for every $G \in H$,

$$\lim_{n \to \infty} T^n G = G - F^*,$$

where F^* is the best approximation to G from $\overline{\mathcal{M}}$.

Our proof of Theorem 9.5 is a variation of a proof from Reich [1983], where we find Theorem 9.4 without relaxation parameters.

A linear operator T defined on H is said to be *strongly non-expansive* if it is of norm at most 1 and whenever $\{G^{(n)}\}$ is a bounded sequence in H, and

$$\lim_{n \to \infty} \|G^{(n)}\| - \|TG^{(n)}\| = 0,$$

then

$$\lim_{n \to \infty} G^{(n)} - TG^{(n)} = 0.$$

This term was coined by Bruck and Reich [1977]. We first prove that our T is strongly non-expansive.

Proposition 9.6 *The T in the statement of Theorem 9.5 is strongly non-expansive.*

Proof We first claim that $I - \mu P$ is strongly non-expansive, where P is any best approximation operator and $\mu \in [0, 2)$. The result trivially holds for $\mu = 0$. Assume $\mu \in (0, 2)$, $\{G^{(n)}\}$ is a bounded sequence in H, and

$$\lim_{n \to \infty} \|G^{(n)}\| - \|(I - \mu P)G^{(n)}\| = 0.$$

Thus

$$\lim_{n \to \infty} \|G^{(n)}\|^2 - \|(I - \mu P)G^{(n)}\|^2 = 0.$$

Now

$$
\begin{aligned}
\|G^{(n)}\|^2 - \|(I - \mu P)G^{(n)}\|^2 &= \|G^{(n)}\|^2 - [\|G^{(n)}\|^2 - \mu(2 - \mu)\|PG^{(n)}\|^2] \\
&= \mu(2 - \mu)\|PG^{(n)}\|^2.
\end{aligned}
$$

Therefore

$$\lim_{n \to \infty} \|PG^{(n)}\| = 0,$$

and

$$\lim_{n \to \infty} \|G^{(n)} - (I - \mu P)G^{(n)}\| = \mu \lim_{n \to \infty} \|PG^{(n)}\| = 0.$$

This proves the claim.

We will now prove that each L of the form

$$L = I - \sum_{i=1}^{r} \mu_i P_i,$$

is strongly non-expansive if $\mu_i \in [0, 2)$, $i = 1, \dots, r$, and $\sum_{i=1}^{r} \mu_i < 2$. We prove this as follows. Assume $\sum_{i=1}^{r} \mu_i = c$. If $c = 0$, there is nothing to prove. As such, assume that $c \in (0, 2)$. Set $\lambda_i := \mu_i/c$. Thus $\lambda_i \geq 0$ and $\sum_{i=1}^{r} \lambda_i = 1$. We write L in the form

$$L = I - \sum_{i=1}^{r} \mu_i P_i = \sum_{i=1}^{r} \lambda_i (I - cP_i).$$

From the triangle inequality

$$\|G\| - \|LG\| \geq \|G\| - \sum_{i=1}^{r} \lambda_i \|(I - cP_i)G\| = \sum_{i=1}^{r} \lambda_i [\|G\| - \|(I - cP_i)G\|].$$

Recall that the summands on the right-hand side are non-negative. Thus, if $\{G^{(n)}\}$ is a bounded sequence in H, and

$$\lim_{n \to \infty} \|G^{(n)}\| - \|LG^{(n)}\| = 0,$$

then

$$\lim_{n \to \infty} \|G^{(n)}\| - \|(I - cP_i)G^{(n)}\| = 0,$$

for those i where $\lambda_i > 0$. Since $I - cP_i$ is strongly non-expansive we have, for those same i, that

$$\lim_{n \to \infty} G^{(n)} - (I - cP_i)G^{(n)} = 0,$$

and therefore

$$\lim_{n \to \infty} G^{(n)} - LG^{(n)} = 0.$$

Finally, a product of strongly non-expansive linear operators is strongly non-expansive. Assume L_1, L_2 are strongly non-expansive linear operators and set $T = L_2 L_1$. We write

$$\|G^{(n)}\| - \|TG^{(n)}\| = \|G^{(n)}\| - \|L_1 G^{(n)}\| + \|L_1 G^{(n)}\| - \|L_2 L_1 G^{(n)}\|.$$

If

$$\lim_{n \to \infty} \|G^{(n)}\| - \|TG^{(n)}\| = 0,$$

then, since L_1 and L_2 are linear operators of norm at most 1, it follows that

$$\lim_{n \to \infty} \|G^{(n)}\| - \|L_1 G^{(n)}\| = 0$$

and

$$\lim_{n \to \infty} \|L_1 G^{(n)}\| - \|L_2 L_1 G^{(n)}\| = 0.$$

As L_1 and L_2 are strongly non-expansive we have that

$$\lim_{n \to \infty} G^{(n)} - L_1 G^{(n)} = 0$$

and

$$\lim_{n \to \infty} L_1 G^{(n)} - L_2 L_1 G^{(n)} = 0,$$

whence

$$\lim_{n \to \infty} G^{(n)} - TG^{(n)} = 0.$$

This implies that the T, as defined in the statement of Theorem 9.5, is strongly non-expansive. $\qquad\square$

In proving Theorem 9.5 we will apply the following result.

Proposition 9.7 *Assume T is a linear operator of norm at most 1. If $G \in H$ is an element for which*

$$\lim_{n \to \infty} \|T^n G - T^{n+1} G\| = 0 \tag{9.2}$$

then the sequence $\{T^n G\}$ converges to a fixed point of T.

Proof From (9.2) it follows that, for each fixed i, we have

$$\lim_{n \to \infty} \|T^n G - T^{n+i} G\| = 0. \tag{9.3}$$

As T is a linear operator of norm at most 1, we have that $\{\|T^n G\|\}$ is non-increasing in n. Thus

$$\lim_{n \to \infty} \|T^n G\| = d \tag{9.4}$$

exists.

We claim that $\|T^n G + T^m G\| \geq 2d$ for all n and m. To this end, note that

$$2d \leq 2\|T^n G\| \leq \|T^n G + T^{n+i} G\| + \|T^n G - T^{n+i} G\|.$$

From (9.3) it therefore follows that

$$\lim_{n \to \infty} \|T^n G + T^{n+i} G\| \geq 2d.$$

As T is a linear operator of norm at most 1, we have that $\{\|T^n G + T^{n+i} G\|\}$ is non-increasing in n. Therefore $\|T^n G + T^{n+i} G\| \geq 2d$ for all n and i, whence $\|T^n G + T^m G\| \geq 2d$ for all n and m.

From the triangle inequality and (9.4) it therefore follows that

$$\lim_{n,m \to \infty} \|T^n G + T^m G\| = 2d,$$

and thus

$$\lim_{n,m \to \infty} (T^n G, T^m G) = d^2.$$

This then implies that

$$\lim_{n,m \to \infty} \|T^n G - T^m G\| = 0.$$

We have proven that $\{T^n G\}$ is a Cauchy sequence and thus converges. If $T^n G$ converges to G^*, then $T^{n+1} G$ converges to $TG^* = G^*$, i.e., to a fixed point of T. $\qquad \square$

We now can prove Theorem 9.5.

Proof of Theorem 9.5 As T is a linear operator of norm at most 1, we have that for each $G \in H$ the sequence $\|T^n G\|$ is non-increasing. Therefore

$$\lim_{n \to \infty} \|T^n G\| - \|T^{n+1} G\| = 0.$$

From Proposition 9.6 we have that T is strongly non-expansive. Let $G^{(n)} = T^n G$. Thus, from the property of being strongly non-expansive we obtain

$$\lim_{n \to \infty} T^n G - T^{n+1} G = \lim_{n \to \infty} G^{(n)} - TG^{(n)} = 0.$$

Applying Proposition 9.7 it follows that T^nG converges to a fixed point of T. Since $T^nG = G - F_n$ for some $F_n \in \mathcal{M}$ we have that T^nG must converge to $G - F^*$, where $F^* \in \overline{\mathcal{M}}$, and

$$T(G - F^*) = G - F^*.$$

We claim that F^* is the best approximation to G from $\overline{\mathcal{M}}$. T is a product of linear operators of norm 1, and thus

$$\|G - F^*\| = \|T(G - F^*)\| = \|L_N \cdots L_1(G - F^*)\| \leq \|L_{N-1} \cdots L_1(G - F^*)\|$$

$$\leq \cdots \leq \|L_1(G - F^*)\| \leq \|G - F^*\|.$$

We must therefore have equality throughout this series of inequalities. From the form of L_1 we see that

$$\|L_1(G - F^*)\| = \left\| \left(I - \sum_{i=1}^{r} \mu_i^{(1)} P_i \right) (G - F^*) \right\| = \|G - F^*\|.$$

Applying Lemma 9.1 it follows that $P_i(G - F^*) = 0$ for all i for which $\mu_i^{(1)} > 0$, and $L_1(G - F^*) = G - F^*$. We now consider $L_2(G - F^*)$. Since $L_1(G - F^*) = G - F^*$ we have

$$\|L_2(G - F^*)\| = \|G - F^*\|,$$

and we can apply the same analysis as previously. By assumption, for each $i \in \{1, \ldots, r\}$ there exists a $k \in \{1, \ldots, N\}$ with $0 < \mu_i^{(k)}$. We therefore obtain that $P_i(G - F^*) = 0$ for $i = 1, \ldots, r$, and as a consequence, see Lemma 9.2, F^* is the best approximation to G from $\overline{\mathcal{M}}$. $\qquad\square$

The General Deterministic Case One would expect that the result of Theorem 9.5 could be generalized to the case where we do not repeatedly iterate the same operator. However, it seems that such a result is still unknown without assuming that $\mathcal{M}$ is closed. Recall that the closedness of the $\mathcal{M}^i$ does not imply the closedness of $\mathcal{M}$, see Chapter 7. The closedness of $\mathcal{M}$ finds its expression in the following fundamental result, see Browder [1967] (also in Bauschke and Borwein [1996]).

Theorem 9.8 *Let $\mathcal{M}^i$, $i = 1, \ldots, r$, be closed linear subspaces of a Hilbert space H, and $\mathcal{M} := \mathcal{M}^1 + \cdots + \mathcal{M}^r$. Let P_i denote the best approximation operator from $\mathcal{M}^i$, $i = 1, \ldots, r$, and let P denote the best approximation operator from $\overline{\mathcal{M}}$. If $\mathcal{M}$ is closed, then there exists a $\kappa > 0$ such that*

$$\|PG\| \leq \kappa \max_{i=1,\ldots,r} \|P_i G\|$$

for all $G \in H$.

Proof We first note that it suffices to prove this result for $G \in \mathcal{M}$. For since $\mathcal{M}$ is closed we have $H = \mathcal{M} \oplus \mathcal{M}^{\perp}$. Each G may therefore be written in the form $G = H_1 + H_2$, where $H_1 \in \mathcal{M}$ and $H_2 \in \mathcal{M}^{\perp}$. As $\mathcal{M}^{\perp} = \cap_{i=1}^{r}(\mathcal{M}^i)^{\perp}$ we have $PH_2 = P_1 H_2 = \cdots = P_r H_2 = 0$. Thus we need only prove the desired inequality for $G \in \mathcal{M}$.

Introduce the norm

$$\|(m_1, \ldots, m_r)\| := \|m_1\| + \cdots + \|m_r\|$$

on $\mathcal{M}^1 \times \cdots \times \mathcal{M}^r$. Let

$$L : \mathcal{M}^1 \times \cdots \times \mathcal{M}^r \to \mathcal{M}^1 + \cdots + \mathcal{M}^r = \mathcal{M}$$

be the linear map given by

$$L(m_1, \ldots, m_r) := m_1 + \cdots + m_r.$$

This map is continuous and onto $\mathcal{M}$. Since $\mathcal{M}$ is complete, it follows from the Open Mapping Theorem that there exists a $\kappa > 0$ such that for each $G \in \mathcal{M}$ there exists $(m_1, \ldots, m_r) \in \mathcal{M}^1 \times \cdots \times \mathcal{M}^r$ such that $L(m_1, \ldots, m_r) = G$ and $\|(m_1, \ldots, m_r)\| \leq \kappa \|G\|$, i.e.,

$$\|m_1\| + \cdots + \|m_r\| \leq \kappa \|m_1 + \cdots + m_r\|.$$

Let $G \in \mathcal{M}$, with $G = m_1 + \cdots + m_r$ and associated κ, as above. Then

$$\|G\|^2 = (G, G) = \left(\sum_{i=1}^{r} m_i, G\right) = \sum_{i=1}^{r}(m_i, G) = \sum_{i=1}^{r}(P_i m_i, G)$$

$$= \sum_{i=1}^{r}(m_i, P_i G) \leq (\|m_1\| + \cdots + \|m_r\|) \max_{i=1,\ldots,r} \|P_i G\| \leq \kappa \|G\| \max_{i=1,\ldots,r} \|P_i G\|.$$

Thus

$$\|G\| \leq \kappa \max_{i=1,\ldots,r} \|P_i G\|.$$

Since $PG = G$ this proves the result. $\qquad\square$

With this closure property we can prove convergence for general iterations of families of algorithms of the form (9.1). We recall that

$$L_n = I - \sum_{i=1}^{r} \mu_i^{(n)} P_i,$$

where $\mu_i^{(n)} \in [0,2]$, $i = 1, \ldots, r$, and $\sum_{i=1}^{r} \mu_i^{(n)} \leq 2$. We set

$$E_n := L_n \cdots L_1,$$

and ask what happens to

$$\lim_{n \to \infty} E_n G$$

for any element $G \in H$. For each n we let $E_n G = G - F_n$ where, by construction, $F_n \in \mathcal{M}$.

We will critically use Theorem 9.8 and the following estimates, which may be found in Bauschke and Borwein [1996], Lemma 3.2.

Proposition 9.9 *Let* $G^{(1)} := G \in H$ *and* $G^{(n+1)} := E_n G$, *for* $n = 1, 2, \ldots$ *Assume that for each* n *we have* $\mu_i^{(n)} \in [0,2]$, $i = 1, \ldots, r$, *and* $\sum_{i=1}^{r} \mu_i^{(n)} \leq 2$. *Then*

$$\|G^{(n)}\|^2 - \|G^{(n+1)}\|^2 \geq \left(2 - \sum_{j=1}^{r} \mu_j^{(n)} \right) \sum_{i=1}^{r} \mu_i^{(n)} \|P_i G^{(n)}\|^2, \qquad (9.5)$$

and

$$\|G^{(n)} - G^{(n+1)}\| \leq \sum_{i=1}^{r} \mu_i^{(n)} \|P_i G^{(n)}\|. \qquad (9.6)$$

Proof The proof is based on a series of elementary calculations. Let

$$H^{(n)} := \sum_{i=1}^{r} \mu_i^{(n)} P_i G^{(n)}.$$

Then $G^{(n+1)} = L_n G^{(n)} = G^{(n)} - H^{(n)}$ and (9.6) immediately follows from the triangle inequality.

To prove (9.5) we write

$$\|G^{(n)}\|^2 - \|G^{(n+1)}\|^2 = \|G^{(n)}\|^2 - \|G^{(n)} - H^{(n)}\|^2 = 2(G^{(n)}, H^{(n)}) - \|H^{(n)}\|^2.$$

Now

$$(G^{(n)}, H^{(n)}) = \left(G^{(n)}, \sum_{i=1}^{r} \mu_i^{(n)} P_i G^{(n)} \right) = \sum_{i=1}^{r} \mu_i^{(n)} (G^{(n)}, P_i G^{(n)})$$

$$= \sum_{i=1}^{r} \mu_i^{(n)} \|P_i G^{(n)}\|^2,$$

since, by the orthogonality, $(G^{(n)}, P_i G^{(n)}) = \|P_i G^{(n)}\|^2$.

We calculate $\|H^{(n)}\|^2$ as follows. Firstly

$$\|H^{(n)}\|^2 = \sum_{i,j=1}^{r} \mu_i^{(n)} \mu_j^{(n)} (P_i G^{(n)}, P_j G^{(n)}).$$

Now

$$2(P_i G^{(n)}, P_j G^{(n)}) = \|P_i G^{(n)}\|^2 + \|P_j G^{(n)}\|^2 - \|P_i G^{(n)} - P_j G^{(n)}\|^2.$$

Thus it easily follows that

$$\|H^{(n)}\|^2 = \sum_{i=1}^{r} \mu_i^{(n)} \|P_i G^{(n)}\|^2 \left(\sum_{i=1}^{r} \mu_j^{(n)} \right) - \sum_{i<j} \mu_i^{(n)} \mu_j^{(n)} \|P_i G^{(n)} - P_j G^{(n)}\|^2.$$

Applying these estimates we obtain

$$\|G^{(n)}\|^2 - \|G^{(n+1)}\|^2 = 2\sum_{i=1}^{r} \mu_i^{(n)} \|P_i G^{(n)}\|^2$$

$$- \sum_{i=1}^{r} \mu_i^{(n)} \|P_i G^{(n)}\|^2 \left(\sum_{i=1}^{r} \mu_j^{(n)} \right) + \sum_{i<j} \mu_i^{(n)} \mu_j^{(n)} \|P_i G^{(n)} - P_j G^{(n)}\|^2$$

$$= \left(2 - \sum_{j=1}^{r} \mu_j^{(n)} \right) \sum_{i=1}^{r} \mu_i^{(n)} \|P_i G^{(n)}\|^2 + \sum_{i<j} \mu_i^{(n)} \mu_j^{(n)} \|P_i G^{(n)} - P_j G^{(n)}\|^2.$$

Since the last term in non-negative, the desired inequality follows immediately.
□

Remark 9.10 Estimate (9.5) also holds if we replace the left-hand side of the equation by

$$\|G^{(n)} - \widehat{G}\|^2 - \|G^{(n+1)} - \widehat{G}\|^2,$$

where $\widehat{G}$ is any element of $\mathcal{M}^\perp = \cap_{i=1}^{r} \mathcal{M}^{i\perp}$, since $P_i(G^{(n)} - \widehat{G}) = P_i G^{(n)}$, $i = 1, \dots, r$, or alternatively, as is easily seen, since

$$\|G^{(n)} - \widehat{G}\|^2 - \|G^{(n+1)} - \widehat{G}\|^2 = \|G^{(n)}\|^2 - \|G^{(n+1)}\|^2.$$

(In the optimization literature $\{G^{(n)}\}$ having this property is said to be a *Fejér monotone sequence* with respect to $\mathcal{M}^\perp$.) Assume F^* is the best approximation to G from $\mathcal{M}$. Then $G - F^* \in \mathcal{M}^\perp$. Substituting $\widehat{G} := G - F^*$ in the above, and recalling that $G^{(n+1)} = G - F_n$ where $F_n \in \mathcal{M}$ we get from (9.5)

$$\|F^* - F_{n-1}\|^2 - \|F^* - F_n\|^2 \geq \left(2 - \sum_{j=1}^{r} \mu_j^{(n)} \right) \sum_{i=1}^{r} \mu_i^{(n)} \|P_i G^{(n)}\|^2. \quad (9.7)$$

This estimate will prove useful in what follows.

The closedness property and the associated $\kappa > 0$ of Theorem 9.8 will also permit us to prove results on rates of convergence. Assume $G \in H$ and F^* is the best approximation to G from $\overline{\mathcal{M}}$. Let $E_n G := G - F_n$, where $F_n \in \mathcal{M}$. Then we say that the rate of convergence of the algorithm is *geometric* if there exist constants C and θ, where $C > 0, 0 \le \theta < 1$, such that

$$\|F^* - F_n\| \le C\theta^n$$

for all $n \in \mathbb{Z}_+$. In the optimization literature this is called *linear convergence*.

A careful consideration of Proposition 9.9 gives us this next result. We make the following assumptions.

(a)

$$\liminf_{n \to \infty} 2 - \sum_{j=1}^{r} \mu_j^{(n)} > 0.$$

(b) There exist a positive integer p and an $\alpha > 0$ such that for each $i \in \{1, \ldots, r\}$ and for any $s \in \mathbb{Z}_+$ there exists a $k_\ell \in \{s+1, \ldots, s+p\}$, dependent upon i, such that

$$\mu_i^{(k_\ell)} \ge \alpha > 0.$$

In the optimization literature, an assumption such as (b) is often called *intermittent*.

These assumptions suffice to prove the following.

Theorem 9.11 *Under the above assumptions (a) and (b), and if $\mathcal{M}$ is closed, then the algorithm, as described above, is such that the $G^{(n)}$ converge to $G - F^*$, where $F^* \in \mathcal{M}$ is the best approximation to G from $\mathcal{M}$. If, in addition, $\liminf_{n \to \infty} \sum_{i=1}^{r} \mu_i^{(n)} > 0$, then the convergence is geometric.*

Proof As the $\|G^{(n)}\|$ is a non-increasing sequence we have $\lim_{n \to \infty} \|G^{(n)}\|^2 - \|G^{(n+1)}\|^2 = 0$ and thus from (9.5)

$$\lim_{n \to \infty} \left(2 - \sum_{j=1}^{r} \mu_j^{(n)} \right) \sum_{i=1}^{r} \mu_i^{(n)} \|P_i G^{(n)}\|^2 = 0.$$

By assumption (a) it therefore follows that

$$\lim_{n \to \infty} \sum_{i=1}^{r} \mu_i^{(n)} \|P_i G^{(n)}\|^2 = 0.$$

Recall that $0 \leq \mu_i^{(n)} \leq 2$ for all i and n. Thus, applying the Cauchy–Schwarz inequality, we obtain

$$\lim_{n \to \infty} \sum_{i=1}^{r} \mu_i^{(n)} \|P_i G^{(n)}\| = 0.$$

Fix $j \in \{1, \ldots, r\}$. We wish to prove that

$$\lim_{n \to \infty} \|P_j G^{(n)}\| = 0.$$

As a consequence of assumption (b) there exists a sequence $\{k_\ell\}_{\ell=1}^{\infty}$, dependent upon j, with $k_{\ell+1} - k_\ell \leq p$ on which $\mu_j^{(k_\ell)} \geq \alpha > 0$, and therefore

$$\lim_{\ell \to \infty} \|P_j G^{(k_\ell)}\| = 0.$$

We also note from (9.6) that if $n < m$, then

$$\|G^{(n)} - G^{(m)}\| \leq \sum_{s=n}^{m-1} \sum_{i=1}^{r} \mu_i^{(s)} \|P_i G^{(s)}\|.$$

Given n there exists, by assumption (b), a k_ℓ in the above-determined sequence, with $n < k_\ell$ and $k_\ell - n \leq 2p$. Thus

$$\|P_j G^{(n)}\| \leq \|P_j (G^{(n)} - G^{(k_\ell)})\| + \|P_j G^{(k_\ell)}\| \leq \|G^{(n)} - G^{(k_\ell)}\| + \|P_j G^{(k_\ell)}\|$$

$$\leq \sum_{s=n}^{k_\ell-1} \sum_{i=1}^{r} \mu_i^{(s)} \|P_i G^{(s)}\| + \|P_j G^{(k_\ell)}\| \leq \sum_{s=n}^{n+2p-1} \sum_{i=1}^{r} \mu_i^{(s)} \|P_i G^{(s)}\| + \|P_j G^{(k_\ell)}\|.$$

As $n \to \infty$ we have that $k_\ell \to \infty$, and both terms on the right-hand side of this inequality tend to zero. Thus

$$\lim_{n \to \infty} \|P_j G^{(n)}\| = 0.$$

Let P denote the orthogonal projector onto $\mathcal{M}$. Then $PG = F^*$, and from Theorem 9.8 there exists a $\kappa > 0$ such that for every $G \in H$

$$\|PG\| \leq \kappa \max_{i=1,\ldots,r} \|P_i G\|.$$

This then implies, by the above, that

$$\lim_{n \to \infty} \|PG^{(n)}\| = 0.$$

Note that $\{G^{(n+1)}\}$ is a bounded sequence in H. Now $PG^{(n+1)} = PG - PF_n = F^* - F_n$. Thus

$$\lim_{n \to \infty} \|F^* - F_n\| = \lim_{n \to \infty} \|PG^{(n+1)}\| = 0,$$

and

$$\lim_{n \to \infty} \|G^{(n+1)} - (G - F^*)\| = \lim_{n \to \infty} \|(G - F_n) - (G - F^*)\| = 0,$$

which proves the desired convergence.

To obtain geometric convergence we additionally assume that

$$\liminf_{n \to \infty} \sum_{i=1}^{r} \mu_i^{(n)} > 0.$$

From (9.7) we have

$$\|F^* - F_{n-1}\|^2 - \|F^* - F_n\|^2 \geq \left(2 - \sum_{j=1}^{r} \mu_j^{(n)}\right) \sum_{i=1}^{r} \mu_i^{(n)} \|P_i G^{(n)}\|^2.$$

By assumption, there exist $\beta, \gamma > 0$ and $N \in \mathbb{Z}_+$ such that, for all $n > N$, we have

$$2 - \sum_{j=1}^{r} \mu_j^{(n)} \geq \beta > 0$$

and

$$\sum_{i=1}^{r} \mu_i^{(n)} \geq \gamma > 0.$$

In addition $\|F^* - F_{n-1}\| = \|PG^{(n)}\| \leq \kappa \|P_i G^{(n)}\|$ for all n and i. For $n > N$ this implies that

$$
\begin{aligned}
\|F^* - F_{n-1}\|^2 - \|F^* - F_n\|^2 &\geq \left(2 - \sum_{j=1}^{r} \mu_j^{(n)}\right) \sum_{i=1}^{r} \mu_i^{(n)} \|P_i G^{(n)}\|^2 \\
&\geq \beta \sum_{i=1}^{r} \mu_i^{(n)} \|P_i G^{(n)}\|^2 \geq \frac{\beta}{\kappa} \sum_{i=1}^{r} \mu_i^{(n)} \|PG^{(n)}\|^2 \\
&\geq \frac{\beta \gamma}{\kappa} \|PG^{(n)}\|^2 = \frac{\beta \gamma}{\kappa} \|F^* - F_{n-1}\|^2.
\end{aligned}
$$

Thus $0 < \beta\gamma/\kappa < 1$ and

$$\|F^* - F_n\| \leq \left(1 - \frac{\beta \gamma}{\kappa}\right)^{1/2} \|F^* - F_{n-1}\|$$

for all n, and therefore

$$\|F^* - F_n\| \leq C \left(1 - \frac{\beta \gamma}{\kappa}\right)^{n/2} \|F^*\|,$$

for some $C > 0$ (to compensate for the first N iterations). This is the desired
result.   □

Remark 9.12 If $\mathcal{M}$ is closed, then we always have geometric convergence in
the model as presented in Theorem 9.5, and thus, of course, also in the case of
the alternating algorithm and iterates of a fixed convex combination as defined in
Theorems 9.3 and 9.4. For details on the geometric rate of convergence in the
case of the pure alternating algorithm ($\alpha_i = 1$ for all i), see Deutsch and Hundal
[1997]. Specific rates of convergence, such as those obtained by Smith, Solmon
and Wagner [1977], generally depend upon the angle between subspaces. We note
that the rate of convergence of the alternating algorithm can be arbitrarily slow if
$\mathcal{M}$ is not closed; see, for example, Franchetti and Light [1986] and Deutsch and
Hundal [2010].

What if $\mathcal{M}$ is not closed, but the other conditions of Theorem 9.11 hold? Must
the algorithm necessarily converge? We do not know. What is true is that if it
converges in norm, then it must converge to the desired limit.

Proposition 9.13 *Assume that the assumptions (a) and (b) hold as in Theorem*
9.11 except that $\mathcal{M}$ is not closed. If the algorithm has a norm cluster point then
the $G^{(n)}$ necessarily converge $G - F^*$, where F^* is the best approximation to G
from $\overline{\mathcal{M}}$.

Proof From the proof of Theorem 9.11 we have that

$$\lim_{n \to \infty} \|P_i G^{(n)}\| = 0,$$

for each $i = 1, \ldots, r$. Assume the algorithm has a norm cluster point. That is,
on some subsequence $\{\ell_k\}$ we have that $G^{(\ell_k)}$ converges in norm to a $\widetilde{G}$. Now
$G^{(\ell_k)} = G - F_{\ell_k - 1}$, where $F_{\ell_k - 1} \in \mathcal{M}$. This implies that $\widetilde{G} = G - \widetilde{F}$, where
$\widetilde{F} \in \overline{\mathcal{M}}$, and $F_{\ell_k - 1}$ converges in norm to $\widetilde{F}$. Since

$$\lim_{n \to \infty} \|P_i G^{(\ell_k)}\| = 0,$$

we have $P_i(\widetilde{G}) = 0$, $i = 1, \ldots, r$. Thus, by Lemma 9.2, $\widetilde{F}$ is the best approximation to G from $\overline{\mathcal{M}}$. In other words, $\widetilde{F} = F^*$. Thus any norm cluster point is
necessarily $G - F^*$.

It remains to prove that the full sequence $\{G^{(n)}\}$ converges to $G - F^*$. Equivalently, we wish to prove that the sequence $\{F_n\}$ converges to F^*. From (9.7) we
see that $\{\|F_n - F^*\|\}$ is a non-increasing sequence in n. Thus for all $n > \ell_k$

$$\|F_n - F_{\ell_k}\| \leq \|F_n - F^*\| + \|F_{\ell_k} - F^*\| \leq 2\|F_{\ell_k} - F^*\|.$$

As

$$\lim_{k \to \infty} \|F_{\ell_k} - F^*\| = 0$$

we have

$$\lim_{n \to \infty} \|F_n - F^*\| = 0. \qquad \square$$

To the best of our knowledge there are no known examples of the conditions of Theorem 9.11 holding and the algorithm not converging to $G - F^*$.

It should be noted that there are other more specific algorithms for this general problem to be found in the literature that are neither discussed nor described here, see, for example, Bauschke [1996].

9.2 A Greedy-Type Algorithm

We now discuss a different strategy which does not quite fall within the set of algorithms as described in Section 9.1. We consider what might be called a greedy-type algorithm. (In the optimization literature this is called a *remotest set* algorithm.) We will prove the desired convergence independently of the closedness of the sum of the subspaces. In addition, the algorithm converges for both a finite and infinite number of subspaces. At the end of this section we return to the case of a finite number of subspaces and prove geometric convergence when the sum of the subspaces is closed.

Let Ω_d be any given set, finite or infinite, of $d \times n$ real matrices. Set

$$\mathcal{M}(\Omega_d) := \text{span}\{f(A\mathbf{x}) : A \in \Omega_d, f : \mathbb{R}^d \to \mathbb{R}\},$$

where f runs over the set of all functions for which $f(A\mathbf{x}) \in L^2(K)$, some appropriate $K \subset \mathbb{R}^n$. As noted in previous chapters, $\mathcal{M}(\Omega_d)$ may be closed or not, and its closure may or may not be all of $L^2(K)$. On the assumption that Ω_d is the set of all $d \times n$ real matrices, and thus $\overline{\mathcal{M}(\Omega_d)} = L^2(K)$, an algorithm for approximating G from elements of $\mathcal{M}(\Omega_d)$ was developed in the statistical literature with the name of *projection pursuit*. It was suggested back in the 1960s and was revitalized in Friedman and Stuetzle [1981]; see the survey article by Huber [1985]. It does not attempt to construct a best approximation from any union of subspaces. Rather, it provides a method of obtaining a sequence $\{f_i(A^i\mathbf{x})\}_{i=1}^{\infty}$ such that the partial sums $\sum_{i=1}^{r} f_i(A^i\mathbf{x})$ converge to the given function G in the $L^2(K)$ norm.

We will consider this method of approximation from a more general perspective. Again, this method is not ridge function dependent. We assume that we are given $\mathcal{M}^j, j \in J$, where each $\mathcal{M}^j$ is a fixed closed subspace in our Hilbert space

H, and J is some counting set. We also assume that P_j is the best approximation operator from $\mathcal{M}^j$, and that for each $G \in H$ we can determine $P_j G$. Set

$$\mathcal{M} := \sum_{j \in J} \mathcal{M}^j.$$

Since $\overline{\mathcal{M}}$, the closure of $\mathcal{M}$, is also a linear subspace, the best approximation operator P on $\overline{\mathcal{M}}$ is well-defined, and $PG = 0$ if and only if $P_j G = 0$ for all $j \in J$.

We analyse the following algorithm for finding the best approximation to G from $\overline{\mathcal{M}}$. For $G \in H$, set $G^{(1)} := G$. At step n we consider the values

$$\|G^{(n)} - P_j G^{(n)}\|, \quad j \in J.$$

We would like to take an $\ell_n \in J$ such that $P_{\ell_n} G^{(n)}$ best approximates $G^{(n)}$ from among all the $P_j G^{(n)}$. That is, an $\ell_n \in J$ for which

$$\|G^{(n)} - P_{\ell_n} G^{(n)}\| = \inf_{j \in J} \|G^{(n)} - P_j G^{(n)}\|, \tag{9.8}$$

and then upgrade accordingly. Finding this infimum, if it exists, is generally a difficult task. Since $P_j G^{(n)}$ is the best approximation to $G^{(n)}$ from $\mathcal{M}^j$ in a Hilbert space, we have

$$\|G^{(n)} - P_j G^{(n)}\|^2 = \|G^{(n)}\|^2 - \|P_j G^{(n)}\|^2. \tag{9.9}$$

As such we do the following. From (9.9) we see that (9.8) is equivalent to finding $\ell_n \in J$ satisfying

$$\|P_{\ell_n} G^{(n)}\| = \sup_{j \in J} \|P_j G^{(n)}\|.$$

Let $\rho_n \in (0, 1]$ and assume we have chosen any $\ell_n \in J$ satisfying

$$\|P_{\ell_n} G^{(n)}\| \geq \rho_n \sup_{j \in J} \|P_j G^{(n)}\|. \tag{9.10}$$

We now set

$$G^{(n+1)} := G^{(n)} - P_{\ell_n} G^{(n)}. \tag{9.11}$$

This is our algorithm. It is a variation on what is called in the literature a "weak greedy algorithm".

By construction $G^{(n)} = G - F_n$, where $F_n \in \mathcal{M}$. The hope, as usual, is that under suitable conditions on the $\{\rho_n\}$ these $G^{(n)}$ will converge to $G - F^*$, where F^* is the best approximation to G from $\overline{\mathcal{M}}$. We will prove the following result.

Theorem 9.14 *Let* $\{\rho_n\}_{n=1}^{\infty}$ *be any fixed values in* $(0, 1]$ *satisfying*

$$\sum_{n=1}^{\infty} \frac{\rho_n}{n} = \infty.$$

Then, in the above algorithm, we have

$$\lim_{n \to \infty} G^{(n)} = G - F^*,$$

where F^* *is the best approximation to G from* $\overline{\mathcal{M}}$.

Remark 9.15 Note that if $\overline{\mathcal{M}} = H$, then in the above theorem $\|G^{(n)}\|$ converges to zero. In other words,

$$\sum_{n=1}^{\infty} P_{\ell_n} G^{(n)}$$

converges to G in norm. This theorem, for ridge functions with all possible directions (where $\overline{\mathcal{M}} = H$), and $\rho_n = \rho \in (0, 1]$ for all n, was first proved by Jones [1987]. It was generalized to the case of the ρ_n, as in the statement of the theorem, in Temlyakov [2000], see also Temlyakov [2011]. The proof of Temlyakov is a refinement of that of Jones. It transpires that this same proof, with minor modifications, is valid in this more general setting.

We first present some ancillary lemmas in order to make the proof of Theorem 9.14 more accessible.

Lemma 9.16 *For all* $n, m \in \mathbb{Z}_+$ *we have*

$$|(P_{\ell_m} G^{(m)}, G^{(n)})| \le \frac{\|P_{\ell_m} G^{(m)}\| \, \|P_{\ell_n} G^{(n)}\|}{\rho_n}.$$

Proof Since P_{ℓ_m} is an orthogonal projector, we have

$$|(P_{\ell_m} G^{(m)}, G^{(n)})| = |(P_{\ell_m} G^{(m)}, P_{\ell_m} G^{(n)})| \le \|P_{\ell_m} G^{(m)}\| \, \|P_{\ell_m} G^{(n)}\|.$$

From (9.10)

$$\|P_{\ell_n} G^{(n)}\| \ge \rho_n \sup_{j \in J} \|P_j G^{(n)}\| \ge \rho_n \|P_{\ell_m} G^{(n)}\|$$

and thus

$$|(P_{\ell_m} G^{(m)}, G^{(n)})| \le \frac{\|P_{\ell_m} G^{(m)}\| \, \|P_{\ell_n} G^{(n)}\|}{\rho_n}. \qquad \square$$

Lemma 9.17 *If $s_j \geq 0$ for all j, and*

$$\sum_{j=1}^{\infty} s_j^2 < \infty, \qquad \sum_{n=1}^{\infty} \frac{\rho_n}{n} = \infty,$$

then

$$\lim_{n \to \infty} \frac{s_n}{\rho_n} \sum_{j=1}^{n-1} s_j = 0.$$

Proof We have, by the Cauchy–Schwarz inequality,

$$\sum_{n=1}^{\infty} \frac{\rho_n}{n} \frac{s_n}{\rho_n} \sum_{j=1}^{n-1} s_j = \sum_{n=1}^{\infty} s_n \frac{\sum_{j=1}^{n-1} s_j}{n} \leq \left(\sum_{n=1}^{\infty} s_n^2 \right)^{1/2} \left(\sum_{n=1}^{\infty} \left(\frac{\sum_{j=1}^{n-1} s_j}{n} \right)^2 \right)^{1/2}.$$

By Hardy's Inequality, see Hardy, Littlewood and Pólya [1952], p. 239,

$$\sum_{n=1}^{\infty} \left(\frac{\sum_{j=1}^{n-1} s_j}{n} \right)^2 \leq 4 \sum_{n=1}^{\infty} s_n^2,$$

and since, by assumption, $\sum_{n=1}^{\infty} s_n^2 < \infty$, it follows that

$$\sum_{n=1}^{\infty} \frac{\rho_n}{n} \frac{s_n}{\rho_n} \sum_{j=1}^{n-1} s_j < \infty.$$

Furthermore, we are given

$$\sum_{n=1}^{\infty} \frac{\rho_n}{n} = \infty,$$

which then implies that

$$\lim_{n \to \infty} \frac{s_n}{\rho_n} \sum_{j=1}^{n-1} s_j = 0. \qquad \square$$

Proof of Theorem 9.14 The sequence $\{\|G^{(n)}\|\}_{n=1}^{\infty}$ is non-increasing in n. Furthermore from (9.9) and (9.11) we see that

$$\|G^{(n)}\|^2 = \|G\|^2 - \sum_{k=1}^{n-1} \|P_{\ell_k} G^{(k)}\|^2,$$

which implies

$$\sum_{k=1}^{\infty} \|P_{\ell_k} G^{(k)}\|^2 \leq \|G\|^2 < \infty. \qquad (9.12)$$

Setting

$$s_k := \|P_{\ell_k} G^{(k)}\|,$$

we have $\sum_{k=1}^{\infty} s_k^2 < \infty$.

For $m < n$ we have, from (9.11),

$$G^{(m)} - G^{(n)} = \sum_{k=m}^{n-1} P_{\ell_k} G^{(k)},$$

and

$$\|G^{(m)} - G^{(n)}\|^2 = \|G^{(m)}\|^2 - \|G^{(n)}\|^2 - 2(G^{(m)} - G^{(n)}, G^{(n)}). \qquad (9.13)$$

Set

$$\theta_{m,n} := |(G^{(m)} - G^{(n)}, G^{(n)})|.$$

From Lemma 9.16

$$\theta_{m,n} = \left| \left(\sum_{k=m}^{n-1} P_{\ell_k} G^{(k)}, G^{(n)} \right) \right| \leq \sum_{k=m}^{n-1} \frac{\|P_{\ell_k} G^{(k)}\| \, \|P_{\ell_n} G^{(n)}\|}{\rho_n} \leq \frac{s_n}{\rho_n} \sum_{k=1}^{n-1} s_k.$$

Thus, from Lemma 9.17, we obtain

$$\lim_{n \to \infty} \theta_{m,n} = 0,$$

and since the bound on $\theta_{m,n}$ is independent of m (aside from $m < n$) we in fact have

$$\lim_{n \to \infty} \max_{m < n} \theta_{m,n} = 0, \qquad (9.14)$$

where the maximum is taken over m.

We wish to prove that $G^{(n)}$ converges in norm to $G - F^*$, where F^* is the best approximation to G from $\overline{\mathcal{M}}$. We first prove that $\{G^{(n)}\}_{n=1}^{\infty}$ is a Cauchy sequence. If $\{G^{(n)}\}_{n=1}^{\infty}$ is not a Cauchy sequence then there exists a $C > 0$ such that for every $K_1 > 0$ there exist $N > K_1$ and $M > 0$ such that

$$\|G^{(N)} - G^{(N+M)}\| > C. \qquad (9.15)$$

In addition, since the $\{\|G^{(n)}\|\}$ converges, given $\varepsilon > 0$ there exists $K_2 > 0$ such that for all $n, m > K_2$

$$\|G^{(m)}\|^2 - \|G^{(n)}\|^2 < \varepsilon.$$

Finally, from (9.14), there exists an $R > N + M$ for which

$$\theta_{m,R} < \varepsilon$$

for all $m < R$. Let $K = \max\{K_1, K_2\}$ and assume $R > N + M > N > K$

are chosen such that R, N and M satisfy the above inequalities. From (9.15) we must have either

$$\|G^{(R)} - G^{(N)}\| > \frac{C}{2}$$

or

$$\|G^{(R)} - G^{(N+M)}\| > \frac{C}{2}.$$

Assume, without loss of generality, that

$$\|G^{(R)} - G^{(N)}\| > \frac{C}{2}.$$

Then from (9.13)

$$\frac{C^2}{4} < \|G^{(R)} - G^{(N)}\|^2 \leq \|G^{(R)}\|^2 - \|G^{(N)}\|^2 + 2\theta_{N,R} < \varepsilon + 2\varepsilon = 3\varepsilon.$$

As ε can be chosen arbitrarily small, we have arrived at a contradiction.

Since $\{G^{(n)}\}_{n=1}^{\infty}$ is a Cauchy sequence, it must converge. The definition of the algorithm implies that

$$G^{(n)} = G - F_n$$

for some $F_n \in \mathcal{M}$. Thus

$$\lim_{n \to \infty} G^{(n)} = G - \widetilde{F}$$

where $\widetilde{F} \in \overline{\mathcal{M}}$. Assume that $\widetilde{F}$ is not the best approximation to G from $\overline{\mathcal{M}}$. There must therefore exist a $k \in J$ for which

$$\|P_k(G - \widetilde{F})\| = c > 0.$$

Since $G^{(n)}$ converges to $G - \widetilde{F}$ there exists an N such that for all $n > N$ we have

$$\sup_{j \in J} \|P_j G^{(n)}\| > \frac{c}{2},$$

and thus, from (9.10),

$$\|P_{\ell_n} G^{(n)}\| \geq \rho_n \frac{c}{2}$$

for all $n > N$. From (9.12) it therefore follows that

$$\sum_{n=1}^{\infty} \rho_n^2 < \infty.$$

But from the Cauchy–Schwarz inequality we then have

$$\sum_{n=1}^{\infty} \frac{\rho_n}{n} \leq \left(\sum_{n=1}^{\infty} \frac{1}{n^2}\right)^{1/2} \left(\sum_{n=1}^{\infty} \rho_n^2\right)^{1/2} < \infty,$$

which contradicts our assumption. $\qquad\square$

Remark 9.18 Nothing seems to be known about rates of convergence in this general case. However, there is a variation on this algorithm called a "Relaxed Greedy Algorithm", where convergence rates are obtained. This algorithm is discussed in Jones [1992] and Temlyakov [2011].

Remark 9.19 In the previous section we mentioned relaxation parameters; see, for example, Theorem 9.3. One can also generalize Theorem 9.14 to include such parameters $\{\alpha_n\}$. That is, replace (9.11) by

$$G^{(n+1)} := G^{(n)} - \alpha_n P_{\ell_n} G^{(n)}.$$

Recall that for $\alpha_n \in (0,2)$ we have

$$\|G^{(n+1)}\|^2 = \|G^{(n)}\|^2 - \alpha_n(2 - \alpha_n)\|P_{\ell_n}G^{(n)}\|^2.$$

It is easily verified that if $\alpha_n \in (0,2)$ and neither 0 nor 2 is a cluster point of the sequence $\{\alpha_n\}_{n=1}^{\infty}$, then with these relaxation parameters Theorem 9.14 remains valid.

Assume, as in Section 9.1, that we have only a finite number of subspaces $\mathcal{M}^j$, $j = 1, \ldots, r$, and that $\rho_n = 1$ for all n. This is a reasonable assumption in this setting. From Theorem 9.14 we have the desired convergence of the algorithm. In addition, under the assumption that $\mathcal{M}$ is closed, we obtain geometric convergence.

Theorem 9.20 *Assume we are given a finite number of subspaces $\mathcal{M}^j$, $j = 1, \ldots, r$, and $\mathcal{M} := \mathcal{M}^1 + \cdots + \mathcal{M}^r$ is closed. Then the rate of convergence of the algorithm as given in Theorem 9.14, with $\rho_n = 1$ for all n, is geometric.*

Proof Let P denote the orthogonal projector onto $\mathcal{M}$. Thus $PG = F^*$, where F^* is the best approximation to G from $\mathcal{M}$. From Theorem 9.8 there exists a $\kappa > 0$ such that for every $G \in H$

$$\|PG\| \leq \kappa \max_{j=1,\ldots,r} \|P_j G\|.$$

From the definition of $F^* \in \mathcal{M}$ we have that $P_j(G - F^*) = 0$ for $j = 1, \ldots, r$. Thus, from (9.9) and (9.11), and since $G - F^* \in \mathcal{M}^{\perp} = \cap_{j=1}^r (\mathcal{M}^j)^{\perp}$,

$$\|P_{\ell_n}G^{(n)}\|^2 = \|G^{(n)}\|^2 - \|G^{(n+1)}\|^2 = \|G^{(n)} - (G-F^*)\|^2 - \|G^{(n+1)} - (G-F^*)\|^2.$$

Since $\|P_{\ell_n}G^{(n)}\| = \max_{j=1,\ldots,r} \|P_j G^{(n)}\|$, we obtain

$$\frac{1}{\kappa^2}\|PG^{(n)}\|^2 \leq \|P_{\ell_n}G^{(n)}\|^2 = \|G^{(n)} - (G-F^*)\|^2 - \|G^{(n+1)} - (G-F^*)\|^2.$$

Now $G^{(n)} - (G - F^*) = G - F_n - (G - F^*) = F^* - F_n = PG^{(n)}$, and $G^{(n+1)} - (G - F^*) = F^* - F_{n+1}$. We therefore have

$$\frac{1}{\kappa^2}\|F^* - F_n\|^2 \le \|F^* - F_n\|^2 - \|F^* - F_{n+1}\|^2.$$

From this estimate geometric convergence easily follows. $\qquad\square$

9.3 Fixed Directions in Smooth Banach Spaces

As in Section 9.1, let us assume that $\mathcal{M}^1, \ldots, \mathcal{M}^r$ are fixed, closed, infinite or finite-dimensional linear subspaces. Moreover, we here assume that they lie in a uniformly convex and uniformly smooth Banach space X. In Section 8.1 we defined uniform convexity. A normed linear space is *smooth* if to each $G \in X$ there exists a unique $\ell \in X^*$ satisfying $\|\ell\| = 1$ and $\ell(G) = \|G\|$. There are various equivalent definitions of uniform smoothness. We will use the fact that X is uniformly smooth if and only if X^* is uniformly convex. The classical L^p spaces, $p \in (1, \infty)$, are both uniformly convex and uniformly smooth.

Let P_i denote the best approximation operator to $\mathcal{M}^i$, $i = 1, \ldots, r$. That is, to each $G \in X$ the element $P_i G$ is the unique best approximation to G from $\mathcal{M}^i$. As X is uniformly convex and $\mathcal{M}^i$ is closed, these P_i are well-defined; see Chapter 8 and Cheney [1966], p. 22. We set

$$\mathcal{M} := \mathcal{M}^1 + \cdots + \mathcal{M}^r,$$

and will prove that if $\mathcal{M}$ is closed, then the alternating algorithm converges to the best approximation from $\mathcal{M}$. (The proof in the case $r = 2$ is due to Deutsch [1979], while this more general case may be found in Pinkus [2015]. If the P_i are linear, which is rare indeed, then this result for any finite r, and without demanding the closure of $\mathcal{M}$, is in Reich [1982].) We recall that the alternating algorithm is defined by setting

$$E := (I - P_r) \cdots (I - P_1)$$

and considering

$$\lim_{s \to \infty} E^s G.$$

It is to be expected that more general results paralleling Theorems 9.5, 9.11 and 9.14 should hold. However, for $r \ge 3$ this algorithm is, at the moment, the only generalization of the results of Section 9.1 to a non-Hilbert space setting of which we are aware. We also know that this algorithm cannot converge, as desired, in every normed linear space, see, for example, Deutsch [1979]. In any normed linear space X that is not smooth, one can construct two linear subspaces $\mathcal{M}^1$ and $\mathcal{M}^2$, and a $G \in X$ for which $P_i G = 0$, $i = 1, 2$, and yet the zero element is not a best approximation to G from $\mathcal{M}^1 + \mathcal{M}^2$. That is, knowing P_1G and P_2G tells us nothing about a best approximation from $\mathcal{M}^1 + \mathcal{M}^2$.

Theorem 9.21 *Assume the* $\mathcal{M}^i$, $i = 1, \ldots, r$, *are closed linear subspaces in a uniformly convex and uniformly smooth Banach space* X. *Let* P_i *denote the best approximation operator from* $\mathcal{M}^i$, $i = 1, \ldots, r$. *If* $\mathcal{M}$ *is closed, then the alternating algorithm converges as desired.*

We will use the following ancillary result in the proof of Theorem 9.21. Its proof is the second paragraph in the proof of Theorem 9.8.

Lemma 9.22 *Let* X *be a Banach space. Assume*

$$\mathcal{M} = \mathcal{M}^1 + \cdots + \mathcal{M}^r,$$

where $\mathcal{M}, \mathcal{M}^1, \ldots, \mathcal{M}^r$ *are closed linear subspaces of* X. *Then there exists a* $\kappa > 0$ *such that each* $m \in \mathcal{M}$ *has a representation of the form*

$$m = m_1 + \cdots + m_r,$$

where $m_j \in \mathcal{M}^j$, $j = 1, \ldots, r$, *and*

$$\|m_1\| + \cdots + \|m_r\| \leq \kappa \|m\|.$$

Proof of Theorem 9.21 As previously noted, the P_j are well-defined. In addition,

$$\|(I - P_j)G\| \leq \|G\|. \tag{9.16}$$

Set

$$H^{(sr+j)} := (I - P_j) \cdots (I - P_1)E^s$$

for $j \in \{1, \ldots, r\}$ and $s \in \mathbb{Z}_+$. Note that $H^{(sr+r)} = E^{s+1}$. Let

$$G^{(k)} := H^{(k)}G =: G - F_k,$$

where $F_k \in \mathcal{M}$. Furthermore, from (9.16)

$$\|G^{(k)}\| \leq \|G^{(k-1)}\| \tag{9.17}$$

for all k. As such

$$\lim_{k \to \infty} \|G^{(k)}\|$$

exists. If

$$\lim_{k \to \infty} \|G^{(k)}\| = 0$$

then there is nothing to prove since this implies that $G \in \mathcal{M}$, by our assumption of closure, and F_k converges to G. As such, we assume that

$$\lim_{k \to \infty} \|G^{(k)}\| = C > 0.$$

For each $k \in \mathbb{Z}_+$, let ϕ_k be the (unique) linear functional on X (see Section 8.1) satisfying

(a) $\|\phi_k\| = \|G^{(k)}\|$,
(b) $\phi_k(G^{(k)}) = \|G^{(k)}\|^2$.

For $k = sr + j$, $j \in \{1, \ldots, r\}$, we also have from the best approximation property and the definition of $H^{(sr+j)}$ that

(c) $\phi_{sr+j}(m_j) = 0$ all $m_j \in \mathcal{M}^j$, $j \in \{1, \ldots, r\}$.

Note that

$$G^{(sr+j)} - G^{(sr+j-1)} \in \mathcal{M}^j,$$

and thus

$$\phi_{sr+j}(G^{(sr+j-1)}) = \phi_{sr+j}(G^{(sr+j)}) = \|G^{(sr+j)}\|^2.$$

We first claim that for every $j, k \in \{1, \ldots, r\}$ we have

$$\lim_{s \to \infty} \|\phi_{sr+j} - \phi_{sr+k}\| = 0.$$

It obviously suffices to prove that

$$\lim_{s \to \infty} \|\phi_{sr+j} - \phi_{sr+j-1}\| = 0$$

for $j \in \{2, \ldots, r\}$. Now

$$
\begin{aligned}
\frac{\|\phi_{sr+j} + \phi_{sr+j-1}\|}{2} &\geq \frac{(\phi_{sr+j} + \phi_{sr+j-1})(G^{(sr+j-1)})}{2\|G^{(sr+j-1)}\|} \\
&= \frac{\phi_{sr+j}(G^{(sr+j-1)}) + \phi_{sr+j-1}(G^{(sr+j-1)})}{2\|G^{(sr+j-1)}\|} \\
&= \frac{\|G^{(sr+j)}\|^2 + \|G^{(sr+j-1)}\|^2}{2\|G^{(sr+j-1)}\|} \\
&\geq \|G^{(sr+j)}\| \\
&= \|\phi_{sr+j}\|.
\end{aligned}
$$

Thus

$$\frac{\|\phi_{sr+j} + \phi_{sr+j-1}\|}{2} \geq \|\phi_{sr+j}\|. \tag{9.18}$$

Furthermore

$$\lim_{s \to \infty} \|\phi_{sr+j}\| = \lim_{s \to \infty} \|G^{(sr+j)}\| = C > 0.$$

The Banach space X is uniformly smooth if and only if X^* is uniformly convex. Thus the *modulus of uniform convexity* defined by

$$\delta(\varepsilon) := \inf \left\{ 1 - \frac{\|f + g\|}{2} : f, g \in X^*, \|f\| = \|g\| = 1, \|f - g\| \geq \varepsilon \right\}$$

is strictly positive for $\varepsilon > 0$. ($\delta(\varepsilon)$ is, by definition, a non-decreasing function of $\varepsilon \in (0, 2]$ that decreases to zero as ε decreases to zero.)

Set

$$f_s = \frac{\phi_{sr+j}}{\|\phi_{sr+j-1}\|}, \quad g_s = \frac{\phi_{sr+j-1}}{\|\phi_{sr+j-1}\|}$$

and $\varepsilon = \|f_s - g_s\|$. Since $\|f_s\| \leq \|g_s\| = 1$, we have

$$\delta(\varepsilon) \leq 1 - \frac{\|f_s + g_s\|}{2},$$

which, when substituting for ε, f_s and g_s, gives us

$$\|\phi_{sr+j-1}\| \, \delta \left(\frac{\|\phi_{sr+j} - \phi_{sr+j-1}\|}{\|\phi_{sr+j-1}\|} \right) \leq \|\phi_{sr+j-1}\| - \frac{\|\phi_{sr+j} + \phi_{sr+j1}\|}{2}.$$

From (9.18) we obtain

$$\|\phi_{sr+j-1}\| \, \delta \left(\frac{\|\phi_{sr+j} - \phi_{sr+j-1}\|}{\|\phi_{sr+j-1}\|} \right) \leq \|\phi_{sr+j-1}\| - \|\phi_{sr+j}\|.$$

From (9.17) and (a) the right-hand side tends to zero as s tends to ∞. Since $\|\phi_{sr+j-1}\|$ is bounded away from zero we must have, by the definition of the modulus of convexity,

$$\lim_{s \to \infty} \|\phi_{sr+j} - \phi_{sr+j-1}\| = 0.$$

We therefore obtain

$$\lim_{s \to \infty} \|\phi_{sr+j} - \phi_{sr+k}\| = 0$$

for every $j, k \in \{1, \ldots, r\}$.

We recall that

$$G^{(sr+j)} = H^{(sr+j)} G = G - F_{sr+j}.$$

We can write

$$G - H^{(sr+j)} G = F_{sr+j} = \widetilde{m}_1 + \cdots + \widetilde{m}_r$$

for some $\widetilde{m}_\ell \in \mathcal{M}^\ell$, $\ell = 1, \ldots, r$ (these elements also depend upon s and j) where, by Lemma 9.22, for some fixed $\kappa > 0$,

$$\|\widetilde{m}_1\| + \cdots + \|\widetilde{m}_r\| \leq \kappa \|F_{sr+j}\| \leq \kappa [\|G\| + \|H^{(sr+j)} G\|] \leq 2\kappa \|G\|.$$

Let F be any element of $\mathcal{M}$ satisfying $\|G - F\| \leq \|G\|$. Set

$$F = m_1 + \cdots + m_r$$

where $m_\ell \in \mathcal{M}^\ell$, $\ell = 1, \ldots, r$, and

$$\|m_1\| + \cdots + \|m_r\| \leq \kappa\|F\| \leq 2\kappa\|G\|,$$

for $\kappa > 0$ as in Lemma 9.22. Now, for F as above,

$$
\begin{aligned}
\|H^{(sr+j)}G\|^2 &= \phi_{sr+j}(H^{(sr+j)}G) = \phi_{sr+j}(G - F_{sr+j}) \\
&= \phi_{sr+j}\left(G - \sum_{k=1}^{r} \widetilde{m}_k\right) \\
&= \phi_{sr+j}(G - F) + \phi_{sr+j}\left(F - \sum_{k=1}^{r} \widetilde{m}_k\right) \\
&= \phi_{sr+j}(G - F) + \phi_{sr+j}\left(\sum_{k=1}^{r}(m_k - \widetilde{m}_k)\right).
\end{aligned}
$$

Since $\phi_{sr+k}(m_k) = 0$ for all $m_k \in \mathcal{M}^k$ we have

$$
\begin{aligned}
\|G^{(sr+j)}\|^2 &= \phi_{sr+j}(G - F) + \sum_{k=1}^{r}(\phi_{sr+j} - \phi_{sr+k})(m_k - \widetilde{m}_k) \\
&\leq \|\phi_{sr+j}\|\,\|G - F\| + \sum_{k=1}^{r}\|\phi_{sr+j} - \phi_{sr+k}\|\,\|m_k - \widetilde{m}_k\| \\
&\leq \|\phi_{sr+j}\|\,\|G - F\| + \sum_{k=1}^{r}\|\phi_{sr+j} - \phi_{sr+k}\|\,4\kappa\|G\| \\
&= \|G^{(sr+j)}\|\,\|G - F\| + 4\kappa\|G\|\sum_{k=1}^{r}\|\phi_{sr+j} - \phi_{sr+k}\|.
\end{aligned}
$$

Let $s \to \infty$ and recall that we have

$$\lim_{s\to\infty}\|\phi_{sr+j} - \phi_{sr+k}\| = 0$$

for $j, k \in \{1, \ldots, r\}$. Furthermore

$$\lim_{s\to\infty}\|G^{(sr+j)}\| = C > 0.$$

Thus, we obtain

$$\lim_{s\to\infty}\|G^{(sr+j)}\| \leq \|G - F\|$$

for every $F \in \mathcal{M}$ satisfying $\|G - F\| \le \|G\|$, and therefore

$$\lim_{s \to \infty} \|G - F_{sr+j}\| \le \min_{F \in \mathcal{M}} \|G - F\| = \|G - F^*\|,$$

where F^* is the best approximation to G from $\mathcal{M}$. It easily follows from the definition of uniform convexity that F_{sr+j} must converge to F^* in X as $s \to \infty$. This is valid for each $j \in \{1, \ldots, r\}$. $\qquad\square$

In this setting nothing is known with regards to rates of convergence.

9.4 The Diliberto–Straus Algorithm

The Diliberto–Straus algorithm is a particular case of the alternating algorithm in $C(K)$, where K is a compact, convex set in $\mathbb{R}^n$, equipped with the uniform norm. It has various drawbacks. One major drawback is that it converges to the desired result only when considering two directions. As such, our discussion of this algorithm will be brief.

Assume we are given two matrices A and B. We set

$$\mathcal{M}(A, B) := \text{span}\{f(A\mathbf{x}) + g(B\mathbf{x})\},$$

where f and g are continuous functions on the appropriate domains so that $f(A\mathbf{x})$ and $g(B\mathbf{x})$ are in $C(K)$. Our goal is to find an algorithmic method of constructing a best approximation to $G \in C(K)$ from $\mathcal{M}(A, B)$.

The best approximation operator from $\mathcal{M}(A)$, in the uniform norm, is not uniquely defined. However, there is a simple and natural best approximation operator. It is the operator that defines $\widetilde{f}(\mathbf{y})$ to be the constant that best approximates the function G for all $\mathbf{y}$ in the intersection of the hyperplane $\{\mathbf{x} : A\mathbf{x} = A\mathbf{y}\}$ with K. In the uniform norm this $\widetilde{f}(\mathbf{y})$ is just the average of the maximum and minimum of G on this hyperplane. That is, for each $\mathbf{y} \in K$ we define

$$\widetilde{f}(\mathbf{y}) = P_A G(\mathbf{y}) := \frac{1}{2} \left[\max_{\{\mathbf{x} : A\mathbf{x} = A\mathbf{y}\} \cap K} G(\mathbf{x}) + \min_{\{\mathbf{x} : A\mathbf{x} = A\mathbf{y}\} \cap K} G(\mathbf{x}) \right].$$

Note that on K we have $\widetilde{f}(\mathbf{y}) = f(A\mathbf{y})$ for some f. Similarly, for $\mathbf{y} \in K$ we define

$$\widetilde{g}(\mathbf{y}) = P_B G(\mathbf{y}) := \frac{1}{2} \left[\max_{\{\mathbf{x} : B\mathbf{x} = B\mathbf{y}\} \cap K} G(\mathbf{x}) + \min_{\{\mathbf{x} : B\mathbf{x} = B\mathbf{y}\} \cap K} G(\mathbf{x}) \right],$$

and we have $\widetilde{g}(\mathbf{y}) = g(B\mathbf{y})$ for some g. One problem with these operators is that the resulting f and g need not, for general K, be continuous. For this reason we demand that K be convex. For convex K the minimum and maximum over parallel hyperplanes are continuous functions, and thus for $G \in C(K)$ the resulting f and g are also continuous.

Let us now explain how the Diliberto–Straus algorithm works. The Diliberto–Straus algorithm is given by repeated iterations of the above two operations. That is, we set

$$EG := (I - P_B)(I - P_A)G,$$

and then iterate E. In other words, as with the alternating algorithm, we first set $G^{(1)} := G$. We then define $G^{(2)} := G^{(1)} - P_A G^{(1)}$. At the next step we define $G^{(3)} := G^{(2)} - P_B G^{(2)}$, etc. In general, $G^{(2n)} := G^{(2n-1)} - P_A G^{(2n-1)}$ and $G^{(2n+1)} := G^{(2n)} - P_B G^{(2n)}$ for all n. Note that, for every n,

$$G^{(n)} = G - f_n - g_n,$$

where $f_n \in \mathcal{M}(A)$ and $g_n \in \mathcal{M}(B)$.

This Diliberto–Straus algorithm was introduced in Diliberto and Straus [1951]. They proved therein that for $K = [a, b] \times [c, d]$

$$\lim_{n \to \infty} \|G - f_n - g_n\| = \inf_{m \in \mathcal{M}(\mathbf{e}^1, \mathbf{e}^2)} \|G - m\|.$$

That is, the norm of the iterations converges as desired. They left open the question of the convergence of the sequence $\{f_n + g_n\}$ (they only had convergence on subsequences). It was later proved by Aumann [1959] that this sequence of functions converges uniformly to a continuous best approximation to G from $\mathcal{M}(\mathbf{e}^1, \mathbf{e}^2)$. The proof of convergence of the norm of the iterations was later generalized by Golomb [1959] to the case where P_A and P_B are, as coined in Golomb [1959], "central extremals", or as termed in Light and Cheney [1985], Chapter 4, "central proximity maps". We will use this latter term.

Definition 9.23 A best approximation operator P from a Banach space X onto a linear subspace M is said to be a *central proximity map* if for all $G \in X$ and $m \in M$ we have

$$\|G - PG + m\| = \|G - PG - m\|.$$

Since K is compact, it is easily verified that both P_A and P_B are central proximity maps onto $\mathcal{M}(A)$ and $\mathcal{M}(B)$, respectively. This follows from the fact that on each set $\{\mathbf{x} : A\mathbf{x} = \mathbf{z}\}$ we have $\min\{(G - P_A G)(\mathbf{x})\} = -\max\{(G - P_A G)(\mathbf{x})\}$, and every $m \in \mathcal{M}(A)$ is a constant function on this set.

From Light and Cheney [1985], Chapter 4, we have the following.

Theorem 9.24 *Let K be a compact, convex subset of $\mathbb{R}^n$. Let A and B be as above. Then, assuming that $\mathcal{M}(A, B)$ is closed in $C(K)$, it follows that*

$$\lim_{n \to \infty} \|G - f_n - g_n\| = \inf_{m \in \mathcal{M}(A,B)} \|G - m\|.$$

What is still unclear is whether we have convergence of the $f_n + g_n$ to a best approximation to G from $\mathcal{M}(A, B)$. It is true in the case proved in Aumann [1959], as mentioned above.

It is also not known whether the closure of $\mathcal{M}(A, B)$ is necessary. However, all the proofs of the Diliberto–Straus algorithm, as found in the literature, use this fact, either explicitly or implicitly. Necessary and sufficient conditions for when subspaces of the form $\mathcal{M}(A, B)$ are closed in $C(K)$ may be found in Section 7.4.

There have been attempts and claims for generalizations of the Diliberto–Straus algorithm to more then two directions. But the algorithm in the case of more than two directions need not converge. The following is an example of the non-effectiveness of the Diliberto–Straus algorithm when approximating from more than two directions. This example is from Medvedev [1992]; see also Khavinson [1997], Chapter 3, §3, for notes thereon. This negative phenomenon was first noted in Aumann [1963]. In fact, in this example we have that the zero function is the best approximation to a function G from each of three ridge function linear subspaces given by linearly independent directions, and yet the zero function is not a best approximation from the sum of these subspaces. Thus, no algorithm, and not only the Diliberto–Straus algorithm, that is based only on knowledge of these best approximation operators P_x, P_y and P_z can converge to a best approximation from the sum of the subspaces.

Example 9.1 Set $I = [0, 1]$, and let $G \in C(I^3)$. We are interested in the problem of approximating G from $\mathcal{M}(\mathbf{e}^1, \mathbf{e}^2, \mathbf{e}^3)$, where $\mathbf{e}^j$ is the jth unit vector. That is, we want to approximate $G(x, y, z)$ in the uniform norm on $[0, 1]^3$ by functions of the form $f(x) + g(y) + h(z)$. Define the function k on $[0, 3]$ by

$$k(t) := \begin{cases} -1, & 0 \le t \le 1 \\ 2t - 3, & 1 \le t \le 2 \\ 1, & 2 \le t \le 3, \end{cases}$$

and let $G \in C(I^3)$ satisfy

$$G(x, y, z) := k(x + y + z).$$

For given $G \in C(I^3)$ we set, as previously,

$$f(x) := P_x G(x, y, z) := \frac{1}{2} \left[\max_{y,z \in I} G(x, y, z) + \min_{y,z \in I} G(x, y, z) \right]$$

and similarly define $g(y) := P_y G(x, y, z)$ and $h(z) := P_z G(x, y, z)$. Note that these P_x, P_y and P_z are best approximation operators to $\mathcal{M}(\mathbf{e}^j)$, $j = 1, 2, 3$, respectively, in the uniform norm. The Diliberto–Straus algorithm, in this setting, is given by defining

$$E\,G := (I - P_z)(I - P_y)(I - P_x)G,$$

and then considering

$$\lim_{s \to \infty} E^s G.$$

Now, for any $x \in I$ we have

$$\max_{y,z \in I} G(x, y, z) = G(x, 1, 1) = k(x + 2) = 1$$

and

$$\min_{y,z \in I} G(x, y, z) = G(x, 0, 0) = k(x) = -1.$$

Thus

$$P_x G(x, y, z) = 0$$

for all $x \in I$. From symmetry considerations we also have $P_y G(x, y, z) = P_z G(x, y, z) = 0$. Thus $E\,G = G$. On the other hand,

$$H(x, y, z) := x + y + z - \frac{3}{2}$$

is obviously a function in $\mathcal{M}(e^1, e^2, e^3)$, i.e., it is of the form $f(x) + g(y) + h(z)$. It is also easily verified that

$$|G(x, y, z) - H(x, y, z)| \le \frac{1}{2}$$

for all $x, y, z \in I$. (In fact it can be shown that H is a best approximation to G from $\mathcal{M}(e^1, e^2, e^3)$.) Thus the best approximation to $G(x, y, z)$ in $C(I^3)$ from $\mathcal{M}(e^1, e^2, e^3)$ is not the zero function, and yet the Diliberto–Straus algorithm, or any other algorithm based on P_x, P_y and P_z, can not converge to a best approximation from $\mathcal{M}(e^1, e^2, e^3)$.

Another normed linear space of interest is L^1. Here we present a simple example showing that, in this setting, the alternating algorithm does not work even in the case of two directions. This example is from Light, McCabe, Phillips and Cheney [1982]. It may also be found in Light and Cheney [1985] in Chapter 7, where conditions are given whereby the Diliberto–Straus algorithm with two directions does converge in L^1 (albeit conditions difficult to verify). These positive results are from Light and Holland [1984].

Before presenting this example, let us briefly recall the fundamental result characterizing best approximations in L^1. Let K be any set, Σ a σ-field of subsets of K, and ν a positive measure on Σ. For $G \in L^1(K, \Sigma, \nu)$, let sgn $G(x)$ denote the sign of $G(x)$, i.e., 1, -1 or 0, as $G(x)$ is positive, negative or zero, respectively. In addition, let

$$Z(G) := \{x : G(x) = 0\}$$

define the zero set of G. Then we have the following.

Theorem 9.25 *Assume* $G \in L^1(K, \Sigma, \nu) \backslash \overline{M}$, *where* M *is a linear subspace of* $L^1(K, \Sigma, \nu)$. *Then* h^* *is a best approximation to* G *from* M *in the* $L^1(K, \Sigma, \nu)$ *norm if and only if*

$$\left| \int_K \text{sgn}(G - h^*) m \, d\nu \right| \leq \int_{Z(G-h^*)} |m| \, d\nu$$

for all $m \in M$.

Using this characterization we now present an example of where the best approximation to a $G \in L^1$ from both $\mathcal{M}(\mathbf{e}^1)$ and $\mathcal{M}(\mathbf{e}^2)$ is the zero function, and yet the zero function is not a best approximation from $\mathcal{M}(\mathbf{e}^1, \mathbf{e}^2)$.

Example 9.2 Set $I = [-1, 1]$, and let $L^1(I^2)$ be the usual L^1 space with Lebesgue measure thereon. We are interested in the problem of approximating $G \in L^1(I^2)$ from $\mathcal{M}(\mathbf{e}^1, \mathbf{e}^2)$, where $\mathbf{e}^j$ is the jth unit vector, $j = 1, 2$. That is, we want to approximate $G(x, y)$ in the usual L^1 norm on $[-1, 1]^2$ by functions of the form $f(x) + g(y)$. Let

$$G(x, y) := \begin{cases} xy, & x, y > 0 \\ -xy, & x, y < 0 \\ 0, & \text{otherwise.} \end{cases}$$

We first claim that the zero function is a best $L^1(I^2)$ approximation to G from each of $\mathcal{M}(\mathbf{e}^1)$ and $\mathcal{M}(\mathbf{e}^2)$. Considering $\mathcal{M}(\mathbf{e}^1)$, then this result is an immediate consequence of Theorem 9.25 since for each fixed $x \in (-1, 1)$ we have

$$\left| \int_{-1}^1 \text{sgn}(G) \, dy \right| = \int_{Z(G)} dy = 1.$$

In fact, it is easily verified that the zero function is the unique best $L^1(I^2)$ approximation to G from $\mathcal{M}(\mathbf{e}^1)$. From symmetry considerations this same result holds with respect to $\mathcal{M}(\mathbf{e}^2)$. We now claim that the zero function is not a best $L^1(I^2)$ approximation to G from $\mathcal{M}(\mathbf{e}^1, \mathbf{e}^2)$. Consider $h(x + y) := x + y$. Obviously this function is in $\mathcal{M}(\mathbf{e}^1, \mathbf{e}^2)$. Moreover

$$\left| \int_{I^2} \text{sgn}(G) h \, dx \, dy \right| > \int_{Z(G)} |h| \, dx \, dy, \tag{9.19}$$

which contradicts the fact that the zero function is a best $L^1(I^2)$ approximation to G from $\mathcal{M}(e^1, e^2)$. (The inequality (9.19) implies that $\|G - ch\|_{L^1(I^2)} < \|G\|_{L^1(I^2)}$ for some constant c.) To verify (9.19) note that, by a change of variable, we have

$$\int_{I^2} \operatorname{sgn}(G) h \, dx \, dy = 2 \int_0^1 \int_0^1 x + y \, dx \, dy$$

while

$$\int_{Z(G)} |h| \, dx \, dy = 2 \int_0^1 \int_0^1 |x - y| \, dx \, dy,$$

and on the interior of the first quadrant we have $x + y > |x - y|$.

10

Integral Representations

In this chapter we consider integral representations of functions using kernels that are ridge functions. The most commonly used integral representation with a ridge function kernel is that given by the Fourier transform. The function $\psi_{\mathbf{w}} := e^{i\mathbf{x}\cdot\mathbf{w}}$ is, for each fixed $\mathbf{w}$, a ridge function. Under suitable assumptions on an f defined on $\mathbb{R}^n$, we have

$$f(\mathbf{x}) = \frac{1}{(2\pi)^n} \int (f, \overline{\psi_{\mathbf{w}}})\psi_{\mathbf{w}}(\mathbf{x})\, d\mathbf{w}.$$

For example, the above holds if $f \in L^1(\mathbb{R}^n) \cap C(\mathbb{R}^n)$ and $\widehat{f} \in L^1(\mathbb{R}^n)$. While we have drifted into the complex plane, we can easily rewrite the above using only real-valued functions.

Another integral representation with a ridge function kernel may be found in John [1955], p. 11. We present it here without proof. Assume $f \in C_0^1(\mathbb{R}^n)$, i.e., f and its first partial derivatives are continuous functions, and f has compact support. Let $\Delta_{\mathbf{x}}$ denote the Laplacian with respect to the variables $x_1, \ldots, x_n$, i.e.,

$$\Delta_{\mathbf{x}} := \sum_{i=1}^{n} \frac{\partial^2}{\partial x_i^2}.$$

Let S^{n-1} denote the unit sphere in $\mathbb{R}^n$, and let da be uniform measure on S^{n-1} of total measure equal to the surface area of the unit sphere S^{n-1}, i.e., of total measure

$$\omega_n := \frac{2\pi^{n/2}}{\Gamma(n/2)}. \tag{10.1}$$

For n and k odd positive integers, we have

$$f(\mathbf{x}) = [\Delta_{\mathbf{x}}]^{(n+k)/2} \frac{1}{4(2\pi i)^{n-1}k!} \int_{\mathbb{R}^n} \left(\int_{S^{n-1}} f(\mathbf{y})|(\mathbf{y}-\mathbf{x})\cdot\mathbf{a}|^k da \right) d\mathbf{y}.$$

For n an even positive integer and k any even non-negative integer, we have

$$f(\mathbf{x}) = [\Delta_{\mathbf{x}}]^{(n+k)/2} \frac{-1}{(2\pi i)^n k!} \int_{\mathbb{R}^n} \left(\int_{S^{n-1}} f(\mathbf{y})((\mathbf{y} - \mathbf{x}) \cdot \mathbf{a})^k \right.$$

$$\left. \times \ln \left[\frac{1}{i}(\mathbf{y} - \mathbf{x}) \cdot \mathbf{a} \right] d\mathbf{a} \right) d\mathbf{y}.$$

The relationship between these integral formulæ and the inverse Radon transform can be found in John [1955], together with other similar integral representations.

In this chapter we review two additional integral representations. The first, using an orthogonal decomposition in terms of Gegenbauer polynomials is from Petrushev [1998]. The second is based upon ridgelets and was presented by Candès [1998] in his doctoral thesis, see also Candès [1999].

As integrals are limits of sums this provides a theoretical basis for the construction of ridge function approximation methods fundamentally different from those presented in Chapter 9. Both Petrushev and Candès do much more than what is presented here. They discuss discretizations of their representations with an eye towards obtaining approximations that are constructive, qualitative and stable. The interested reader should consult those references.

10.1 Gegenbauer Ridge Polynomials

One approach to integral representations of functions with ridge function kernels is due to Petrushev [1998]. He considers functions in $L^2(B^n)$, where B^n is the unit ball in $\mathbb{R}^n$, i.e.,

$$B^n := \{\mathbf{x} : \|\mathbf{x}\|_2 \leq 1\}.$$

The integral representation given by Petrushev is based on an orthogonal decomposition in terms of Gegenbauer ridge polynomials.

We first catalog various facts concerning Gegenbauer polynomials. As the proofs of these facts would lead us too far afield we simply state them here. Their proofs and more detailed results may be found, for example, in Erdélyi [1953], and Stein and Weiss [1971].

Gegenbauer polynomials, also called ultraspherical polynomials, are generally denoted $\{C_m^\lambda\}_{m=0}^\infty$, $\lambda > 0$. These C_m^λ are univariate algebraic polynomials of degree m, and are orthogonal on $[-1, 1]$ with respect to the weight function $(1 - t^2)^{\lambda-1/2}$, i.e.,

$$\int_{-1}^{1} C_m^\lambda(t) C_k^\lambda(t)(1 - t^2)^{\lambda-1/2} dt = \delta_{m,k} h_{m,\lambda},$$

where

$$h_{m,\lambda} := \frac{\sqrt{\pi}\,(2\lambda)_m \Gamma(\lambda + 1/2)}{(m + \lambda) m!\,\Gamma(\lambda)}.$$

The $(a)_k$ is the usual Pochhammer symbol, namely $(a)_0 := 1$ and $(a)_k := a(a + 1) \cdots (a+k-1)$ for k any positive integer. Gegenbauer polynomials are particular cases of Jacobi polynomials, and special cases of the Gegenbauer polynomials are the Legendre polynomials ($\lambda = 1/2$), and the Chebyshev polynomials of the second kind ($\lambda = 1$). There are various methods of characterizing these $\{C_m^\lambda\}_{m=0}^\infty$. They may be given via the generating function

$$\frac{1}{(1 - 2tx + x^2)^\lambda} = \sum_{m=0}^\infty C_m^\lambda(t) x^m,$$

via the recurrence relation

$$C_m^\lambda(t) = \frac{1}{m} \left[2t(m + \lambda - 1) C_{m-1}^\lambda(t) - (m + 2\lambda - 2) C_{m-2}^\lambda(t) \right],$$

with $C_0^\lambda(t) := 1$, $C_1^\lambda(t) := 2\lambda t$, as a solution to the ordinary differential equation

$$(1 - t^2) y'' - (2\lambda + 1) t\, y' + m(m + 2\lambda) y = 0$$

with suitable boundary conditions, or can be explicitly written in the form

$$C_m^\lambda(t) := \sum_{j=0}^{\lfloor m/2 \rfloor} \frac{(-1)^j (\lambda)_{m-j}}{(m-j)!} \binom{m-j}{m-2j} (2t)^{m-2j}.$$

From the above we obtain

$$C_m^\lambda(-t) = (-1)^m C_m^\lambda(t),$$

i.e., C_m^λ is even or odd depending on the parity of m, and

$$C_m^\lambda(1) = \frac{(2\lambda)_m}{m!}.$$

We will mainly use the orthonormally normalized Gegenbauer polynomials with $\lambda = n/2$. That is, we set

$$U_m := \frac{C_m^{n/2}}{\sqrt{h_{m,n/2}}},$$

and thus

$$\int_{-1}^1 U_m(t) U_k(t) (1 - t^2)^{(n-1)/2} dt = \delta_{m,k}.$$

An important property of this choice of λ is that

$$\int_{B^n} p(\mathbf{x}) U_m(\mathbf{a} \cdot \mathbf{x}) \, d\mathbf{x} = 0 \tag{10.2}$$

for every $\mathbf{a} \in S^{n-1}$ and $p \in \Pi_{m-1}^n$. In addition, the U_m satisfy the following two fundamental identities. For $\mathbf{a}, \mathbf{b} \in S^{n-1}$, we have

$$\int_{B^n} U_m(\mathbf{a} \cdot \mathbf{x}) \, U_m(\mathbf{b} \cdot \mathbf{x}) \, d\mathbf{x} = \frac{U_m(\mathbf{a} \cdot \mathbf{b})}{U_m(1)}, \tag{10.3}$$

and for each $\mathbf{b} \in S^{n-1}$, we have

$$\int_{S^{n-1}} U_m(\mathbf{a} \cdot \mathbf{x}) \, U_m(\mathbf{a} \cdot \mathbf{b}) \, d\mathbf{a} = \frac{U_m(1)}{\nu_m} U_m(\mathbf{b} \cdot \mathbf{x}), \tag{10.4}$$

where

$$\nu_m := \frac{(m+1)_{n-1}}{2(2\pi)^{n-1}}.$$

Let SH_m^n denote the space of spherical harmonics of degree m on S^{n-1}. That is, SH_m^n is the restriction to S^{n-1} of H_m^n, the homogeneous algebraic polynomials of degree m, that are also harmonic on $\mathbb{R}^n$. The spherical harmonics of degree m are orthogonal (over S^{n-1}) to the spherical harmonics of degree k for $m \neq k$. Let

$$N(n, m) := \dim SH_m^n.$$

Then

$$N(n, m) = \binom{n-1+m}{n-1} - \binom{n-3+m}{n-1}$$

for $m \geq 2$, while $N(n, 0) = 1$ and $N(n, 1) = n$. Set

$$K_m(t) := \frac{N(n, m)}{\omega_n C_m^{(n-2)/2}(1)} C_m^{(n-2)/2}(t),$$

where ω_n is defined in (10.1). The polynomial $K_m(\mathbf{a} \cdot \mathbf{b})$ is the reproducing kernel for SH_m^n, i.e., $K_m(\mathbf{a} \cdot \mathbf{b}) \in SH_m^n$ as a function of $\mathbf{b}$ for each choice of $\mathbf{a} \in S^{n-1}$, and

$$\int_{S^{n-1}} S(\mathbf{b}) K_m(\mathbf{a} \cdot \mathbf{b}) \, d\mathbf{b} = S(\mathbf{a})$$

for every $S \in SH_m^n$ and $\mathbf{a} \in S^{n-1}$. For $\varepsilon = 0$ if m is even, and $\varepsilon = 1$ if m is odd, we have

$$K_m(t) + K_{m-2}(t) + \cdots + K_\varepsilon(t) = \frac{\nu_m U_m(t)}{U_m(1)}.$$

Thus, from the orthogonality of the SH_m^n for different m, it follows that we have that $\nu_m U_m(\mathbf{a} \cdot \mathbf{b})/U_m(1)$ is the reproducing kernel for

$$SH_m^n \oplus SH_{m-2}^n \oplus \cdots \oplus SH_\varepsilon^n,$$

i.e., for each $\mathbf{a} \in S^{n-1}$ we have that $U_m(\mathbf{a} \cdot \mathbf{b}) \in SH_m^n \oplus SH_{m-2}^n \oplus \cdots \oplus SH_\varepsilon^n$, and

$$\int_{S^{n-1}} S(\mathbf{b}) \frac{\nu_m U_m(\mathbf{a} \cdot \mathbf{b})}{U_m(1)} \, d\mathbf{b} = S(\mathbf{a}) \tag{10.5}$$

for every $S \in SH_m^n \oplus SH_{m-2}^n \oplus \cdots \oplus SH_\varepsilon^n$ and $\mathbf{a} \in S^{n-1}$.

Let $(\cdot, \cdot)$ denote the usual inner product on $L^2(B^n)$, i.e.,

$$(f, g) := \int_{B^n} f(\mathbf{x}) g(\mathbf{x}) \, d\mathbf{x}.$$

With these preliminaries, we can now prove the basic reproducing formula from Petrushev [1998].

Theorem 10.1 *Let $f \in L^2(B^n)$. Then f has a unique representation of the form*

$$f(\mathbf{x}) = \sum_{m=0}^{\infty} \nu_m \int_{S^{n-1}} (f, U_m(\mathbf{a}\cdot)) U_m(\mathbf{a} \cdot \mathbf{x}) \, d\mathbf{a}.$$

Proof Let $f \in L^2(B^n)$, $n \geq 2$. Since $U_m(\mathbf{a} \cdot \mathbf{x}) \in \Pi_m^n$, as a function of $\mathbf{x}$, it follows that

$$Q_m(f, \mathbf{x}) := \nu_m \int_{S^{n-1}} (f, U_m(\mathbf{a}\cdot)) U_m(\mathbf{a} \cdot \mathbf{x}) \, d\mathbf{a} \tag{10.6}$$

is in Π_m^n for each m. From (10.3) we have for $\mathbf{a}, \mathbf{b} \in S^{n-1}$ that

$$(U_m(\mathbf{b}\cdot), U_m(\mathbf{a}\cdot)) = \frac{U_m(\mathbf{a} \cdot \mathbf{b})}{U_m(1)}.$$

Thus, for $f = U_m(\mathbf{b}\cdot)$ we have from (10.4)

$$Q_m(f, \mathbf{x}) = \nu_m \int_{S^{n-1}} \frac{U_m(\mathbf{a} \cdot \mathbf{b})}{U_m(1)} U_m(\mathbf{a} \cdot \mathbf{x}) \, d\mathbf{a} = U_m(\mathbf{b} \cdot \mathbf{x}) = f(\mathbf{x}).$$

From (10.6), and since Q_m is the identity on $Y_m := \text{span}\{U_m(\mathbf{b}\cdot) : \mathbf{b} \in S^{n-1}\}$, it follows that $Q_m^2 = Q_m$. Furthermore, for any $p \in \Pi_{m-1}^n$ we have from (10.2) that

$$\int_{B^n} Q_m(f, \mathbf{x}) p(\mathbf{x}) \, d\mathbf{x} = \nu_m \int_{S^{n-1}} (f, U_m(\mathbf{a}\cdot)) \left(\int_{B^n} p(\mathbf{x}) U_m(\mathbf{a} \cdot \mathbf{x}) \, d\mathbf{x} \right) d\mathbf{a}$$
$$= 0.$$

Thus Q_m is the linear projector onto Y_m, and Y_m is a subspace of $\Pi_m^n \cap (\Pi_{m-1}^n)^\perp$. Furthermore, from (10.2), the Y_m are pairwise orthogonal subspaces. If we can prove that $Y_m = \Pi_m^n \cap (\Pi_{m-1}^n)^\perp$, then since Q_m is the linear projector onto Y_m, and $\oplus_{m=0}^k Y_m = \Pi_k^n$ for each k, it then follows that

$$f(\mathbf{x}) = \sum_{m=0}^{\infty} Q_m(f, \mathbf{x}),$$

as claimed. As Y_m is a subspace of $\Pi_m^n \cap (\Pi_{m-1}^n)^\perp$, to prove equality it suffices to verify that

$$\dim Y_m = \dim(\Pi_m^n \cap (\Pi_{m-1}^n)^\perp) = \dim H_m^n = \binom{n-1+m}{n-1}.$$

For each $\mathbf{a} \in S^{n-1}$, we have that $U_m(\mathbf{a} \cdot \mathbf{b}) \in SH_m^n \oplus SH_{m-2}^n \oplus \cdots \oplus SH_\varepsilon^n$, as a function of $\mathbf{b}$. It therefore follows that

$$A_m(f, \mathbf{a}) := (f, U_m(\mathbf{a} \cdot))$$

is also in $SH_m^n \oplus SH_{m-2}^n \oplus \cdots \oplus SH_\varepsilon^n$. Note that $A_m(f, \mathbf{a})$ is a linear operator that maps Y_m into $SH_m^n \oplus SH_{m-2}^n \oplus \cdots \oplus SH_\varepsilon^n$. Now Q_m, as a linear operator, is a map from $SH_m^n \oplus SH_{m-2}^n \oplus \cdots \oplus SH_\varepsilon^n$ onto Y_m. Moreover, for $\mathbf{b} \in S^{n-1}$ and by (10.3) and (10.5),

$$\int_{B^n} Q_m(f, \mathbf{x}) U_m(\mathbf{b} \cdot \mathbf{x}) \, d\mathbf{x} = \int_{S^{n-1}} A_m(f, \mathbf{a}) \nu_m \int_{B^n} U_m(\mathbf{a} \cdot \mathbf{x}) U_m(\mathbf{b} \cdot \mathbf{x}) \, d\mathbf{x} \, d\mathbf{a}$$

$$= \int_{S^{n-1}} A_m(f, \mathbf{a}) \nu_m \frac{U_m(\mathbf{a} \cdot \mathbf{b})}{U_m(1)} \, d\mathbf{a} = A_m(f, \mathbf{b}).$$

Thus A_m is a linear operator with Q_m as its inverse. Therefore

$$\begin{aligned}
\dim Y_m &= \dim(SH_m^n \oplus SH_{m-2}^n \oplus \cdots \oplus SH_\varepsilon^n) \\
&= \sum_{j=0}^{[m/2]} N(n, m-2j) = \binom{n-1+m}{n-1},
\end{aligned}$$

which is as desired. $\qquad\square$

Remark 10.2 It should be noted that the best approximation to $f \in L^2(B^n)$ from Π_k^n is given by

$$\sum_{m=0}^{k} \nu_m \int_{S^{n-1}} (f, U_m(\mathbf{a} \cdot)) U_m(\mathbf{a} \cdot \mathbf{x}) \, d\mathbf{a}.$$

In Petrushev [1998] we also find the following Parseval identity.

Theorem 10.3 *Let* $f \in L^2(B^n)$. *Then*

$$\|f\|_{L^2(B^n)}^2 = \sum_{m=0}^{\infty} \nu_m \|(f, U_m(\mathbf{a} \cdot))\|_{L^2(S^{n-1})}^2.$$

Proof Since $Q_m(f) \in \Pi_m^n \cap (\Pi_{m-1}^n)^\perp$, the $\{Q_m\}$ are orthogonal and thus

$$\|f\|_{L^2(B^n)}^2 = \sum_{m=0}^{\infty} \|Q_m(f)\|_{L^2(B^n)}^2.$$

From (10.3) we have

$$\int_{B^n} Q_m(f, \mathbf{x})^2 \, d\mathbf{x}$$

$$= \nu_m^2 \int_{S^{n-1}} \int_{S^{n-1}} \int_{B^n} (f, U_m(\mathbf{a} \cdot))(f, U_m(\mathbf{b} \cdot)) U_m(\mathbf{a} \cdot \mathbf{x}) U_m(\mathbf{b} \cdot \mathbf{x}) \, d\mathbf{x} \, d\mathbf{a} \, d\mathbf{b}$$

$$= \nu_m^2 \int_{S^{n-1}} \int_{S^{n-1}} (f, U_m(\mathbf{a} \cdot))(f, U_m(\mathbf{b} \cdot)) \frac{U_m(\mathbf{a} \cdot \mathbf{b})}{U_m(1)} \, d\mathbf{a} \, d\mathbf{b}.$$

Since $(f, U_m(\mathbf{b} \cdot)) \in SH_m^n \oplus SH_{m-2}^n \oplus \cdots \oplus SH_\varepsilon^n$ we can now use (10.5) to obtain

$$\int_{B^n} Q_m(f, \mathbf{x})^2 \, d\mathbf{x} = \nu_m \int_{S^{n-1}} (f, U_m(\mathbf{a} \cdot))^2 d\mathbf{a}.$$

This completes the proof. $\qquad\qquad\square$

Of particular interest is the case $n = 2$ where, since we set $\lambda = 1$, we have that the U_m are the Chebyshev polynomials of the second kind.

10.2 Ridgelets

In this section we describe a construction due to Candès [1998]. We recall the definition of ridgelets as defined in Section 6.5, but for normalization and notational purposes we will index these ridgelets in a different way.

Let $(\cdot, \cdot)$ denote the usual inner product on $L^2(\mathbb{R}^n)$, i.e.,

$$(f, g) := \int_{\mathbb{R}^n} f(\mathbf{x}) g(\mathbf{x}) \, d\mathbf{x}.$$

Set

$$\Gamma = \mathbb{R}_+ \times S^{n-1} \times \mathbb{R} = \{\gamma = (\lambda, \mathbf{a}, b) : \lambda, b \in \mathbb{R}, \lambda > 0, \mathbf{a} \in S^{n-1}\},$$

i.e., **a** is on the unit sphere in $\mathbb{R}^n$. For a given univariate function ψ defined on all of $\mathbb{R}$, and $\gamma \in \Gamma$, set

$$\psi_\gamma(\mathbf{x}) := \frac{1}{\sqrt{\lambda}} \, \psi\left(\frac{\mathbf{a} \cdot \mathbf{x} - b}{\lambda}\right).$$

Let $\mu(d\gamma)$ on Γ be the measure defined by

$$\mu(d\gamma) := \frac{d\lambda}{\lambda^{n+1}} \, da \, db,$$

where da is, as previously, the uniform measure on S^{n-1} of total measure equal to the surface area of the unit sphere S^{n-1}, i.e., of total measure ω_n.

We assume, in what follows, that $\psi \in \mathcal{S}(\mathbb{R})$, the Schwartz space of rapidly decreasing functions on $\mathbb{R}$. That is, $\psi \in C^\infty(\mathbb{R})$ and

$$\sup_t |t^n \psi^{(n)}(t)| < \infty$$

for all $n \in \mathbb{Z}_+$. In addition, we assume that

$$K_\psi := \int_{-\infty}^\infty \frac{|\widehat{\psi}(\xi)|^2}{|\xi|^n} \, d\xi < \infty.$$

The fundamental result that is the basis for ridgelet theory is the following reproducing formula.

Theorem 10.4 *Let $f, \widehat{f} \in L^1(\mathbb{R}^n)$. If ψ satisfies the above assumptions, then*

$$f(\mathbf{x}) = c_\psi \int (f, \psi_\gamma) \psi_\gamma(\mathbf{x}) \, \mu(d\gamma),$$

where

$$c_\psi := \frac{1}{2(2\pi)^{n-1} K_\psi}.$$

Proof We use the Radon transform

$$(R_\mathbf{a} f)(t) := \int_{\mathbf{a} \cdot \mathbf{x} = t} f(\mathbf{x}) \, d\mathbf{x} = \int_{\mathbf{a} \cdot \mathbf{y} = 0} f(t\mathbf{a} + \mathbf{y}) \, d\mathbf{y}.$$

(Recall that $\mathbf{a} \in S^{n-1}$.) It is well-known, see, for example, Helgason [1980], p. 4, or Natterer [1986], p. 11, that

$$\left(\widehat{R_\mathbf{a} f}\right)(\xi) = \widehat{f}(\xi \mathbf{a}), \qquad \xi \in \mathbb{R}.$$

Since we have assumed that $\widehat{f} \in L^1(\mathbb{R}^n)$, we have $\widehat{R_\mathbf{a} f} \in L^1(\mathbb{R})$.

We will slightly abuse notation by setting $\psi_\lambda(t) := \lambda^{-1/2}\psi(t/\lambda)$ for $t \in \mathbb{R}$ and $\lambda > 0$. Thus

$$\psi_\gamma(\mathbf{x}) = \psi_\lambda(\mathbf{a} \cdot \mathbf{x} - b).$$

In addition, set $\widetilde{\psi}(t) = \psi(-t)$. Let

$$
\begin{aligned}
w_{\lambda,\mathbf{a}}(b) &= \left(\widetilde{\psi}_\lambda * R_\mathbf{a}f\right)(b) = \int_{-\infty}^{\infty} \frac{1}{\sqrt{\lambda}}\psi\left(\frac{t-b}{\lambda}\right)\left(\int_{\mathbf{a}\cdot\mathbf{x}=t} f(\mathbf{x})d\mathbf{x}\right)dt \\
&= \int_{\mathbb{R}^n} f(\mathbf{x})\frac{1}{\sqrt{\lambda}}\psi\left(\frac{\mathbf{a}\cdot\mathbf{x}-b}{\lambda}\right)d\mathbf{x} = (f,\psi_\gamma).
\end{aligned}
$$

Thus we can write

$$
\begin{aligned}
I(\mathbf{x}) &:= \int (f,\psi_\gamma)\psi_\gamma(\mathbf{x})\,\mu(d\gamma) \\
&= \int \psi_\lambda(\mathbf{a}\cdot\mathbf{x}-b)w_{\lambda,\mathbf{a}}(b)\frac{d\lambda}{\lambda^{n+1}}\,d\mathbf{a}\,db \\
&= \int \psi_\lambda(\mathbf{a}\cdot\mathbf{x}-b)\left(\widetilde{\psi}_\lambda * R_\mathbf{a}f\right)(b)\frac{d\lambda}{\lambda^{n+1}}\,d\mathbf{a}\,db \\
&= \int \left(\psi_\lambda * \left(\widetilde{\psi}_\lambda * R_\mathbf{a}f\right)\right)(\mathbf{a}\cdot\mathbf{x})\frac{d\lambda}{\lambda^{n+1}}\,d\mathbf{a}\,db.
\end{aligned}
$$

As $\left(\psi_\lambda * \left(\widetilde{\psi}_\lambda * R_\mathbf{a}f\right)\right) \in L^1(\mathbb{R})$, and its Fourier transform is given by

$$\lambda|\widehat{\psi}(\lambda\xi)|^2\widehat{f}(\xi\mathbf{a}),$$

it follows that

$$I(\mathbf{x}) = \frac{1}{2\pi}\int e^{i\xi\mathbf{a}\cdot\mathbf{x}}\widehat{f}(\xi\mathbf{a})\lambda|\widehat{\psi}(\lambda\xi)|^2\frac{d\lambda}{\lambda^{n+1}}\,d\mathbf{a}\,d\xi.$$

For every real-valued g we have $\overline{\widehat{g}(-\xi)} = \widehat{g}(\xi)$ and thus

$$I(\mathbf{x}) = \frac{1}{\pi}\int e^{i\xi\mathbf{a}\cdot\mathbf{x}}\widehat{f}(\xi\mathbf{a})|\widehat{\psi}(\lambda\xi)|^2 1_{\{\xi>0\}}\frac{d\lambda}{\lambda^n}\,d\mathbf{a}\,d\xi,$$

where

$$1_{\{\xi>0\}} := \begin{cases} 1, & \xi > 0 \\ 0, & \xi \le 0. \end{cases}$$

Now, by Fubini's Theorem, we obtain

$$
\begin{aligned}
I(\mathbf{x}) &= \frac{1}{\pi}\int e^{i\xi\mathbf{a}\cdot\mathbf{x}}\widehat{f}(\xi\mathbf{a})\left\{\int \frac{|\widehat{\psi}(\lambda\xi)|^2}{\lambda^n}d\lambda\right\}1_{\{\xi>0\}}\,d\mathbf{a}\,d\xi \\
&= \frac{1}{\pi}\int e^{i\xi\mathbf{a}\cdot\mathbf{x}}\widehat{f}(\xi\mathbf{a})K_\psi\xi^{n-1}1_{\{\xi>0\}}\,d\mathbf{a}\,d\xi.
\end{aligned}
$$

Let $\mathbf{y} = \xi\mathbf{a}$. Since $\xi \in \mathbb{R}_+$ and $\mathbf{a} \in S^{n-1}$, we have that $\mathbf{y}$ runs over $\mathbb{R}^n$ and thus

$$I(\mathbf{x}) = \frac{K_\psi}{\pi} \int_{\mathbb{R}^n} e^{i\mathbf{y}\cdot\mathbf{x}} \widehat{f}(\mathbf{y}) \, d\mathbf{y} = \frac{K_\psi}{\pi}(2\pi)^n f(\mathbf{x}),$$

which proves the theorem. □

The associated Parseval identity is the following result.

Theorem 10.5 *Let $f \in L^1(\mathbb{R}^n) \cap L^2(\mathbb{R}^n)$. If ψ satisfies the previous assumptions, then*

$$\|f\|_{L^2(\mathbb{R}^n)}^2 = c_\psi \int |(f, \psi_\gamma)|^2 \mu(d\gamma).$$

Proof As in the proof of Theorem 10.4, set

$$w_{\lambda,\mathbf{a}}(b) = \left(\widetilde{\psi}_\lambda * R_\mathbf{a} f\right)(b) = (f, \psi_\gamma).$$

Thus

$$\int |(f, \psi_\gamma)|^2 \mu(d\gamma) = \int |w_{\lambda,\mathbf{a}}(b)|^2 \frac{d\lambda}{\lambda^{n+1}} \, d\mathbf{a} \, db.$$

Using Fubini's Theorem for positive functions

$$\int |w_{\lambda,\mathbf{a}}(b)|^2 \frac{d\lambda}{\lambda^{n+1}} \, d\mathbf{a} \, db = \int \|w_{\lambda,\mathbf{a}}\|_{L^2(\mathbb{R})}^2 \frac{d\lambda}{\lambda^{n+1}} \, d\mathbf{a}.$$

Now, $w_{\lambda,\mathbf{a}}$ is integrable as it is a convolution of two integrable functions. It also belongs to $L^2(\mathbb{R})$ since

$$\|w_{\lambda,\mathbf{a}}\|_{L^2(\mathbb{R})} \le \|f\|_{L^1(\mathbb{R}^n)} \|\psi_\lambda\|_{L^2(\mathbb{R})}.$$

Thus its Fourier transform is well-defined and

$$\widehat{w}_{\lambda,\mathbf{a}}(\xi) = \widehat{f}(\xi\mathbf{a})\overline{\widehat{\psi}_\lambda(\xi)}.$$

Furthermore,

$$\|w_{\lambda,\mathbf{a}}\|_{L^2(\mathbb{R})}^2 = \int |w_{\lambda,\mathbf{a}}(b)|^2 db = \frac{1}{2\pi} \int |\widehat{w}_{\lambda,\mathbf{a}}(\xi)|^2 d\xi,$$

and therefore

$$
\begin{aligned}
\int \|w_{\lambda,\mathbf{a}}\|_{L^2(\mathbb{R})}^2 \frac{d\lambda}{\lambda^{n+1}} \, d\mathbf{a} &= \frac{1}{2\pi} \int |\widehat{f}(\xi\mathbf{a})|^2 |\widehat{\psi}_\lambda(\xi)|^2 \frac{d\lambda}{\lambda^{n+1}} \, d\mathbf{a} \, d\xi \\
&= \frac{2}{2\pi} \int |\widehat{f}(\xi\mathbf{a})|^2 |\widehat{\psi}(\lambda\xi)|^2 1_{\{\xi>0\}} \frac{d\lambda}{\lambda^n} \, d\mathbf{a} \, d\xi.
\end{aligned}
$$

As

$$\int \frac{|\widehat{\psi}(\lambda\xi)|^2}{\lambda^n} d\lambda = K_\psi |\xi|^{n-1},$$

we continue the above to

$$= \frac{2K_\psi}{2\pi} \int |\widehat{f}(\xi \mathbf{a})|^2 \xi^{n-1} 1_{\{\xi>0\}} d\mathbf{a} \, d\xi = \frac{K_\psi}{\pi} (2\pi)^n \|f\|^2_{L^2(\mathbb{R}^n)},$$

which is the desired result. □

In Murata [1996] a parallel analysis is to be found. It is, in one sense, more general as it introduces ψ_γ^1 and ψ_γ^2 and obtains a formula of the form

$$c_{1,2} \int (f, \psi_\gamma^1) \psi_\gamma^2(\mathbf{x}) \, \mu(d\gamma)$$

for reproducing f. On the other hand, under the conditions therein this integral may be divergent and thus a convergence factor is included. Furthermore, no Parseval identity is provided.

11

Interpolation at Points

In this chapter we consider the following questions. *Can we characterize those points* $\mathbf{x}^1, \ldots, \mathbf{x}^k \in \mathbb{R}^n$ *(any finite k) such that for every choice of data* $b_1, \ldots, b_k$ *($b_j \in \mathbb{R}$, $j = 1, \ldots, k$), there exists a function* $G \in \mathcal{M}(A^1, \ldots, A^r)$ *satisfying*

$$G(\mathbf{x}^j) = b_j, \qquad j = 1, \ldots, k?$$

That is, for given fixed $d \times n$ matrices $A^1, \ldots, A^r$, do there exist functions $f_1, \ldots, f_r : \mathbb{R}^d \to \mathbb{R}$ for which

$$\sum_{i=1}^{r} f_i(A^i \mathbf{x}^j) = b_j, \qquad j = 1, \ldots, k?$$

For $r = 1$ this problem has a simple solution. Given a $d \times n$ matrix A, we want to know conditions on the points $\{\mathbf{x}^j\}_{j=1}^k$ in $\mathbb{R}^n$ such that for every choice of $b_1, \ldots, b_k$ there exists a function $f : \mathbb{R}^d \to \mathbb{R}$ (depending on the $\mathbf{x}^j$ and b_j) such that

$$f(A\mathbf{x}^j) = b_j, \qquad j = 1, \ldots, k.$$

Obviously such a function exists if and only if

$$A\mathbf{x}^s \neq A\mathbf{x}^t$$

for all $s \neq t$, $s, t \in \{1, \ldots, k\}$. And, in general, if for some $i \in \{1, \ldots, r\}$, the values $A^i \mathbf{x}^j$, $j = 1, \ldots, k$, are all distinct, then it easily follows that we can interpolate as desired, independent of and without using the other A^ℓ, $\ell \neq i$. The problem becomes more interesting and more difficult when, for each i, the k values $A^i \mathbf{x}^j$, $j = 1, \ldots, k$, are not all distinct.

In Section 11.1 we state some general, elementary results concerning interpolation at points. In Section 11.2 we detail necessary and sufficient conditions for when we can interpolate in the case of two directions, i.e., $r = 2$. In Section 11.3 we consider the case of $r \geq 3$ directions, but only in $\mathbb{R}^2$, and present an exact geometric characterization for a large (but not the complete) set of points where interpolation is not always possible. We also state a definitive result providing a geometric characterization of sets of points where interpolation is not possible for three directions in $\mathbb{R}^2$.

11.1 General Results

Let us first introduce some notation.

Definition 11.1 Given $d \times n$ matrices $\{A^i\}_{i=1}^r$, we say that the set of points $\{\mathbf{x}^j\}_{j=1}^k$ in $\mathbb{R}^n$ has the *NI-property* (non-interpolation property) with respect to the $\{A^i\}_{i=1}^r$ if there exist $\{b_j\}_{j=1}^k \subset \mathbb{R}$ for which we *cannot* find $f_i : \mathbb{R}^d \to \mathbb{R}$, $i = 1, \ldots, r$, satisfying

$$\sum_{i=1}^r f_i(A^i \mathbf{x}^j) = b_j, \qquad j = 1, \ldots, k.$$

We say that the set of points $\{\mathbf{x}^j\}_{j=1}^k$ in $\mathbb{R}^n$ has the *MNI-property* (minimal non-interpolation property) with respect to the $\{A^i\}_{i=1}^r$, if $\{\mathbf{x}^j\}_{j=1}^k$ has the NI-property and no proper subset of the $\{\mathbf{x}^j\}_{j=1}^k$ has the NI-property.

In other words, set

$$\mathcal{N} := \{(G(\mathbf{x}^1), \ldots, G(\mathbf{x}^k)) : G \in \mathcal{M}(A^1, \ldots, A^r)\}. \qquad (11.1)$$

$\mathcal{N}$ is a linear subspace of $\mathbb{R}^k$. The set $\{\mathbf{x}^j\}_{j=1}^k$ has the NI-property with respect to the $\{A^i\}_{i=1}^r$ if and only if $\mathcal{N}$ is a proper subspace of $\mathbb{R}^k$. The following result, essentially to be found in Braess and Pinkus [1993], easily follows from this fact and the above definitions.

Proposition 11.2 *The set of points* $\{\mathbf{x}^j\}_{j=1}^k$ *in* $\mathbb{R}^n$ *has the NI-property with respect to the* $d \times n$ *matrices* $\{A^i\}_{i=1}^r$ *if and only if there exists a vector* $\boldsymbol{\beta} = (\beta_1, \ldots, \beta_k) \in \mathbb{R}^k \backslash \{\mathbf{0}\}$ *such that*

$$\sum_{j=1}^k \beta_j f_i(A^i \mathbf{x}^j) = 0 \qquad (11.2)$$

for all $f_i : \mathbb{R}^d \to \mathbb{R}$ *and each* $i = 1, \ldots, r$. *The set of points* $\{\mathbf{x}^j\}_{j=1}^k$ *in* $\mathbb{R}^n$ *has the MNI-property if and only if the vector* $\boldsymbol{\beta} \in \mathbb{R}^k \backslash \{\mathbf{0}\}$ *satisfying (11.2) is unique, up to multiplication by a constant, and has no zero component.*

Proof Let $\mathcal{N}$ be as given in (11.1). Since $\mathcal{N}$ is a linear subspace of $\mathbb{R}^k$, it does *not* equal $\mathbb{R}^k$ if and only if there exists a $\beta \in \mathbb{R}^k \backslash \{\mathbf{0}\}$ such that

$$\sum_{j=1}^{k} \beta_j G(\mathbf{x}^j) = 0$$

for all $G \in \mathcal{M}(A^1, \ldots, A^r)$. Obviously this is equivalent to (11.2). If $\beta_\ell = 0$ for some ℓ, then we can delete $\mathbf{x}^\ell$ from the $\{\mathbf{x}^j\}_{j=1}^k$ and the remaining points have the NI-property. Thus the fact that the MNI-property is equivalent to the uniqueness of the β, up to multiplication by a constant, with no zero component, easily follows. □

Remark 11.3 Note that the existence of $\beta \neq \mathbf{0}$ satisfying (11.2) is the existence of a non-trivial linear functional supported on the points $\{\mathbf{x}^j\}_{j=1}^k$ annihilating the linear subspace $\mathcal{M}(A^1, \ldots, A^r)$.

We can squeeze out more information from this elementary approach. Set

$$\Lambda_i := \{A^i \mathbf{x}^j \ : \ j = 1, \ldots, k\}$$

for each $i = 1, \ldots, r$. Assume Λ_i contains s_i distinct points in $\mathbb{R}^d$, $1 \leq s_i \leq k$. Denote these distinct points by $\mathbf{c}_1^i, \ldots, \mathbf{c}_{s_i}^i$, i.e.,

$$\Lambda_i = \{\mathbf{c}_1^i, \ldots, \mathbf{c}_{s_i}^i\}, \qquad i = 1, \ldots, r,$$

and $\mathbf{c}_t^i \neq \mathbf{c}_v^i$ for $t \neq v$, $t, v \in \{1, \ldots, s_i\}$. For each $\ell = 1, \ldots, s_i$, let $h_i^\ell : \mathbb{R}^d \to \mathbb{R}$ satisfy

$$h_i^\ell(\mathbf{c}_t^i) = \delta_{\ell t}, \qquad t = 1, \ldots, s_i.$$

Thus

$$\sum_{j=1}^{k} \beta_j f_i(A^i \mathbf{x}^j) = 0$$

for all $f_i : \mathbb{R}^d \to \mathbb{R}$ if and only if

$$\sum_{j=1}^{k} \beta_j h_i^\ell(A^i \mathbf{x}^j) = 0$$

for $\ell = 1, \ldots, s_i$, and $i = 1, \ldots, r$. From Proposition 11.2, the set of points $\{\mathbf{x}^j\}_{j=1}^k$ has the NI-property if and only if there exists a $\beta \in \mathbb{R}^k \backslash \{\mathbf{0}\}$ such that

$$\sum_{j=1}^{k} \beta_j h_i^\ell(A^i \mathbf{x}^j) = 0, \tag{11.3}$$

$\ell = 1, \ldots, s_i, i = 1, \ldots, r$. The equations (11.3) can also be rewritten in the form

$$\sum_{\{j \,:\, A^i \mathbf{x}^j = \mathbf{c}\}} \beta_j = 0 \tag{11.4}$$

for all $\mathbf{c} \in \mathbb{R}^d$, and each $i = 1, \ldots, k$. That is, we sum over the j for which

$$\mathbf{x}^j \in \Gamma_{A^i}(\mathbf{c}) := \{\mathbf{x} : A^i \mathbf{x} = \mathbf{c}\}.$$

(We understand that the sum over the empty set is zero.)

Returning to (11.3), we observe that we have reduced the interpolation problem to the matrix problem

$$\beta C = \mathbf{0},$$

where β is a vector in $\mathbb{R}^k$ and C is a $k \times s$ matrix, $s = \sum_{i=1}^r s_i$. The important property of C is that all its entries, i.e., the $h_i^\ell(A^i \mathbf{x}^j)$, are 0s and 1s (no row or column of which is identically zero). Note that if $s_i = k$ for some i, then there is no non-zero β satisfying (11.3). This is the situation, as previously noted, where the values $A^i \mathbf{x}^j$, $j = 1, \ldots, k$, are all distinct for some i.

The above analysis implies the following result from Weinmann [1994].

Proposition 11.4 *Let C be the $k \times s$ matrix, $s := \sum_{i=1}^r s_i$, as constructed above. Then for the given $d \times n$ matrices $\{A^i\}_{i=1}^r$, the set $\{\mathbf{x}^j\}_{j=1}^k$ in $\mathbb{R}^n$ has the NI-property with respect to the $\{A^i\}_{i=1}^r$ if and only if*

$$\operatorname{rank} C < k.$$

Remark 11.5 Note that if the equation

$$\beta C = \mathbf{0}$$

has a non-trivial solution β, and since all entries of C are integers, then there necessarily exists a non-trivial solution β', all of whose entries are integers.

Based on the above we also obtain a result of Sun [1993]. In what follows, $\#$ counts the number of elements in a set.

Proposition 11.6 *Assume there exists a subset $\{\mathbf{x}^{j_1}, \ldots, \mathbf{x}^{j_s}\}$ of the point set $\{\mathbf{x}^1, \ldots, \mathbf{x}^k\}$ with the property that the sum, over i, of the number of distinct values of $\{A^i \mathbf{x}^{j_t}\}_{t=1}^s$ is at most $s + r - 2$, i.e.,*

$$\sum_{i=1}^r \#\{A^i \mathbf{x}^{j_t}\}_{t=1}^s \leq s + r - 2.$$

Then the set of points $\{\mathbf{x}^j\}_{j=1}^k$ in $\mathbb{R}^n$ has the NI-property with respect to the $\{A^i\}_{i=1}^r$.

Proof Consider the equations (11.4) restricted to the indices $j_1, \ldots, j_s$, i.e., the equations

$$\sum_{\{j_t \,:\, A^i \mathbf{x}^{j_t} = \mathbf{c}\}} \beta_{j_t} = 0 \tag{11.5}$$

for each $i = 1, \ldots, r$. By assumption there are $p \leq s + r - 2$ such non-trivial equations in s unknowns. However, for each $i \in \{1, \ldots, r\}$,

$$\sum_{\mathbf{c}} \sum_{\{j_t \,:\, A^i \mathbf{x}^{j_t} = \mathbf{c}\}} \beta_{j_t} = \sum_{t=1}^{s} \beta_{j_t}.$$

Thus we have among the equations of (11.5) at least $r - 1$ that are redundant. The number of essential equations is therefore at most $p - r + 1 \leq s - 1$. Since there are fewer equations than unknowns there exists a non-trivial solution to (11.5) and thus to (11.4) (setting $\beta_j = 0$ for $j \notin \{j_1, \ldots, j_s\}$). $\qquad \square$

If $B = CC^T$, then $B = \{b_{jt}\}_{j,t=1}^{k}$ is a $k \times k$ positive semi-definite matrix. Furthermore for $j, t \in \{1, \ldots, k\}$,

$$b_{jt} = \sum_{i=1}^{r} \sum_{\ell=1}^{s_i} h_i^{\ell}(A^i \mathbf{x}^j) h_i^{\ell}(A^i \mathbf{x}^t)$$

$$= \#\{i : A^i \mathbf{x}^j = A^i \mathbf{x}^t\}. \tag{11.6}$$

Note that $b_{jj} = r$ for $j = 1, \ldots, k$. Sun [1993] calls this matrix a "characteristic matrix". From the above we obtain this next result originally due to Sun [1993].

Proposition 11.7 *Let B be the positive semi-definite $k \times k$ matrix, as constructed above in (11.6). Then, for the given $d \times n$ matrices $\{A^i\}_{i=1}^{r}$, the set $\{\mathbf{x}^j\}_{j=1}^{k}$ in $\mathbb{R}^n$ has the NI-property with respect to the $\{A^i\}_{i=1}^{r}$ if and only if B is singular, i.e., $\operatorname{rank} B < k$.*

In the paper Sun [1993] can also be found a discussion regarding classes of functions in $\mathcal{M}(A^1, \ldots, A^r)$ from which we can find appropriate interpolants, assuming the NI-property does not hold.

A simple application of Proposition 11.7 is the following, also due to Sun [1993]. We recall, see Section 5.4, that for a $d \times n$ matrix A we let $L(A)$ denote the span of the rows of A.

Proposition 11.8 *Assume we are given $(n-1) \times n$ matrices $\{A^i\}_{i=1}^{r}$ of rank $n-1$ such that $L(A^i) \neq L(A^j)$ for all $i \neq j$. If $\{\mathbf{x}^j\}_{j=1}^{k}$ are distinct points in $\mathbb{R}^n$ and $r > k$, then the above matrix B is non-singular.*

Proof As each A^i is of rank $n - 1$ it follows that the vectors $\mathbf{c}^i \in \mathbb{R}^n \backslash \{\mathbf{0}\}$ satisfying $A^i \mathbf{c}^i = \mathbf{0}$ are unique, up to multiplication by constants. As $L(A^i) \neq L(A^j)$ we have that the vectors $\{\mathbf{c}^i\}_{i=1}^r$ are pairwise linearly independent.

By construction $b_{jj} = r$ for $j = 1, \ldots, k$. We claim that $b_{jt} \in \{0, 1\}$ for $j \neq t$. Recall from (11.6) that

$$b_{jt} = \#\{i : A^i \mathbf{x}^j = A^i \mathbf{x}^t\}.$$

If $A^i \mathbf{x}^j = A^i \mathbf{x}^t$ and $A^\ell \mathbf{x}^j = A^\ell \mathbf{x}^t$ for $i \neq \ell$, then we have $A^i(\mathbf{x}^j - \mathbf{x}^t) = A^\ell(\mathbf{x}^j - \mathbf{x}^t) = 0$. But $\mathbf{x}^j - \mathbf{x}^t$ is thus a non-zero multiple of both $\mathbf{c}^i$ and $\mathbf{c}^\ell$, a contradiction.

As is known, any $k \times k$ positive semi-definite matrix with r ($r > k$) on the diagonal and off-diagonal entries 1s or 0s is non-singular, e.g., from diagonal dominance or the Gershgorin Theorem. $\square$

Note also the connection with Proposition 5.34.

11.2 Closed Paths: $r = 2$

The results of Section 11.1 were analytic in nature. One would like, if possible, to provide a geometric characterization of points satisfying the NI-property. Such an approach is possible in a few instances. We start with the case of two directions in $\mathbb{R}^n$, where a geometric solution to this problem is relatively simple. We will use the concept of a *closed path*, as introduced in Definition 8.5. Some authors use the term lightning bolt, or trip rather than closed path. See Khavinson [1997], p. 55, for many references to where this concept is used. It is also to be found in Dyn, Light and Cheney [1989], which is a paper concerned with interpolation at the points $\{\mathbf{x}^j\}_{j=1}^k$ using linear combinations of the functions $\{\|\mathbf{x} - \mathbf{x}^j\|_1\}_{j=1}^k$ (where $\|\cdot\|_1$ is the usual ℓ_1 norm on $\mathbb{R}^2$). From this problem the authors were naturally led to a consideration of interpolation by functions of the form

$$g(x, y) = f_1(x) + f_2(y).$$

In other words, they considered the two directions $\mathbf{e}^1 = (1, 0)$ and $\mathbf{e}^2 = (0, 1)$. Moreover given any two distinct directions $\mathbf{a}^1$ and $\mathbf{a}^2$, a non-singular linear transformation takes $\mathbf{e}^1$ and $\mathbf{e}^2$ to $\mathbf{a}^1$ and $\mathbf{a}^2$ in $\mathbb{R}^2$. Here we will deal with generalized ridge functions in $\mathbb{R}^n$. This result may be further generalized, see Section 12.1.

We recall the definition of a closed path, see Definition 8.5.

Definition 11.9 The sequence of points $\{\mathbf{v}^i\}_{i=1}^p$ is a *closed path* with respect to the distinct directions A^1 and A^2 if $p = 2q$, and for some permutation of the

$\{\mathbf{v}^i\}_{i=1}^{2q}$ (which we assume to be as given) we have

$$A^1\mathbf{v}^{2j-1} = A^1\mathbf{v}^{2j}, \qquad j = 1,\ldots,q,$$

and

$$A^2\mathbf{v}^{2j} = A^2\mathbf{v}^{2j+1}, \qquad j = 1,\ldots,q,$$

where we set $\mathbf{v}^{2q+1} = \mathbf{v}^1$.

Geometrically this simply says that the points $\mathbf{v}^1,\ldots,\mathbf{v}^p$, and $\mathbf{v}^1$ again, form the vertices of a closed path with edges in directions parallel to $\{\mathbf{x} : A^i\mathbf{x} = 0\}$, $i = 1, 2$. An example in $\mathbb{R}^2$ with $d = 1$, directions parallel to the axes and $p = 10$, is given in Figure 11.1.

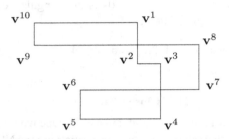

Figure 11.1

In this case of two directions, i.e., $r = 2$, in $\mathbb{R}^n$ a set of points has the NI-property if and only if a subset thereof forms a closed path. The full theorem is the following.

Theorem 11.10 *Assume we are given two distinct $d \times n$ matrices A^1 and A^2. Then the following are equivalent.*
(a) The set of points $\{\mathbf{x}^j\}_{j=1}^k$ has the NI-property with respect to the A^1 and A^2.
(b) There exists a subset $\{\mathbf{y}^j\}_{j=1}^s$ of the $\{\mathbf{x}^j\}_{j=1}^k$ such that

$$\left|\Gamma_{A^i}(\mathbf{c}) \cap \{\mathbf{y}^j\}_{j=1}^s\right| \neq 1$$

for $i = 1, 2$ and every $\mathbf{c} \in \mathbb{R}$.
(c) There exists a subset of the $\{\mathbf{x}^j\}_{j=1}^k$ which forms a closed path.
(d) There exists a subset $\{\mathbf{z}^j\}_{j=1}^t$ of the $\{\mathbf{x}^j\}_{j=1}^k$ and $\varepsilon_j \in \{-1,1\}$, $j = 1,\ldots,t$, such that

$$\sum_{j=1}^{t} \varepsilon_j f_i(A^i\mathbf{z}^j) = 0$$

for every $f_i : \mathbb{R}^d \to \mathbb{R}$ and $i = 1, 2$.

Proof (a)⇒(b). Assume the set of points $\{\mathbf{x}^j\}_{j=1}^k$ has the NI-property with respect to A^1 and A^2. From Proposition 11.2 there exists a $\beta \in \mathbb{R}^k\backslash\{\mathbf{0}\}$ such that

$$\sum_{j=1}^{k} \beta_j f_i(A^i \mathbf{x}^j) = 0$$

for all $f_i : \mathbb{R}^d \to \mathbb{R}$, and $i = 1, 2$. Let $\{\mathbf{y}^\ell\}_{\ell=1}^s$ denote the subset of the $\{\mathbf{x}^j\}_{j=1}^k$ for which $\beta_j \neq 0$. That is, after renumbering

$$\sum_{\ell=1}^{s} \beta_\ell' f_i(A^i \mathbf{y}^\ell) = 0$$

for all $f_i : \mathbb{R}^d \to \mathbb{R}$ and $i = 1, 2$, and $\beta_\ell' \neq 0$, $\ell = 1, \ldots, s$. Recall that $\Gamma_{A^i}(\mathbf{c}) = \{\mathbf{x} : A^i\mathbf{x} = \mathbf{c}\}$. If $\Gamma_{A^i}(\mathbf{c}) \cap \{\mathbf{y}^\ell\}_{\ell=1}^s$ is not empty for some $\mathbf{c} \in \mathbb{R}^d$, then it follows from (11.4) that $\sum_\ell \beta_\ell' = 0$, where ℓ runs over the set of indices for which $\mathbf{y}^\ell \in \Gamma_{A^i}(\mathbf{c})$. Hence the set contains at least two points.

(b)⇒(c). We are given $\{\mathbf{y}^j\}_{j=1}^s$ satisfying (b). Set $\mathbf{z}^1 := \mathbf{y}^1$. By assumption, there exists a $\mathbf{y}^{\ell_2}$, $\ell_2 \neq 1$, such that

$$A^1 \mathbf{y}^{\ell_2} = A^1 \mathbf{z}^1.$$

Set $\mathbf{z}^2 := \mathbf{y}^{\ell_2}$. By assumption, there exists a $\mathbf{y}^{\ell_3}$, $\ell_3 \neq \ell_2$, such that

$$A^2 \mathbf{y}^{\ell_3} = A^2 \mathbf{z}^2.$$

Set $\mathbf{z}^3 := \mathbf{y}^{\ell_3}$. Continue in this fashion alternating the directions A^i at each step.

Since we can continue this process indefinitely, but there are only s distinct $\mathbf{y}^1, \ldots, \mathbf{y}^s$, we must reach a stage where

$$\mathbf{z}^v \in \{\mathbf{z}^1, \ldots, \mathbf{z}^{v-1}\}.$$

Assume $\mathbf{z}^u = \mathbf{z}^v$ where $u < v$.

If u and v have the same parity, then the set $\{\mathbf{z}^u, \ldots, \mathbf{z}^{v-1}\}$ is a closed path with respect to A^1 and A^2. If, on the other hand, u and v have opposite parity, then the set $\{\mathbf{z}^{u+1}, \ldots, \mathbf{z}^{v-1}\}$ is a closed path with respect to A^1 and A^2.

(c)⇒(d). Let $\{\mathbf{z}^j\}_{j=1}^{2q}$ form a closed path (with vertices ordered as in the definition of a closed path). Then

$$\sum_{j=1}^{2q} (-1)^j f_i(A^i \mathbf{z}^j) = 0$$

for all $f_i : \mathbb{R}^d \to \mathbb{R}$, and $i = 1, 2$. For example, for $i = 1$ we have

$$A^1 \mathbf{z}^{2j-1} = A^1 \mathbf{z}^{2j}, \qquad j = 1, \ldots, q.$$

Thus

$$-f_1(A^1\mathbf{z}^{2j-1}) + f_1(A^1\mathbf{z}^{2j}) = 0, \qquad j = 1, \ldots, q$$

for any $f_1 : \mathbb{R}^d \to \mathbb{R}$, and

$$\sum_{j=1}^{2q} (-1)^j f_1(A^1\mathbf{z}^j) = 0.$$

The similar argument holds for $i = 2$.

(d)$\Rightarrow$(a). This is a consequence of Proposition 11.2.   □

Remark 11.11 If the $\{\mathbf{z}^j\}_{j=1}^t$ are a subset of the $\{\mathbf{x}^j\}_{j=1}^k$ which form a closed path then, see Proposition 11.6,

$$\sum_{i=1}^{2} \#\{A^i\mathbf{z}^j\}_{j=1}^t \leq t.$$

In this case of two distinct directions the converse also holds. See Sun [1993], Theorem 9, for details.

11.3 Difference Commensurable Points

In this section we consider the interpolation problem in $\mathbb{R}^2$, and provide a complete geometric characterization for a large (but not the complete) set of points satisfying the NI-property. The results of this section are taken from Braess and Pinkus [1993].

Assume that we are given r pairwise linearly independent directions $\mathbf{a}^1, \ldots, \mathbf{a}^r$ in $\mathbb{R}^2$. For notational ease we assume in this section that the point $\mathbf{a}^i$ are of the form $\mathbf{a}^i = (\sin\theta_i, -\cos\theta_i)$, where $0 = \theta_1 < \theta_2 < \cdots < \theta_r < \pi$, and $\mathbf{x} = (x, y)$. This simply means that

$$\mathbf{a}^i \cdot \mathbf{x} = x\sin\theta_i - y\cos\theta_i$$

is a constant along any straight line which intersects the x-axis with positive angle θ_i.

We first define what we mean by a *brick*. A brick is a set of 2^r vertices that will be determined by the directions $\mathbf{a}^1, \ldots, \mathbf{a}^r$ and sides of length $\sigma_1, \ldots, \sigma_r$, ($\sigma_i > 0$, $i = 1, \ldots, r$). It is a set of 2^r points (vertices) in $\mathbb{R}^2$ with the NI-property with respect to the $\{\mathbf{a}^i\}_{i=1}^r$. (In certain non-generic cases, it is possible that some of these 2^r points might be equal.) It is constructed as follows, up to translation.

Take the point $\mathbf{x}^1 = (0, 0)$ and project it a distance σ_1 in the $\mathbf{a}^1$ direction.

That is, shift it by $(\sigma_1 \cos \theta_1, \sigma_1 \sin \theta_1)$ (which in this case is $(\sigma_1, 0)$). Let $\mathbf{x}^2 = (\sigma_1, 0)$. Now project the two points $\mathbf{x}^1$ and $\mathbf{x}^2$ a distance σ_2 in the $\mathbf{a}^2$ direction. That is, shift them by $(\sigma_2 \cos \theta_2, \sigma_2 \sin \theta_2)$ to obtain the new points $\mathbf{x}^3$ and $\mathbf{x}^4$. Note that $\mathbf{a}^1 \cdot \mathbf{x}^1 = \mathbf{a}^1 \cdot \mathbf{x}^2, \mathbf{a}^1 \cdot \mathbf{x}^3 = \mathbf{a}^1 \cdot \mathbf{x}^4, \mathbf{a}^2 \cdot \mathbf{x}^1 = \mathbf{a}^2 \cdot \mathbf{x}^3, \mathbf{a}^2 \cdot \mathbf{x}^2 = \mathbf{a}^2 \cdot \mathbf{x}^4$, and $\|\mathbf{x}^1 - \mathbf{x}^2\| = \|\mathbf{x}^3 - \mathbf{x}^4\| = \sigma_1$, while $\|\mathbf{x}^1 - \mathbf{x}^3\| = \|\mathbf{x}^2 - \mathbf{x}^4\| = \sigma_2$, where $\| \cdot \|$ is the Euclidean norm. That is, the $\mathbf{x}^1, \mathbf{x}^2, \mathbf{x}^3, \mathbf{x}^4$ are the four vertices of a parallelogram. We now project these four points a distance σ_3 in the direction $\mathbf{a}^3$ to get eight points. That is, we shift them by $(\sigma_3 \cos \theta_3, \sigma_3 \sin \theta_3)$. We continue this process. For $r = 3$, the eight points form the vertices of a figure which looks like a drawing of a projection of a parallelepiped. Hence the term "brick".

Analytically the $\{\mathbf{x}^j\}_{j=1}^{2^r}$, as defined above, are given as follows. For $j \in \{1, 2, \ldots, 2^r\}$ consider the representation of $j - 1$ as a binary number

$$j - 1 := \sum_{\ell=1}^{r} d_\ell 2^{\ell-1}, \tag{11.7}$$

where $d_\ell := d_\ell(j) \in \{0, 1\}$, and set

$$\mathbf{x}^j := \sum_{\ell=1}^{r} d_\ell(j) \sigma_\ell \mathbf{b}^\ell,$$

where $\mathbf{b}^\ell := (\cos \theta_\ell, \sin \theta_\ell), \ell = 1, \ldots, r$. This is a brick with a vertex at $\mathbf{x}^1 = (0, 0)$. A brick, in general, is a translate of these 2^r points, i.e., $\{\mathbf{y}^j\}_{j=1}^{2^r}$ where $\mathbf{y}^j = \mathbf{x}^j + \mathbf{c}, j = 1, \ldots, 2^r$, for some arbitrary $\mathbf{c}$, and where the $\{\mathbf{x}^j\}_{j=1}^{2^r}$ form a brick with a vertex at $(0, 0)$.

We now alternately associate with each of the 2^r vertices $\{\mathbf{x}^j\}_{j=1}^{2^r}$ values $\varepsilon_j \in \{-1, 1\}$. This can easily be done in an alternate fashion. For example, in the above construction give $\mathbf{x}^1$ the value 1 and $\mathbf{x}^2$ the value -1. Give the projection of $\mathbf{x}^1$ in the $\mathbf{a}^2$ direction, namely $\mathbf{x}^3$, the value -1, and $\mathbf{x}^4$, the projection of $\mathbf{x}^2$ in the $\mathbf{a}^2$ direction, the value 1. Continue in this fashion. That is, each time one doubles the number of points (due to a projection in a new direction), switch the signs. Referring to the binary decomposition (11.7), we set $\varepsilon_j := (-1)^{n_j}$, where

$$n_j := \sum_{\ell=1}^{r} d_\ell(j).$$

A brick with these assigned weights will be called a *signed brick*.

As is easily checked, the resulting vector $\boldsymbol{\varepsilon} = (\varepsilon_1, \ldots, \varepsilon_{2^r})$ has the property that

$$\sum_{j=1}^{2^r} \varepsilon_j G(\mathbf{x}^j) = 0$$

for every $G \in \mathcal{M}(\mathbf{a}^1, \ldots, \mathbf{a}^r)$. That is, from Proposition 11.2, the vertices of a brick have the NI-property.

Bricks seem so natural that it is tempting to ask if all sets of points with the NI-property contain a subset which can be obtained by taking a (finite) sum of signed bricks. We first explain what we mean by the above statement.

A signed brick B is determined by 2^r vertices and a vector $\varepsilon \in \{-1, 1\}^{2^r}$, as given above. Given s signed bricks $B_1, \ldots, B_s$ and numbers $\alpha_1, \ldots, \alpha_s$, by

$$\sum_{i=1}^{s} \alpha_i B_i$$

we mean the set of points $\{\mathbf{y}^j\}_{j=1}^p$ with associated values $\{\gamma_j\}_{j=1}^p$, where each $\mathbf{y}^j$ is in at least one of the B_i, $i = 1, \ldots, s$, the value γ_j is the sum of $\alpha_i \varepsilon_\ell^i$ for $i \in \{1, \ldots, s\}$ and $\ell \in \{1, \ldots, 2^r\}$ such that $\mathbf{x}^\ell$ in B_i is $\mathbf{y}^j$, and $\gamma_j \neq 0$. A vertex of a brick is not included if the associated "weight" γ_j is zero. Note two important facts. Firstly

$$\sum_{j=1}^{p} \gamma_j G(\mathbf{y}^j) = 0$$

for all $G \in \mathcal{M}(\mathbf{a}^1, \ldots, \mathbf{a}^r)$, since it is obtained as a sum of such equations. Secondly, among the points $\{\mathbf{y}^j\}_{j=1}^p$ we do *not* include those points for which $\gamma_j = 0$. For example, assume $k = 2$ and we have two bricks $\{\mathbf{x}^j\}_{j=1}^4$ and $\{\mathbf{z}^j\}_{j=1}^4$ as given in Figure 11.2 (with directions parallel to the axes), and the ε as previously defined.

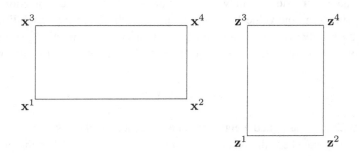

Figure 11.2

If $\mathbf{x}^4 = \mathbf{z}^3$, then the resulting $B_1 + B_2$ is given as in Figure 11.3.

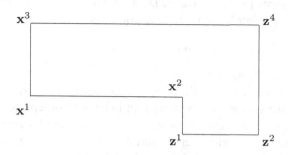

Figure 11.3

If $\mathbf{x}^4 = \mathbf{z}^1$, then $B_1 - B_2$ is given as in Figure 11.4.

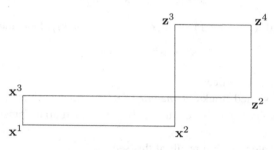

Figure 11.4

In this way we can cancel out points, and always remain with a set of points satisfying the NI-property.

Although we did not explicitly state it in Theorem 11.10, it is not difficult to ascertain that for $r = 2$ and $d = 1$ every set of points with the NI-property contains a subset which is obtained as a sum of signed bricks (in fact, parallelograms). This is intimately related to the idea of a closed path. For $r = 3$ this is not true, see Theorem 11.15. However, for a large class of points $\{\mathbf{x}^j\}_{j=1}^k$ and any $r \geq 3$, every set of points in $\mathbb{R}^2$ with the NI-property does contain a subset obtained by taking sums of signed bricks (of a specific type). In what follows we delineate such a set and prove the result. To explain, we introduce the following definitions.

Definition 11.12 We say that the set of points $\{\mathbf{x}^j\}_{j=1}^k$ is *difference commensurable* (or has the DC-property) with respect to the direction $\mathbf{a}$ with difference δ, if there exists a number $\delta > 0$ and *integers* $\{\mu_{st}\}_{s,t=1}^k$ such that

$$\mathbf{a} \cdot \mathbf{x}^s - \mathbf{a} \cdot \mathbf{x}^t = \mu_{st}\delta$$

for every $s, t = 1, \ldots, k$.

That is, the points $\{\mathbf{x}^j\}_{j=1}^k$ have the DC-property with respect to a with difference δ if all these points lie on the regular grid lines

$$\mathbf{a} \cdot \mathbf{x} = n\delta + \nu$$

for some fixed $\nu \in \mathbb{R}$, and $n \in \mathbb{Z}$.

Given the distinct directions $\mathbf{a}^1, \dots, \mathbf{a}^r$ (as above), there are bricks, the vertices of which have the DC-property with respect to $\mathbf{a}^1$ with difference δ. These are given by the previous construction where σ_1 is arbitrary, but for each of the other σ_is the product $\sigma_i \sin \theta_i$ is an integer multiple of δ. Since we can add bricks, we define *elementary bricks* as translates of those bricks for which $\sigma_i \sin \theta_i = \delta$, $i = 2, \dots, r$ (recall that $0 < \theta_2 < \cdots < \theta_r < \pi$). This implies that for each j,

$$\mathbf{a}^1 \cdot \mathbf{x}^j - \mathbf{a}^1 \cdot \mathbf{x}^1 = n_j \delta \qquad (11.8)$$

for some $n_j \in \{0, 1, \dots, r-1\}$. In fact, $n_j = \sum_{\ell=1}^r d_\ell(j)$. Note that the equation

$$\mathbf{a}^1 \cdot \mathbf{x}^j - \mathbf{a}^1 \cdot \mathbf{x}^1 = (r-1)\delta \qquad (11.9)$$

holds for exactly two vertices.

We call such signed bricks *elementary DC signed bricks with respect to* $\mathbf{a}^1$ *with difference* δ. These bricks are uniquely determined up to translation, and the choice of σ_1.

We can now state the main result of this section.

Theorem 11.13 *We are given pairwise linearly independent directions* $\mathbf{a}^1, \dots, \mathbf{a}^r$ *in* $\mathbb{R}^2$. *Assume that the set of points* $\{\mathbf{x}^j\}_{j=1}^k$ *have the DC-property with respect to* $\mathbf{a}^\ell$, *some* $\ell \in \{1, \dots, r\}$, *with difference* δ. *Then the points* $\{\mathbf{x}^j\}_{j=1}^k$ *have the NI-property with respect to the directions* $\mathbf{a}^1, \dots, \mathbf{a}^r$ *if and only if a subset of these points may be obtained as a finite sum of elementary DC signed bricks with respect to* $\mathbf{a}^\ell$ *with difference* δ.

The proof of Theorem 11.13 is very much based on the following simple lemma.

Lemma 11.14 *Assume that the points* $\{\mathbf{y}^j\}_{j=1}^s$ *have the MNI-property with respect to the pairwise linearly independent directions* $\mathbf{a}^1, \dots, \mathbf{a}^r$. *Further assume that these points have the DC-property with respect to* $\mathbf{a}^1$ *with difference* δ. *Then*

$$\max_{i,j \in \{1,\dots,s\}} \left| \mathbf{a}^1 \cdot \mathbf{y}^i - \mathbf{a}^1 \cdot \mathbf{y}^j \right| \geq (r-1)\delta.$$

Proof Since the $\{\mathbf{y}^j\}_{j=1}^s$ have the MNI-property, then from Proposition 11.2 we have the existence of a vector $\beta \in \mathbb{R}^s \backslash \{\mathbf{0}\}$ such that each of its components is non-zero, and

$$\sum_{j=1}^{s} \beta_j f_i(\mathbf{a}^i \cdot \mathbf{y}^j) = 0$$

for all $f_i : \mathbb{R} \to \mathbb{R}$ and each $i = 1, \ldots, r$. This implies that, for $\Gamma_{\mathbf{a}^i}(\lambda) = \{\mathbf{x} : \mathbf{a}^i \cdot \mathbf{x} = \lambda\}$, we have

$$\left| \Gamma_{\mathbf{a}^i}(\lambda) \cap \{\mathbf{y}^j\}_{j=1}^{s} \right| \neq 1$$

for every $\lambda \in \mathbb{R}$ and $i = 1, \ldots, r$. That is, no line of the form $\mathbf{a}^i \cdot \mathbf{x} = \lambda$ contains exactly one point from $\{\mathbf{y}^j\}_{j=1}^{s}$.

Consider the convex hull $\mathcal{C}$ of the points $\{\mathbf{y}^j\}_{j=1}^{s}$. From the above it follows that this is a polygon with exactly $2r$ sides. Exactly two edges of the polygon are parallel to $\mathbf{b}^i = (\cos\theta_i, \sin\theta_i)$ whenever $i = 1, \ldots, r$. For each $i \in \{1, \ldots, r\}$, there are $\lambda_1^i < \lambda_2^i$ such that $\Gamma_{\mathbf{a}^i}(\lambda_1^i)$ and $\Gamma_{\mathbf{a}^i}(\lambda_2^i)$ contain sides of $\mathcal{C}$. (The $\Gamma_{\mathbf{a}^i}(\lambda_1^i)$ and $\Gamma_{\mathbf{a}^i}(\lambda_2^i)$ are support functionals for $\mathcal{C}$.) Let $\mathcal{C} \cap \Gamma_{\mathbf{a}^i}(\lambda_2^i)$ be the straight line with endpoints $\mathbf{y}_1^i, \mathbf{y}_2^i$, where $\mathbf{a}^1 \cdot \mathbf{y}_2^i > \mathbf{a}^1 \cdot \mathbf{y}_1^i$, $i = 2, \ldots, r$. Since $0 = \theta_1 < \theta_2 < \cdots < \theta_r < \pi$ it follows that $\mathbf{y}_2^i = \mathbf{y}_1^{i+1}$, $i = 2, \ldots, r-1$. Now

$$\mathbf{a}^1 \cdot \mathbf{y}_2^i - \mathbf{a}^1 \cdot \mathbf{y}_1^i \geq \delta$$

since the $\{\mathbf{y}^j\}_{j=1}^{s}$ have the DC-property with respect to $\mathbf{a}^1$ with difference δ. Summing i over $2, \ldots, r$, we obtain that

$$\mathbf{a}^1 \cdot \mathbf{y}_2^r - \mathbf{a}^1 \cdot \mathbf{y}_1^2 \geq (r-1)\delta,$$

which proves our lemma. $\qquad\qquad\square$

Proof of Theorem 11.13 One direction is obvious. If a subset of the point set $\{\mathbf{x}^j\}_{j=1}^{k}$ is obtained as a finite sum of elementary DC signed bricks with respect to $\mathbf{a}^\ell$ (with difference δ), then the points $\{\mathbf{x}^j\}_{j=1}^{k}$ have the NI-property with respect to the directions $\mathbf{a}^1, \ldots, \mathbf{a}^r$.

It remains to prove the converse direction. For convenience, we assume that $\ell = 1$. From Proposition 11.2 we have the existence of a vector $\beta \in \mathbb{R}^k \setminus \{\mathbf{0}\}$ such that

$$\sum_{j=1}^{k} \beta_j f_i(\mathbf{a}^i \cdot \mathbf{x}^j) = 0 \qquad (11.10)$$

for all $f_i : \mathbb{R} \to \mathbb{R}$ and each $i = 1, \ldots, r$.

Let

$$\max\left\{ \mathbf{a}^1 \cdot \mathbf{x}^i - \mathbf{a}^1 \cdot \mathbf{x}^j : i, j \in \{1, \ldots, k\}, \beta_i, \beta_j \neq 0 \right\} = n\delta.$$

From Lemma 11.14, $n \geq r - 1$. For convenience, assume that

$$\min\{\mathbf{a}^1 \cdot \mathbf{x}^i : \beta_i \neq 0\} = 0.$$

Let $i_0, j_0 \in \{1, \ldots, k\}$ be such that $\mathbf{a}^1 \cdot \mathbf{x}^{i_0} = \mathbf{a}^1 \cdot \mathbf{x}^{j_0} = n\delta$, $\beta_{i_0}, \beta_{j_0} \neq 0$, and $\mathbf{x}^{i_0} \neq \mathbf{x}^{j_0}$. Such i_0 and j_0 must exist (see the proof of Lemma 11.14). Let B_{i_0} denote the elementary DC signed brick with respect to $\mathbf{a}^1$ with difference δ, where $\sigma_1 = \|\mathbf{x}^{i_0} - \mathbf{x}^{j_0}\|$, and the points $\mathbf{x}^{i_0}$ and $\mathbf{x}^{j_0}$ are the vertices of the top-most row of B_{i_0}. From (11.8) and (11.9) we conclude that $0 \leq \mathbf{a}^1 \cdot \mathbf{y} < n\delta$ for any other vertex $\mathbf{y}$ in B_{i_0}. We now add $\pm \beta_{i_0} B_{i_0}$ to the $\{\mathbf{x}^1, \ldots, \mathbf{x}^k\}$ in the manner previously indicated, i.e., with respect to (11.10), so that the new coefficient of $\mathbf{x}^{i_0}$ is zero. Since the B_{i_0} has the NI-property, we get a new set of points $\{\mathbf{x}_1^j\}_{j=1}^{k_1}$ with the NI-property. This new set has the following properties.

(a) There exists a $\beta^1 \in \mathbb{R}^{k_1} \backslash \{\mathbf{0}\}$ such that

$$\sum_{j=1}^{k_1} \beta_j^1 f_i(\mathbf{a}^i \cdot \mathbf{x}_1^j) = 0$$

for all $f_i : \mathbb{R} \to \mathbb{R}$ and $i = 1, \ldots, r$.

(b) $\min\limits_{j=1,\ldots,k_1} \{\mathbf{a}^1 \cdot \mathbf{x}_1^j : \beta_j^1 \neq 0\} \geq 0$.

(c) $\max\limits_{j=1,\ldots,k_1} \{\mathbf{a}^1 \cdot \mathbf{x}_1^j : \beta_j^1 \neq 0\} \leq n\delta$.

(d) The set of $\mathbf{x}_1^j$ with $\beta_j^1 \neq 0$ satisfying $\mathbf{a}^1 \cdot \mathbf{x}_1^j = n\delta$ is a strict subset of the set of $\mathbf{x}^j$ with $\beta_j \neq 0$ satisfying $\mathbf{a}^1 \cdot \mathbf{x}^j = n\delta$ in that no new points have been added, and $\mathbf{x}^{i_0}$ is not included.

The new set of points may not have these properties in that we may have all the $\beta_j^1 = 0$. If so, then we are finished and the theorem is proved. We wish to show that this situation must occur after a finite number of steps.

To this end, we continue the above process. Since the number of points $\mathbf{x}^j$ for which $\beta_j \neq 0$ and $\mathbf{a}^1 \cdot \mathbf{x}^j = n\delta$ is finite, we eventually reach a step ℓ_1, after adding in a finite number of elementary DC signed bricks of the above form, where

$$\max_j \{\mathbf{a}^1 \cdot \mathbf{x}_{\ell_1}^j : \beta_j^{\ell_1} \neq 0\} \leq (n-1)\delta.$$

At this stage we add elementary DC signed bricks, as above, whose top-most row lies on the line $\mathbf{a}^1 \cdot \mathbf{x} = (n-1)\delta$. Because of the previous addition of elementary DC signed bricks, the set of points $\mathbf{x}_{\ell_1}^j$ satisfying $\beta_j^{\ell_1} \neq 0$ and $\mathbf{a}^1 \cdot \mathbf{x}_{\ell_1}^j = (n-1)\delta$ may be much larger than it was previously. However, it is still finite, and starting at this stage it decreases in number by at least one point at each step. We continue this process.

Recall that the elementary DC signed brick has r levels (of difference δ). That is, if $\{\mathbf{y}^j\}$ are the vertices of the elementary DC signed brick, and

$$\max_j \mathbf{a}^1 \cdot \mathbf{y}^j \geq (r-1)\delta,$$

then

$$\min_j \mathbf{a}^1 \cdot \mathbf{y}^j \geq 0.$$

This implies that if at step ℓ

$$\max_j \{\mathbf{a}^1 \cdot \mathbf{x}_\ell^j : \beta_j^\ell \neq 0\} \geq (r-1)\delta$$

then we do not, by adding elementary DC signed bricks as in the above process, add vertices $\mathbf{y}^j$ with $\mathbf{a}^1 \cdot \mathbf{y}^j < 0$.

Assuming that we do not at any stage finish this process, we must eventually reach a stage ℓ^* where the set $\{\mathbf{x}_{\ell^*}^j\}_{j=1}^{k_{\ell^*}}$ has the NI-property, and satisfies

$$\max_{j=1,\ldots,k_{\ell^*}} \{\mathbf{a}^1 \cdot \mathbf{x}_{\ell^*}^j : \beta_j^{\ell^*} \neq 0\} \leq (r-2)\delta,$$

and

$$\min_{j=1,\ldots,k_{\ell^*}} \{\mathbf{a}^1 \cdot \mathbf{x}_{\ell^*}^j : \beta_j^{\ell^*} \neq 0\} \geq 0.$$

This contradicts Lemma 11.14. The theorem is proved. □

We mention, without giving the very detailed proof, one additional result that provides a geometric characterization of sets of points with the NI-property. It is due to Braess and Pinkus [1993]. It generalizes Theorem 11.10 to $r = 3$, but only when $n = 2$. That is, it considers the case of three distinct directions in $\mathbb{R}^2$. It provides a complete classification of all sets of points with the NI-property in this particular case. It also shows that the result of Theorem 11.13 is not valid for arbitrary choices of directions and points.

Given three directions $\mathbf{a}^1, \mathbf{a}^2, \mathbf{a}^3$ in $\mathbb{R}^2$ we call a hexagon a *regular hexagon* if its six vertices satisfy the NI-property with respect to $\mathbf{a}^1, \mathbf{a}^2, \mathbf{a}^3$. Regular hexagons do exist and can be easily constructed. It is a *signed regular hexagon* when we assign to its six vertices, alternately, the weights 1 and -1. As previously, when summing signed regular hexagons we give weights to each hexagon and a vertex is not included if the associated sum of weights is zero.

Theorem 11.15 *Let $\mathbf{a}^1, \mathbf{a}^2, \mathbf{a}^3$ be three pairwise linearly independent directions in $\mathbb{R}^2$. Then the set of points $\{\mathbf{x}^j\}_{j=1}^k$ has the NI-property with respect to the $\{\mathbf{a}^i\}_{i=1}^3$ if and only if there is a non-empty subset of the $\{\mathbf{x}^j\}_{j=1}^k$ which may be obtained as a finite sum of signed regular hexagons.*

12

Interpolation on Lines

In this final chapter we discuss the problem of the possibility of interpolation by functions from $\mathcal{M}(\mathbf{a}^1, \ldots, \mathbf{a}^r)$ on straight lines. That is, assume we are given the straight lines $\{t\mathbf{b}^j + \mathbf{c}^j : t \in \mathbb{R}\}$, $\mathbf{b}^j \neq \mathbf{0}$, $j = 1, \ldots, m$. The question we ask is when, for every (or most) choice of data $g_j(t)$, $j = 1, \ldots, m$, do there exist functions $G \in \mathcal{M}(\mathbf{a}^1, \ldots, \mathbf{a}^r)$ satisfying

$$G(t\mathbf{b}^j + \mathbf{c}^j) = g_j(t), \qquad t \in \mathbb{R}, \, j = 1, \ldots, m?$$

Why interpolation on straight lines? Because that seems to be the most natural setting for interpolation from ridge functions.

In Section 12.1 we first show that interpolation by ridge functions on any set X in $\mathbb{R}^n$ is possible if and only if it is possible on every finite point set $\{\mathbf{x}^1, \ldots, \mathbf{x}^k\} \subset X$. In Section 12.2 we show what happens when $r = 1$, i.e., when we have only one direction. We will show that we can interpolate from $\mathcal{M}(\mathbf{a})$ on the straight line $\{t\mathbf{b} + \mathbf{c} : t \in \mathbb{R}\}$ if and only if $\mathbf{a} \cdot \mathbf{b} \neq 0$, while we can never interpolate from $\mathcal{M}(\mathbf{a})$ to all given functions on the union of two straight lines. In Section 12.3 we consider the case of two directions, i.e., interpolation from $\mathcal{M}(\mathbf{a}^1, \mathbf{a}^2)$. We show exact conditions under which we can interpolate on two distinct straight lines. We also show how to reduce these conditions to more meaningful geometric conditions when we are in $\mathbb{R}^2$. In addition, by example, we show that while the data (the G) might be continuous on the union of two straight lines where interpolation from $\mathcal{M}(\mathbf{a}^1, \mathbf{a}^2)$ is possible, this does not imply that the associated f_1 and f_2 in the representation

$$G(\mathbf{x}) = f_1(\mathbf{a}^1 \cdot \mathbf{x}) + f_2(\mathbf{a}^2 \cdot \mathbf{x})$$

can be taken to be continuous. In Section 12.4 we reprove the major result of Section 12.3 by a different method. We then use this proof and an analysis of certain first-order difference equations to prove that it is never possible to interpolate

168

from $\mathcal{M}(\mathbf{a}^1, \mathbf{a}^2)$ to all (most) functions on the union of three straight lines. Most of the material of this chapter is taken from Ismailov and Pinkus [2013].

12.1 Interpolation on a Set

Let $\ell_j := \{t\mathbf{b}^j + \mathbf{c}^j : t \in \mathbb{R}\}$, $\mathbf{b}^j, \mathbf{c}^j \in \mathbb{R}^n$, $\mathbf{b}^j \neq \mathbf{0}$, $j = 1, \ldots, m$, denote a set of m straight lines and $L := \bigcup_{j=1}^m \ell_j$. The problem of interpolation of arbitrary data on the lines $\{\ell_j\}_{j=1}^m$ by linear combinations of ridge functions with fixed directions, i.e., $\mathcal{M}(\mathbf{a}^1, \ldots, \mathbf{a}^k)$, is equivalent to the problem of the representation of an arbitrarily given G defined on L by such combinations. That is, it is equivalent to the question of when each and every function G defined on L is necessarily of the form

$$G(\mathbf{x}) = \sum_{i=1}^r f_i(\mathbf{a}^i \cdot \mathbf{x})$$

for all $\mathbf{x} \in L$ and for some f_i, $i = 1, \ldots, r$. Concerning this problem, we have a result from Ismailov [2008a] that shows that interpolation to every function G defined on L from $\mathcal{M}(\mathbf{a}^1, \ldots, \mathbf{a}^r)$ is possible if and only if it is possible for every finite point set $\{\mathbf{x}^1, \ldots, \mathbf{x}^k\} \subset L$. In other words, the problem of interpolation on an infinite set of points is solvable if and only if it is solvable on every finite subset thereon.

Theorem 12.1 *Let X be any subset of $\mathbb{R}^n$. Then every function G defined on X is of the form*

$$G(\mathbf{x}) = \sum_{i=1}^r f_i(\mathbf{a}^i \cdot \mathbf{x})$$

for some f_i, $i = 1, \ldots, r$, if and only if there is no finite subset $\{\mathbf{x}^j\}_{j=1}^k$ of points in X with the NI-property with respect to the $\{\mathbf{a}^i\}_{i=1}^r$.

In the proof of this theorem we utilize a generalization of ridge functions. We shall replace linear combinations of ridge functions with fixed directions $\mathbf{a}^1, \ldots, \mathbf{a}^r$ by the following. Let $h_i : X \to \mathbb{R}$, $i = 1, \ldots, r$, be r fixed real-valued functions. Set

$$\mathcal{M}(h_1, \ldots, h_r) := \left\{ \sum_{i=1}^r f_i(h_i(\mathbf{x})) : f_i : \mathbb{R} \to \mathbb{R} \right\}.$$

Paralleling what we did with *directions*, we define the following.

Definition 12.2 Given $h_i : X \to \mathbb{R}$, $i = 1, \ldots, r$, we say that the set of points $\{\mathbf{x}^j\}_{j=1}^k$ in $\mathbb{R}^n$ has the *NI-property* (non-interpolation property) with respect to the $\{h_i\}_{i=1}^r$ if there exist $\{b_j\}_{j=1}^k \subset \mathbb{R}$ such that we *cannot* find $f_i : \mathbb{R} \to \mathbb{R}$, $i = 1, \ldots, r$, satisfying

$$\sum_{i=1}^r f_i(h_i(\mathbf{x}^j)) = b_j, \qquad j = 1, \ldots, k.$$

We say that the set of points $\{\mathbf{x}^j\}_{j=1}^k$ in $\mathbb{R}^n$ has the *MNI-property* (minimal non-interpolation property) with respect to the $\{h_i\}_{i=1}^r$, if $\{\mathbf{x}^j\}_{j=1}^k$ has the NI-property and no proper subset of the $\{\mathbf{x}^j\}_{j=1}^k$ has the NI-property.

By an argument totally analogous to that given in the proof of Proposition 11.2 we obtain this next result.

Proposition 12.3 *Given $\{h_i\}_{i=1}^r$, the set of points $\{\mathbf{x}^j\}_{j=1}^k$ in $\mathbb{R}^n$ has the NI-property with respect to the $\{h_i\}_{i=1}^r$ if and only if there exists a vector $\beta = (\beta_1, \ldots, \beta_k) \in \mathbb{R}^k \backslash \{\mathbf{0}\}$ such that*

$$\sum_{j=1}^k \beta_j f_i(h_i(\mathbf{x}^j)) = 0 \qquad \qquad (12.1)$$

for all $f_i : \mathbb{R} \to \mathbb{R}$ and each $i = 1, \ldots, r$. The set of points $\{\mathbf{x}^j\}_{j=1}^k$ in $\mathbb{R}^n$ has the MNI-property if and only if the vector $\beta \in \mathbb{R}^k \backslash \{\mathbf{0}\}$ satisfying (12.1) is unique, up to multiplication by a constant, and has no zero component.

We will prove the following generalization of Theorem 12.1.

Theorem 12.4 *Let X be any subset of $\mathbb{R}^n$. For given $\{h_i\}_{i=1}^r$, every function G defined on X is of the form*

$$G(\mathbf{x}) = \sum_{i=1}^r f_i(h_i(\mathbf{x}))$$

for some f_i, $i = 1, \ldots, r$, if and only if there is no finite subset $\{\mathbf{x}^j\}_{j=1}^k$ of points in X with the NI-property with respect to the $\{h_i\}_{i=1}^r$.

Proof Not permitting the NI-property is obviously necessary. We are interested in the sufficiency. Let us assume that there is no finite subset $\{\mathbf{x}^j\}_{j=1}^k$ of points in X with the NI-property with respect to the $\{h_i\}_{i=1}^r$. We wish to prove that each G, defined on X, has the form

$$G(\mathbf{x}) = \sum_{i=1}^r f_i(h_i(\mathbf{x}))$$

for some f_i, $i = 1, \ldots, r$.

We first prove this result under the assumption that the Y_i, the range of the h_i, $i = 1, \ldots, r$, are disjoint sets. That is, let $Y_i = h_i(X)$, and assume $Y_i \cap Y_j = \emptyset$ for all $i \neq j$.

Let $\mathcal{L}$ denote the sequences $\mathbf{y} = \{y_1, \ldots, y_r\}$ such that there exists a $\mathbf{x} \in X$ for which $h_i(\mathbf{x}) = y_i$, $i = 1, \ldots, r$. Note that for each such $\mathbf{y} = \{y_1, \ldots, y_r\} \in \mathcal{L}$ we have $y_i \neq y_j$ for all $i \neq j$ since the ranges of the h_i are disjoint. Furthermore, we claim that each $\mathbf{y} \in \mathcal{L}$ has a unique preimage. That is, there is a unique $\mathbf{x} \in X$ such that $h_i(\mathbf{x}) = y_i$, $i = 1, \ldots, r$. For if, on the contrary, there exist distinct $\mathbf{x}^1$, $\mathbf{x}^2$ in X such that $h_i(\mathbf{x}^1) = h_i(\mathbf{x}^2) = y_i$, $i = 1, \ldots, r$, then $\{\mathbf{x}^1, \mathbf{x}^2\}$ has the NI-property with respect to the $\{h_i\}_{i=1}^r$, i.e.,

$$\sum_{j=1}^{2} (-1)^j f_i(h_i(\mathbf{x}^j)) = 0$$

for all f_i, $i = 1, \ldots, r$.

We are given $G : X \to \mathbb{R}$. For any positive integer k, real numbers α_j and $\mathbf{y}^j \in \mathcal{L}$, $j = 1, \ldots, k$, we define the linear functional

$$F\left(\sum_{j=1}^{k} \alpha_j \Delta_{\mathbf{y}^j}\right) := \sum_{j=1}^{k} \alpha_j G(\mathbf{x}^j),$$

where $\mathbf{x}^j$ is the unique preimage of $\mathbf{y}^j$. Here we consider $\Delta_{\mathbf{y}}$, for each $\mathbf{y} \in \mathcal{L}$, as the indicator function of $\mathbf{y}$. More precisely

$$\Delta_{\mathbf{y}} := \delta_{y_1} + \cdots + \delta_{y_r},$$

where δ_y is the indicator function of $y \in \mathbb{R}$. We consider

$$\mathcal{S} := \left\{\sum_{j=1}^{k} \alpha_j \Delta_{\mathbf{y}^j}\right\}$$

as a linear space and F as a linear functional on $\mathcal{S}$. We claim that F is well-defined on $\mathcal{S}$. That is, each element of $\mathcal{S}$ has a unique representation of the above form. For if there exist $\alpha_j \in \mathbb{R}$ and $\mathbf{y}^j \in \mathcal{L}$ for which

$$\sum_{j=1}^{k} \alpha_j \Delta_{\mathbf{y}^j} = \sum_{j=1}^{k} \alpha_j \left(\sum_{i=1}^{r} \delta_{y_i^j}\right) = 0,$$

then it follows that

$$\sum_{j=1}^{k} \alpha_j f_i(h_i(\mathbf{x}^j)) = 0,$$

for all $f_i : \mathbb{R} \to \mathbb{R}$, $i = 1, \ldots, r$. By our assumption of no finite subset with the NI-property this implies that $\alpha_j = 0$, $j = 1, \ldots, k$.

We now define the linear space

$$\mathcal{S}' := \left\{ \sum_{j=1}^{k} \alpha_j \delta_{\omega^j} \right\},$$

where k is any positive integer, the α_j are real numbers and $\omega^j \in Y_1 \cup \cdots \cup Y_r$, $j = 1, \ldots, k$. We can consider $\mathcal{S}$ as a subspace of $\mathcal{S}'$ since

$$\Delta_{\mathbf{y}} = \delta_{y_1} + \cdots + \delta_{y_r}$$

for each $\mathbf{y} = \{y_1, \ldots, y_r\}$ in $\mathcal{L}$. As $\mathcal{S}$ is a linear subspace of $\mathcal{S}'$ and F is a linear functional on $\mathcal{S}$, it is well-known and follows by a simple application of Zorn's Lemma that there exists a linear extension F' of F on $\mathcal{S}'$. Set

$$f_i(y) := F'(\delta_y)$$

for $y \in Y_i$, $i = 1, \ldots, r$.

Given G, as above, and $\mathbf{x} \in X$, let $y_i := h_i(\mathbf{x})$, $i = 1, \ldots, r$ and $\mathbf{y} := \{y_1, \ldots, y_r\}$. Thus

$$G(\mathbf{x}) = F(\Delta_{\mathbf{y}}) = F'(\delta_{y_1} + \cdots + \delta_{y_r}) = \sum_{i=1}^{r} F'(\delta_{y_i})$$

$$= \sum_{i=1}^{r} f_i(y_i) = \sum_{i=1}^{r} f_i(h_i(\mathbf{x})).$$

We have proven the theorem under the assumption that the Y_i are disjoint.

Assume now that the Y_i are not disjoint. Choose arbitrary disjoint intervals (a_i, b_i), $i = 1, \ldots, r$, and let

$$\tau_i : \mathbb{R} \to (a_i, b_i), \qquad i = 1, \ldots, r,$$

be any one-to-one mapping of $\mathbb{R}$ onto (a_i, b_i). Define

$$h_i'(\mathbf{x}) := \tau_i(h_i(\mathbf{x})), \qquad i = 1, \ldots, r.$$

By the one-to-one property, it follows that a finite subset $\{\mathbf{x}^j\}_{j=1}^{k}$ of points in X has the NI-property with respect to the $\{h_i\}_{i=1}^{r}$ if and only if it has the NI-property with respect to the $\{h_i'\}_{i=1}^{r}$. By construction and assumption, the ranges of the h_i' are disjoint and no finite subset $\{\mathbf{x}^j\}_{j=1}^{k}$ of points in X has the NI-property with respect to the $\{h_i'\}_{i=1}^{r}$. Thus each G defined on X is of the form

$$G(\mathbf{x}) = \sum_{i=1}^{r} f_i'(h_i'(\mathbf{x})) = \sum_{i=1}^{r} f_i'(\tau_i(h_i(\mathbf{x})))$$

for some f_i', $i = 1, \ldots, r$. Set

$$f_i(y) := f_i'(\tau_i(y)), \qquad i = 1, \ldots, r.$$

This proves the theorem. $\qquad\qquad\qquad\qquad\qquad\qquad\qquad\qquad\qquad\qquad\qquad$ $\square$

12.2 Interpolation from $\mathcal{M}(\mathbf{a})$

Let us first consider the elementary case of one direction, i.e.,

$$\mathcal{M}(\mathbf{a}) = \{f(\mathbf{a} \cdot \mathbf{x}) : f : \mathbb{R} \to \mathbb{R}\}.$$

It is easily shown that interpolation is possible on a straight line $\{t\mathbf{b} + \mathbf{c} : t \in \mathbb{R}\}$ if and only if that straight line is not contained in any of the hyperplanes $\{\mathbf{x} : \mathbf{a} \cdot \mathbf{x} = c\}$ for any $c \in \mathbb{R}$. In other words we must have $\mathbf{a} \cdot \mathbf{b} \neq 0$. Furthermore interpolation to all arbitrary functions on two distinct straight lines is never possible. By this we mean that for most functions g_1 and g_2 defined on $\mathbb{R}$, there does not exist a $G \in \mathcal{M}(\mathbf{a})$ satisfying

$$G(t\mathbf{b}^j + \mathbf{c}^j) = g_j(t), \qquad t \in \mathbb{R}, \, j = 1, 2,$$

where $t\mathbf{b}^j + \mathbf{c}^j$, $j = 1, 2$, define two distinct straight lines in $\mathbb{R}^n$.

Proposition 12.5 *(a) We are given* $\mathbf{b} \in \mathbb{R}^n \backslash \{\mathbf{0}\}$, *the line* $\{t\mathbf{b} + \mathbf{c} : t \in \mathbb{R}\}$, *and an arbitrary function g defined on* $\mathbb{R}$. *Then for any given* $\mathbf{a} \in \mathbb{R}^n \backslash \{\mathbf{0}\}$ *there always exists a univariate function f such that*

$$f(\mathbf{a} \cdot (t\mathbf{b} + \mathbf{c})) = g(t)$$

for all $t \in \mathbb{R}$ *if and only if* $\mathbf{a} \cdot \mathbf{b} \neq 0$.
(b) Given $\mathbf{b}^1, \mathbf{b}^2 \in \mathbb{R}^n \backslash \{\mathbf{0}\}$, *and two distinct lines* $\{t\mathbf{b}^j + \mathbf{c}^j : t \in \mathbb{R}\}$, $j = 1, 2$, *then for almost all arbitrary functions* g_1, g_2 *defined on* $\mathbb{R}$ *there does not exist an f such that*

$$f(\mathbf{a} \cdot (t\mathbf{b}^j + \mathbf{c}^j)) = g_j(t)$$

for all $t \in \mathbb{R}$, *and* $j = 1, 2$.

Proof We start with (a). We are interested in solving the interpolation problem

$$f(\mathbf{a} \cdot (t\mathbf{b} + \mathbf{c})) = g(t).$$

Set $B := \mathbf{a} \cdot \mathbf{b}$ and $C := \mathbf{a} \cdot \mathbf{c}$. Then the above reduces to solving

$$f(tB + C) = g(t)$$

for all t and any given g. Obviously, by a change of variable, this always has a solution f if and only if $B \neq 0$.

The case (b) follows from (a). In (a) we saw that if there is a solution, then it is unique. Thus there is no room to maneuver. One can also prove it directly, as above. That is, assume we are given two lines $t\mathbf{b}^j + \mathbf{c}^j$, $j = 1, 2$, and two arbitrary functions g_1 and g_2. Set $B_j := \mathbf{a}^1 \cdot \mathbf{b}^j$ and $C_j := \mathbf{a}^1 \cdot \mathbf{c}^j$, $j = 1, 2$. The interpolation problem

$$f(\mathbf{a} \cdot (t\mathbf{b}^j + \mathbf{c}^j)) = g_j(t), \qquad j = 1, 2,$$

may be rewritten as

$$f(tB_j + C_j) = g_j(t), \qquad j = 1, 2.$$

If $B_j = 0$ for any j, then we cannot interpolate on that respective line. Assume $B_j \neq 0$, $j = 1, 2$. Thus we have, by a change of variable, that

$$f(s) = g_1((s - C_1)/B_1)$$

and

$$f(s) = g_2((s - C_2)/B_2),$$

implying that we must have

$$g_1((s - C_1)/B_1) = g_2((s - C_2)/B_2).$$

But for most (arbitrary) g_1 and g_2 this does not hold. There are other methods of verifying this simple result. □

The above result illustrates why straight lines seem to be a natural interpolation set for ridge functions. If there exists an interpolant from $\mathcal{M}(\mathbf{a})$ to every function on a straight line, then that interpolant is unique.

12.3 Interpolation from $\mathcal{M}(\mathbf{a}^1, \mathbf{a}^2)$ on Two Straight Lines

We will totally analyze the interpolation/representation problem with two directions on two straight lines. (In the case of only one straight line we can appeal to Proposition 12.5.)

We assume we are given linearly independent directions $\mathbf{a}^1, \mathbf{a}^2$ in $\mathbb{R}^n$, and

$$\mathcal{M}(\mathbf{a}^1, \mathbf{a}^2) = \{f_1(\mathbf{a}^1 \cdot \mathbf{x}) + f_2(\mathbf{a}^2 \cdot \mathbf{x}) : f_i : \mathbb{R} \to \mathbb{R}\}.$$

In addition, we assume that we are given two distinct straight lines $\ell_j := \{t\mathbf{b}^j + \mathbf{c}^j : t \in \mathbb{R}\}$, $j = 1, 2$. Set

$$B_{ij} := \mathbf{a}^i \cdot \mathbf{b}^j, \quad C_{ij} := \mathbf{a}^i \cdot \mathbf{c}^j,$$

for $i, j = 1, 2$. Then we have the following.

Theorem 12.6 *Assume we are given linearly independent directions $\mathbf{a}^1, \mathbf{a}^2$ in $\mathbb{R}^n$, and two distinct straight lines*

$$\ell_j = \{t\mathbf{b}^j + \mathbf{c}^j : t \in \mathbb{R}\}, \qquad j = 1, 2.$$

If any of the following hold then for almost all g_1, g_2 defined on $\mathbb{R}$ there does not exist a $G \in \mathcal{M}(\mathbf{a}^1, \mathbf{a}^2)$ satisfying

$$G(t\mathbf{b}^j + \mathbf{c}^j) = g_j(t), \qquad t \in \mathbb{R}, j = 1, 2.$$

(a) $B_{11}B_{22} + B_{12}B_{21} = 0$.

(b) rank $\begin{bmatrix} B_{11} & B_{12} & C_{12} - C_{11} \\ B_{21} & B_{22} & C_{22} - C_{21} \end{bmatrix} = 1$.

Assuming that (a) and (b) do not hold there always exists a $G \in \mathcal{M}(\mathbf{a}^1, \mathbf{a}^2)$ satisfying

$$G(t\mathbf{b}^j + \mathbf{c}^j) = g_j(t), \qquad t \in \mathbb{R}, j = 1, 2,$$

under the proviso that if $B_{11}B_{22} - B_{12}B_{21} \neq 0$, then we must impose a condition of the form

$$g_1(t_1) = g_2(t_2),$$

where t_1, t_2 satisfy

$$\begin{bmatrix} B_{11} & -B_{12} \\ B_{21} & -B_{22} \end{bmatrix} \begin{bmatrix} t_1 \\ t_2 \end{bmatrix} = \begin{bmatrix} C_{12} - C_{11} \\ C_{22} - C_{21} \end{bmatrix}.$$

We recall that in Definition 11.9 we defined a closed path with respect to two distinct directions, while in Theorem 11.10 we proved that given two directions then interpolation is not possible on a finite point set if and only if there exists a subset of this point set that forms a closed path. We apply Theorem 12.1 to this case to obtain the following result to be used in the proof of Theorem 12.6.

Theorem 12.7 *Assume we are given two linearly independent directions $\mathbf{a}^1$ and $\mathbf{a}^2$ in $\mathbb{R}^n$. Let X be any subset of $\mathbb{R}^n$. Then every given function defined on X is in $\mathcal{M}(\mathbf{a}^1, \mathbf{a}^2)$ if and only if there are no finite set of points in X that form a closed path with respect to the directions $\mathbf{a}^1$ and $\mathbf{a}^2$.*

Proof of Theorem 12.6 Based on Theorem 12.7, we are going to search for closed paths on $L = \ell_1 \bigcup \ell_2$. We will consider, sequentially, two-point, four-point, $2s$-point ($s \geq 3$) closed paths with respect to $\mathbf{a}^1$ and $\mathbf{a}^2$. In fact, we will show that the union of two straight lines cannot contain six-point, eight-point, etc., closed paths with respect to any $\mathbf{a}^1$ and $\mathbf{a}^2$ without containing two-point or four-point closed subpaths. This is a geometric statement, although our proof will be analytic in nature.

Two-point closed paths Firstly, we recall that by definition $\{\mathbf{v}^1, \mathbf{v}^2\}$ is a two-point closed path if and only if

$$\mathbf{a}^i \cdot \mathbf{v}^1 = \mathbf{a}^i \cdot \mathbf{v}^2 \tag{12.2}$$

for both $i = 1$ and $i = 2$. (We assume the points $\mathbf{v}^1$ and $\mathbf{v}^2$ are distinct.)

If the two points $\{\mathbf{v}^1, \mathbf{v}^2\}$ of the closed path lie on the line ℓ_1, then $\mathbf{v}^j = t_j \mathbf{b}^1 + \mathbf{c}^1$, $j = 1, 2$, with $t_1 \neq t_2$, and it easily follows from (12.2) that we must have

$$\mathbf{a}^1 \cdot \mathbf{b}^1 = \mathbf{a}^2 \cdot \mathbf{b}^1 = 0,$$

i.e., $B_{11} = B_{21} = 0$. In this case

$$f_1(\mathbf{a}^1 \cdot (t\mathbf{b}^1 + \mathbf{c}^1)) + f_2(\mathbf{a}^2 \cdot (t\mathbf{b}^1 + \mathbf{c}^1)) = f_1(\mathbf{a}^1 \cdot \mathbf{c}^1) + f_2(\mathbf{a}^2 \cdot \mathbf{c}^1)$$

for all t, i.e., $f_1(\mathbf{a}^1 \cdot \mathbf{x}) + f_2(\mathbf{a}^2 \cdot \mathbf{x})$ is a constant function on the line ℓ_1, and thus cannot interpolate to any non-constant function g_1 thereon. Conversely, if $B_{11} = B_{21} = 0$ then any two distinct points $\{\mathbf{v}^1, \mathbf{v}^2\}$ of ℓ_1 is a two-point closed path. Similarly, the two points $\{\mathbf{v}^1, \mathbf{v}^2\}$ form a closed path on the line ℓ_2 if and only if

$$\mathbf{a}^1 \cdot \mathbf{b}^2 = \mathbf{a}^2 \cdot \mathbf{b}^2 = 0,$$

i.e., $B_{12} = B_{22} = 0$.

Assume that the two points $\{\mathbf{v}^1, \mathbf{v}^2\}$ form a closed path, not on the same line. We assume, without loss of generality, that $\mathbf{v}^1 \in \ell_1$ and $\mathbf{v}^2 \in \ell_2$. Set $\mathbf{v}^1 := t_1 \mathbf{b}^1 + \mathbf{c}^1$ and $\mathbf{v}^2 := t_2 \mathbf{b}^2 + \mathbf{c}^2$. Thus our conditions are:

$$\begin{aligned}
\mathbf{a}^1 \cdot (t_1 \mathbf{b}^1 + \mathbf{c}^1) &= \mathbf{a}^1 \cdot (t_2 \mathbf{b}^2 + \mathbf{c}^2) \\
\mathbf{a}^2 \cdot (t_1 \mathbf{b}^1 + \mathbf{c}^1) &= \mathbf{a}^2 \cdot (t_2 \mathbf{b}^2 + \mathbf{c}^2)
\end{aligned} \tag{12.3}$$

that we rewrite as:

$$\begin{aligned}
B_{11} t_1 + C_{11} &= B_{12} t_2 + C_{12} \\
B_{21} t_1 + C_{21} &= B_{22} t_2 + C_{22}.
\end{aligned} \tag{12.4}$$

When do there exist solutions to this problem with distinct $\mathbf{v}^1$ and $\mathbf{v}^2$?

The first possibility is that the matrix

$$\begin{bmatrix} B_{11} & -B_{12} \\ B_{21} & -B_{22} \end{bmatrix} \tag{12.5}$$

is non-singular. In this case there are unique t_1 and t_2 such that the above ((12.3) or (12.4)) holds. Moreover from (12.3) we see that for any f_1 and f_2

$$f_1(\mathbf{a}^1 \cdot (t_1\mathbf{b}^1 + \mathbf{c}^1)) + f_2(\mathbf{a}^2 \cdot (t_1\mathbf{b}^1 + \mathbf{c}^1)) = f_1(\mathbf{a}^1 \cdot (t_2\mathbf{b}^2 + \mathbf{c}^2)) + f_2(\mathbf{a}^2 \cdot (t_2\mathbf{b}^2 + \mathbf{c}^2)),$$

and thus we get the condition

$$g_1(t_1) = g_2(t_2). \tag{12.6}$$

This is a generic case. That is, in general the g_1 and g_2 are not absolutely arbitrary. There is a condition of the form (12.6) that must be satisfied by the given data. It may be that $\mathbf{v}^1 = \mathbf{v}^2$. For example, in $\mathbb{R}^2$ the matrix (12.5) is non-singular if and only if the two lines ℓ_1 and ℓ_2 are not parallel and meet at the common point $\mathbf{v}^1 = \mathbf{v}^2$ (see the proof of Theorem 12.8). In this case we certainly must have that $g_1(t_1) = g_2(t_2)$. In $\mathbb{R}^n$, $n > 2$, we need not have $\mathbf{v}^1 = \mathbf{v}^2$.

The second possibility is that the matrix (12.5) is singular. Note that since we assume that there does not exist a two-point closed path on either one of the two lines, it then follows that the rank of this matrix is 1. In this case there exists a solution if and only if

$$(C_{12} - C_{11}, C_{22} - C_{21})^T$$

is in the range of the matrix (12.5). And if this is the case, then there is, in fact, an affine set of dimension one of such solutions (t_1, t_2), i.e., we obtain $g_1(t_1 + \alpha s_1) = g_2(t_2 + \alpha s_2)$ for all $\alpha \in \mathbb{R}$ and some $(s_1, s_2) \neq (0,0)$. This is the condition

$$\mathrm{rank} \begin{bmatrix} B_{11} & -B_{12} & C_{12} - C_{11} \\ B_{21} & -B_{22} & C_{22} - C_{21} \end{bmatrix} = 1.$$

To summarize: we have two-point closed paths and definitely cannot interpolate to arbitrarily given functions on ℓ_1 and ℓ_2 if we have any of:

(a1) $B_{11} = B_{21} = 0$,

(a2) $B_{12} = B_{22} = 0$,

(b) $\mathrm{rank} \begin{bmatrix} B_{11} & B_{12} & C_{12} - C_{11} \\ B_{21} & B_{22} & C_{22} - C_{21} \end{bmatrix} = 1$.

If

$$\mathrm{rank} \begin{bmatrix} B_{11} & B_{12} \\ B_{21} & B_{22} \end{bmatrix} = 2$$

then we have a condition of the form

$$g_1(t_1) = g_2(t_2)$$

where (t_1, t_2) satisfy

$$\begin{bmatrix} B_{11} & -B_{12} \\ B_{21} & -B_{22} \end{bmatrix} \begin{bmatrix} t_1 \\ t_2 \end{bmatrix} = \begin{bmatrix} C_{12} - C_{11} \\ C_{22} - C_{21} \end{bmatrix}.$$

We will call this "Condition Z".

Four-point closed paths We assume that (a1), (a2) and (b) do not hold, i.e., there are no two-point closed paths, but there is a four-point closed path with distinct points $\{\mathbf{v}^1, \mathbf{v}^2, \mathbf{v}^3, \mathbf{v}^4\}$. If three of these points lie on the same line ℓ_j, then we claim that there is a two-point closed path of the form (a1) or (a2). To see this, assume without loss of generality that $\mathbf{v}^1$, $\mathbf{v}^2$ and $\mathbf{v}^3$ lie on ℓ_1. Since

$$\mathbf{a}^1 \cdot (t_1 \mathbf{b}^1 + \mathbf{c}^1) = \mathbf{a}^1 \cdot \mathbf{v}^1 = \mathbf{a}^1 \cdot \mathbf{v}^2 = \mathbf{a}^1 \cdot (t_2 \mathbf{b}^1 + \mathbf{c}^1)$$

and $\mathbf{v}^1$ and $\mathbf{v}^2$ are distinct, i.e., $t_1 \neq t_2$, it follows that $B_{11} = \mathbf{a}^1 \cdot \mathbf{b}^1 = 0$. Similarly from

$$\mathbf{a}^2 \cdot \mathbf{v}^2 = \mathbf{a}^2 \cdot \mathbf{v}^3$$

it follows that $B_{21} = \mathbf{a}^2 \cdot \mathbf{b}^1 = 0$. Thus (a1) holds and the two points $\{\mathbf{v}^1, \mathbf{v}^2\}$ are on a two-point closed path. If three points lie on ℓ_2, then (a2) will hold.

By a suitable permutation, we may therefore assume that we have either:

(i) $\mathbf{v}^1, \mathbf{v}^2 \in \ell_1$ and $\mathbf{v}^3, \mathbf{v}^4 \in \ell_2$,
(ii) $\mathbf{v}^1, \mathbf{v}^3 \in \ell_1$ and $\mathbf{v}^2, \mathbf{v}^4 \in \ell_2$.

Assume (i) holds. Then we obtain the equations

$$\begin{aligned}
\mathbf{a}^1 \cdot (t_1 \mathbf{b}^1 + \mathbf{c}^1) &= \mathbf{a}^1 \cdot (t_2 \mathbf{b}^1 + \mathbf{c}^1) \\
\mathbf{a}^2 \cdot (t_2 \mathbf{b}^1 + \mathbf{c}^1) &= \mathbf{a}^2 \cdot (t_3 \mathbf{b}^2 + \mathbf{c}^2) \\
\mathbf{a}^1 \cdot (t_3 \mathbf{b}^2 + \mathbf{c}^2) &= \mathbf{a}^1 \cdot (t_4 \mathbf{b}^2 + \mathbf{c}^2) \\
\mathbf{a}^2 \cdot (t_4 \mathbf{b}^2 + \mathbf{c}^2) &= \mathbf{a}^2 \cdot (t_1 \mathbf{b}^1 + \mathbf{c}^1).
\end{aligned}$$

Consider the first equation. We see that $(t_1 - t_2) B_{11} = 0$. But as $\mathbf{v}^1, \mathbf{v}^2 \in \ell_1$, $\mathbf{v}^1 \neq \mathbf{v}^2$, we have $t_1 - t_2 \neq 0$. Thus $B_{11} = \mathbf{a}^1 \cdot \mathbf{b}^1 = 0$. Similarly from the third equation we obtain $B_{12} = \mathbf{a}^1 \cdot \mathbf{b}^2 = 0$. In this case our original interpolation problem

$$\begin{aligned}
f_1(\mathbf{a}^1 \cdot (t\mathbf{b}^1 + \mathbf{c}^1)) + f_2(\mathbf{a}^2 \cdot (t\mathbf{b}^1 + \mathbf{c}^1)) &= g_1(t) \\
f_1(\mathbf{a}^1 \cdot (t\mathbf{b}^2 + \mathbf{c}^2)) + f_2(\mathbf{a}^2 \cdot (t\mathbf{b}^2 + \mathbf{c}^2)) &= g_2(t),
\end{aligned}$$

reduces to

$$\begin{aligned}
f_1(\mathbf{a}^1 \cdot \mathbf{c}^1) + f_2(\mathbf{a}^2 \cdot (t\mathbf{b}^1 + \mathbf{c}^1)) &= g_1(t) \\
f_1(\mathbf{a}^1 \cdot \mathbf{c}^2) + f_2(\mathbf{a}^2 \cdot (t\mathbf{b}^2 + \mathbf{c}^2)) &= g_2(t).
\end{aligned}$$

Note that the function f_1 does not properly enter into the analysis, and based on the proof of Proposition 12.5 (the case $r = 1$, $m = 2$) it easily follows that we cannot interpolate to almost any given g_1 and g_2. If we assume, say $\mathbf{v}^1, \mathbf{v}^2 \in \ell_2$ and $\mathbf{v}^3, \mathbf{v}^4 \in \ell_1$, then we get $B_{21} = B_{22} = 0$ and the similar analysis holds. Conversely if $B_{11} = B_{12} = 0$ or $B_{21} = B_{22} = 0$, then we can construct many four-point closed paths. Thus we also have the conditions

(a3) $B_{11} = B_{12} = 0$

(a4) $B_{21} = B_{22} = 0$.

Assuming (ii) we have

$$
\begin{aligned}
\mathbf{a}^1 \cdot (t_1 \mathbf{b}^1 + \mathbf{c}^1) &= \mathbf{a}^1 \cdot (t_2 \mathbf{b}^2 + \mathbf{c}^2) \\
\mathbf{a}^2 \cdot (t_2 \mathbf{b}^2 + \mathbf{c}^2) &= \mathbf{a}^2 \cdot (t_3 \mathbf{b}^1 + \mathbf{c}^1) \\
\mathbf{a}^1 \cdot (t_3 \mathbf{b}^1 + \mathbf{c}^1) &= \mathbf{a}^1 \cdot (t_4 \mathbf{b}^2 + \mathbf{c}^2) \\
\mathbf{a}^2 \cdot (t_4 \mathbf{b}^2 + \mathbf{c}^2) &= \mathbf{a}^2 \cdot (t_1 \mathbf{b}^1 + \mathbf{c}^1).
\end{aligned} \tag{12.7}
$$

Subtracting the first from the third equation and the second from the fourth, we obtain

$$
\begin{aligned}
B_{11}(t_3 - t_1) &= B_{12}(t_4 - t_2) \\
B_{21}(t_3 - t_1) &= -B_{22}(t_4 - t_2).
\end{aligned}
$$

Since $\mathbf{v}^1, \mathbf{v}^3 \in \ell_1$, $\mathbf{v}^1 \neq \mathbf{v}^3$, we have $t_3 - t_1 \neq 0$, and similarly $t_4 - t_2 \neq 0$. Thus, if there is a solution (with distinct $\mathbf{v}^j$) then the associated determinant is zero, i.e.,

(a) $B_{11}B_{22} + B_{12}B_{21} = 0$.

If we assume that (a) holds and the B_{ij} are non-zero (the other cases are covered by (a1)–(a4)), then it may be verified that, say, given any t_1 there exist t_2, t_3, t_4 such that (12.7) holds. That is, (a) implies many solutions to (12.7).

$2s$-**point closed paths**, $s > 2$ We claim that the union of two straight lines cannot contain six-point, eight-point, etc., closed paths with respect to any linearly independent $\mathbf{a}^1$ and $\mathbf{a}^2$ without containing two-point or four-point closed paths (satisfying (a) or (b)). We will first prove this for six-point closed paths, and then present the general analysis.

Assume $\mathbf{v}^1, \ldots, \mathbf{v}^6$ form a six-point closed path on ℓ_1 and ℓ_2, but no subset is a two- or four-point closed path (other than satisfying Condition Z). If there are three consecutive points on any one line then, by the previous analysis, both $\mathbf{a}^1$ and $\mathbf{a}^2$ are orthogonal to $\mathbf{b}^1$ or $\mathbf{b}^2$. That is, we either have $B_{11} = B_{21} = 0$ or $B_{12} = B_{22} = 0$, i.e., (a1) or (a2) hold, and we have a two-point closed path. If three consecutive points are not on any one line, but two consecutive points are on one line, then by parity considerations we must have two other consecutive points on one line. These can be on the same line or on different lines. Let us consider both situations. Recall that if we have two consecutive points on the one line, for example, $\mathbf{v}^1, \mathbf{v}^2 \in \ell_1$, then $B_{11} = \mathbf{a}^1 \cdot \mathbf{b}^1 = 0$. Now if we have two pairs of two consecutive points on the same line (but no three consecutive points on one line), then we can assume, up to permutation, that $\mathbf{v}^1, \mathbf{v}^2, \mathbf{v}^4, \mathbf{v}^5 \in \ell_1$. But from $\mathbf{v}^1, \mathbf{v}^2 \in \ell_1$ we get $B_{11} = 0$ and from $\mathbf{v}^4, \mathbf{v}^5 \in \ell_1$ we get $B_{21} = 0$, i.e., (a1) holds. This implies that we have a two-point closed path. If we have two pairs of consecutive points on different lines (but no three consecutive points on one line), and if we have $\mathbf{v}^1, \mathbf{v}^2 \in \ell_1$ then we must have either $\mathbf{v}^3, \mathbf{v}^4 \in \ell_2$ or $\mathbf{v}^5, \mathbf{v}^6 \in \ell_2$. In both cases we obtain $B_{11} = 0$ and $B_{12} = 0$, i.e., (a3) holds and we have a four-point closed path.

What remains is to analyze, up to permutations, the case where $\mathbf{v}^1, \mathbf{v}^3, \mathbf{v}^5 \in \ell_1$ and $\mathbf{v}^2, \mathbf{v}^4, \mathbf{v}^6 \in \ell_2$. Writing down the resulting equations we have

$$
\begin{aligned}
t_1 B_{11} + C_{11} &= t_2 B_{12} + C_{12} \\
t_2 B_{22} + C_{22} &= t_3 B_{21} + C_{21} \\
t_3 B_{11} + C_{11} &= t_4 B_{12} + C_{12} \\
t_4 B_{22} + C_{22} &= t_5 B_{21} + C_{21} \\
t_5 B_{11} + C_{11} &= t_6 B_{12} + C_{12} \\
t_6 B_{22} + C_{22} &= t_1 B_{21} + C_{21}.
\end{aligned}
$$

Since $\mathbf{v}^1, \mathbf{v}^3$ and $\mathbf{v}^5$ are distinct points on ℓ_1, the t_1, t_3 and t_5 are distinct values. Similarly, the t_2, t_4 and t_6 are distinct values. In the above equations take differences of the equations containing the B_{11}, and also those containing the B_{22} to obtain

$$
\begin{aligned}
(t_3 - t_1) B_{11} &= (t_4 - t_2) B_{12} \\
(t_5 - t_1) B_{11} &= (t_6 - t_2) B_{12} \\
(t_5 - t_3) B_{11} &= (t_6 - t_4) B_{12}
\end{aligned}
$$

and

$$
\begin{aligned}
(t_4 - t_2) B_{22} &= (t_5 - t_3) B_{21} \\
(t_6 - t_2) B_{22} &= -(t_3 - t_1) B_{21} \\
(t_6 - t_4) B_{22} &= -(t_5 - t_1) B_{21}.
\end{aligned}
$$

Thus $B_{11} = 0$ if and only if $B_{12} = 0$ and (a3) holds, while $B_{22} = 0$ if and only if $B_{21} = 0$ and (a4) holds. As such, let us assume that $B_{ij} \neq 0$ for all i, j. There are many ways of proving that the above cannot hold. For example, it follows (dividing by B_{11} and B_{22}, as appropriate) that

$$
\begin{aligned}
(t_3 - t_1) &= C(t_5 - t_3) \\
(t_5 - t_1) &= -C(t_3 - t_1) \\
(t_5 - t_3) &= -C(t_5 - t_1)
\end{aligned}
$$

where $C \neq 0$. Multiplying the above equations we obtain $C = 1$. Thus each of the t_1, t_3, t_5 is an average of the other two, contradicting the fact that they are distinct.

What about closed paths of more points? The above argument may be extended as follows. Assume $\mathbf{v}^1, \ldots, \mathbf{v}^{2s}$ form a $2s$-point closed path on ℓ_1 and ℓ_2, $s > 3$, but no subset is a two- or four-point closed path (other than satisfying Condition Z). If there are three consecutive points on any one line then, by the previous analysis, both $\mathbf{a}^1$ and $\mathbf{a}^2$ are orthogonal to $\mathbf{b}^1$ or $\mathbf{b}^2$. That is, we either have $B_{11} = B_{21} = 0$ or $B_{12} = B_{22} = 0$, i.e., (a1) or (a2) hold, and we have a two-point closed path. Assume three consecutive points are not on any one line, but two consecutive points are on one line, namely $\mathbf{v}^1, \mathbf{v}^2 \in \ell_1$. As noted, this implies that $B_{11} = 0$. From parity considerations we must have two other consecutive points on one line. Starting at $\mathbf{v}^3 \in \ell_2$ consider the first time we have $\mathbf{v}^k, \mathbf{v}^{k+1}$ on the same line. If k is even then they lie on ℓ_1 and $B_{21} = 0$. If k is odd then they lie on ℓ_2 and $B_{12} = 0$. Thus it follows that (a1) or (a3) hold, a contradiction.

It remains to analyze, up to permutations, the case where $\mathbf{v}^1, \mathbf{v}^3, \ldots, \mathbf{v}^{2s-1} \in \ell_1$ and $\mathbf{v}^2, \mathbf{v}^4, \ldots, \mathbf{v}^{2s} \in \ell_2$. Writing down the resulting equations we have

$$
\begin{aligned}
t_1 B_{11} + C_{11} &= t_2 B_{12} + C_{12} \\
t_2 B_{22} + C_{22} &= t_3 B_{21} + C_{21} \\
t_3 B_{11} + C_{11} &= t_4 B_{12} + C_{12} \\
\cdots &= \cdots \\
t_{2s-1} B_{11} + C_{11} &= t_{2s} B_{12} + C_{12} \\
t_{2s} B_{22} + C_{22} &= t_1 B_{21} + C_{21}.
\end{aligned}
$$

Since $\mathbf{v}^1, \mathbf{v}^3, \ldots, \mathbf{v}^{2s-1}$ are distinct points on ℓ_1, the $t_1, t_3, \ldots, t_{2s-1}$ are distinct values. Similarly, the $t_2, t_4, \ldots, t_{2s}$ are distinct values. In the above equations take differences of the equations containing the B_{11}, and also those containing the B_{22} to obtain

$$\begin{aligned}
(t_3 - t_1)B_{11} &= (t_4 - t_2)B_{12} \\
(t_5 - t_1)B_{11} &= (t_6 - t_2)B_{12} \\
(t_5 - t_3)B_{11} &= (t_6 - t_4)B_{12} \\
\cdots &= \cdots \\
(t_{2s-1} - t_{2s-3})B_{11} &= (t_{2s} - t_{2s-2})B_{12}
\end{aligned}$$

and

$$\begin{aligned}
(t_4 - t_2)B_{22} &= (t_5 - t_3)B_{21} \\
(t_6 - t_2)B_{22} &= (t_7 - t_3)B_{21} \\
(t_6 - t_4)B_{22} &= (t_7 - t_5)B_{21} \\
\cdots &= \cdots \\
(t_{2s} - t_{2s-2})B_{22} &= -(t_{2s-1} - t_1)B_{21}.
\end{aligned}$$

From here we see that $B_{11} = 0$ if and only if $B_{12} = 0$ and (a3) holds, while $B_{22} = 0$ if and only if $B_{21} = 0$ and (a4) holds. As such, we may assume that $B_{ij} \neq 0$ for all i, j. It now follows (dividing by B_{11} and B_{22}, as appropriate) that

$$\begin{aligned}
(t_3 - t_1) &= C(t_5 - t_3) \\
(t_5 - t_1) &= C(t_7 - t_3) \\
(t_5 - t_3) &= C(t_7 - t_5) \\
\cdots &= \cdots \\
(t_{2s-1} - t_{2s-3}) &= -C(t_{2s-1} - t_1),
\end{aligned}$$

where $C \neq 0$. Multiplying the above equations we obtain $\pm C^k = 1$ for some $\pm$ and k. Thus $C = 1$ or $C = -1$. If $C = -1$, then from the first equation we obtain $t_1 = t_5$ which is a contradiction. If $C = 1$, then each of the t_{2i-1} is an average of t_{2i-3} and t_{2i+1}, $i = 1, \ldots, s$, where $t_{-1} = t_{2s-1}$ and $t_{2s+1} = t_1$, i.e., we consider t_{2i-1} cyclically. In any case, as these t_{2i-1} are all distinct we have arrived at a contradiction.

Applying Theorem 12.7 we have therefore proven Theorem 12.6.   □

In $\mathbb{R}^2$ Theorem 12.6 can be restated in both a simpler and geometric form.

Theorem 12.8 *Assume we are given linearly independent directions* $\mathbf{a}^1, \mathbf{a}^2$ *in* $\mathbb{R}^2$, *and two distinct straight lines*

$$\ell_j := \{t\mathbf{b}^j + \mathbf{c}^j : t \in \mathbb{R}\}, \qquad j = 1, 2.$$

Assume that if ℓ_1 *and* ℓ_2 *intersect, then* g_1 *and* g_2 *agree at this point of intersection. Then for almost all such* g_1, g_2 *defined on* $\mathbb{R}$ *there does not exist a* $G \in \mathcal{M}(\mathbf{a}^1, \mathbf{a}^2)$ *satisfying*

$$G(t\mathbf{b}^j + \mathbf{c}^j) = g_j(t), \qquad t \in \mathbb{R}, \ j = 1, 2,$$

if and only if there exist $(k_1, k_2) \in \mathbb{R}^2 \backslash \{(0,0)\}$ *for which*

$$(k_1 \mathbf{a}^1 - k_2 \mathbf{a}^2) \cdot \mathbf{b}^1 = 0$$

and

$$(k_1 \mathbf{a}^1 + k_2 \mathbf{a}^2) \cdot \mathbf{b}^2 = 0.$$

Proof Let us consider conditions (a) and (b), as well as Condition Z, as they appear in Theorem 12.6. In $\mathbb{R}^2$, as $\mathbf{a}^1$ and $\mathbf{a}^2$ are linearly independent, their span is all of $\mathbb{R}^2$. That is, it cannot be that both $\mathbf{a}^1$ and $\mathbf{a}^2$ are orthogonal to any non-zero vector in $\mathbb{R}^2$. (This implies that neither (a1) nor (a2) can hold.)

We claim that (b) cannot hold. Since the span of $\mathbf{a}^1$ and $\mathbf{a}^2$ is all of $\mathbb{R}^2$, the first two columns of the matrix

$$\begin{bmatrix} B_{11} & B_{12} & C_{12} - C_{11} \\ B_{21} & B_{22} & C_{22} - C_{21} \end{bmatrix},$$

are non-zero. If

$$\text{rank} \begin{bmatrix} B_{11} & B_{12} \\ B_{21} & B_{22} \end{bmatrix} = 1,$$

then $\mathbf{b}^1 = \alpha \mathbf{b}^2$ for some $\alpha \neq 0$. If (b) holds and

$$\text{rank} \begin{bmatrix} B_{11} & B_{12} & C_{12} - C_{11} \\ B_{21} & B_{22} & C_{22} - C_{21} \end{bmatrix} = 1,$$

it now also follows that $\mathbf{c}^2 - \mathbf{c}^1 = \beta \mathbf{b}^2$. Substituting we see that $\ell_1 = \ell_2$, a contradiction.

What about Condition Z? If t_1, t_2 satisfy

$$\begin{bmatrix} B_{11} & -B_{12} \\ B_{21} & -B_{22} \end{bmatrix} \begin{bmatrix} t_1 \\ t_2 \end{bmatrix} = \begin{bmatrix} C_{12} - C_{11} \\ C_{22} - C_{21} \end{bmatrix}.$$

It then follows that both $\mathbf{a}^1$ and $\mathbf{a}^2$ are orthogonal to

$$(t_1 \mathbf{b}^1 + \mathbf{c}^1) - (t_2 \mathbf{b}^2 + \mathbf{c}^2).$$

But in $\mathbb{R}^2$ this implies that

$$t_1 \mathbf{b}^1 + \mathbf{c}^1 = t_2 \mathbf{b}^2 + \mathbf{c}^2.$$

In other words, Condition Z simply says that g_1 and g_2 agree at the point of intersection of the lines ℓ_1 and ℓ_2.

Theorem 12.8 now easily follows since the existence of $(k_1, k_2) \in \mathbb{R}^2 \backslash \{(0,0)\}$ satisfying

$$\begin{aligned}
(k_1 \mathbf{a}^1 - k_2 \mathbf{a}^2) \cdot \mathbf{b}^1 &= 0 \\
(k_1 \mathbf{a}^1 + k_2 \mathbf{a}^2) \cdot \mathbf{b}^2 &= 0
\end{aligned}$$

is equivalent to

$$\det \begin{pmatrix} B_{11} & -B_{12} \\ B_{21} & B_{22} \end{pmatrix} = B_{11} B_{22} + B_{12} B_{21} = 0. \qquad \square$$

The following is an example of where interpolation is always possible from $\mathcal{M}(\mathbf{a}^1, \mathbf{a}^2)$, but for some given continuous (and bounded) g_1 and g_2 there exist no continuous (or bounded) f_1 and f_2 satisfying

$$f_1(\mathbf{a}^1 \cdot (t\mathbf{b}^j + \mathbf{c}^j)) + f_2(\mathbf{a}^2 \cdot (t\mathbf{b}^j + \mathbf{c}^j)) = g_j(t), \qquad t \in \mathbb{R}, \ j = 1, 2. \tag{12.8}$$

Example 12.1 Set $\mathbf{a}^1 := (1, -1)$, $\mathbf{a}^2 := (1, 1)$,

$$\ell_1 := \{t(1, 1/3) : t \in \mathbb{R}\}$$

and

$$\ell_2 := \{t(1, -1/3) + (0, 4/3) : t \in \mathbb{R}\}.$$

Thus, in our terminology, $\mathbf{b}^1 = (1, 1/3)$, $\mathbf{b}^2 = (1, -1/3)$, $\mathbf{c}^1 = (0, 0)$ and $\mathbf{c}^2 = (0, 4/3)$. It is readily verified that neither of the conditions (a) and (b) of Theorem 12.6 hold or, equivalently as we are in $\mathbb{R}^2$, there exist no $(k_1, k_2) \in \mathbb{R}^2 \backslash \{(0,0)\}$ for which

$$(k_1 \mathbf{a}^1 - k_2 \mathbf{a}^2) \cdot \mathbf{b}^1 = 0$$

and

$$(k_1 \mathbf{a}^1 + k_2 \mathbf{a}^2) \cdot \mathbf{b}^2 = 0.$$

Furthermore, the lines ℓ_1 and ℓ_2 intersect at the point $(2, 2/3)$ where $t_1 = t_2 = 2$. Thus for all g_1, g_2 satisfying $g_1(2) = g_2(2)$ we know from Theorem 12.6 that there exists a $G \in \mathcal{M}(\mathbf{a}^1, \mathbf{a}^2)$ satisfying

$$G(t(1, 1/3)) = g_1(t)$$

and

$$G(t(1, -1/3) + (0, 4/3)) = g_2(t).$$

Now

$$G(\mathbf{x}) = f_1(\mathbf{a}^1 \cdot \mathbf{x}) + f_2(\mathbf{a}^2 \cdot \mathbf{x})$$

for some f_1, f_2 defined on $\mathbb{R}$. We construct continuous (and bounded) g_1, g_2 for which the f_1, f_2 satisfying the above cannot be continuous (and bounded) on $\mathbb{R}$.

To this end, let $\{c_n\}_{n=1}^{\infty}$ be any decreasing sequence of positive numbers tending to zero for which

$$\sum_{n=1}^{\infty} c_n = \infty.$$

Set $g_1(t) := 0$ on all $\mathbb{R}$, and define g_2 to satisfy

$$g_2\left(\sum_{k=0}^{2n} \frac{1}{2^k}\right) := c_n,$$

$g_2(t) := 0$ for $t \geq 2$, $g_2(t) := c_1$ for $t \leq 7/4$, and g_2 is continuous and piecewise linear on $[7/4, 2)$. That is, on the interval

$$\left[\sum_{k=0}^{2n} \frac{1}{2^k}, \sum_{k=0}^{2n+2} \frac{1}{2^k}\right]$$

g_2 is a linear function with endpoint values c_n and c_{n+1}. Since the $c_n \downarrow 0$ it follows that g_2 is continuous (and bounded) on all $\mathbb{R}$, and $g_1(2) = g_2(2)$.

Consider the following set of points in $\mathbb{R}^2$. Let

$$\mathbf{x}^n := \left(\sum_{k=0}^{2n-1} \frac{1}{2^k}, \sum_{k=0}^{2n-1} \frac{(-1)^k}{2^k}\right),$$

$n = 1, 2, \ldots$ and

$$\mathbf{y}^n := \left(\sum_{k=0}^{2n} \frac{1}{2^k}, \sum_{k=0}^{2n} \frac{(-1)^k}{2^k}\right),$$

$n = 1, 2, \ldots$. It is a simple exercise to verify that $\mathbf{x}^n \in \ell_1$ and $\mathbf{y}^n \in \ell_2$ for all n, and, in addition, that

$$\mathbf{a}^1 \cdot \mathbf{x}^n = \mathbf{a}^1 \cdot \mathbf{y}^n, \qquad n = 1, 2, \ldots, \tag{12.9}$$

while

$$\mathbf{a}^2 \cdot \mathbf{x}^{n+1} = \mathbf{a}^2 \cdot \mathbf{y}^n, \qquad n = 1, 2, \ldots . \tag{12.10}$$

Assume f_1, f_2 satisfy (12.8). Thus we have

$$f_1(\mathbf{a}^1 \cdot \mathbf{x}^n) + f_2(\mathbf{a}^2 \cdot \mathbf{x}^n) = 0, \qquad n = 1, 2, \ldots,$$

and

$$f_1(\mathbf{a}^1 \cdot \mathbf{y}^n) + f_2(\mathbf{a}^2 \cdot \mathbf{y}^n) = g_2 \left(\sum_{k=0}^{2n} \frac{1}{2^k} \right) = c_n, \qquad n = 1, 2, \dots .$$

From (12.9) and taking differences in the above two equalities we obtain

$$f_2(\mathbf{a}^2 \cdot \mathbf{y}^n) - f_2(\mathbf{a}^2 \cdot \mathbf{x}^n) = c_n, \qquad n = 1, 2, \dots .$$

Thus

$$\sum_{n=1}^{r} \left(f_2(\mathbf{a}^2 \cdot \mathbf{y}^n) - f_2(\mathbf{a}^2 \cdot \mathbf{x}^n) \right) = \sum_{n=1}^{r} c_n.$$

From (12.10) we see that this is a telescoping sum and thus the left-hand side equals

$$f_2(\mathbf{a}^2 \cdot \mathbf{y}^r) - f_2(\mathbf{a}^2 \cdot \mathbf{x}^1).$$

Since $\sum_{n=1}^{\infty} c_n = \infty$, it follows that

$$\lim_{r \to \infty} f_2(\mathbf{a}^2 \cdot \mathbf{y}^r) = \infty.$$

Now $\lim_{r \to \infty} \mathbf{y}^r = (2, 2/3)$ (the intersection point of the lines) and we have that f_2 is unbounded in a neighborhood of $t = 8/3$. As such, f_2 is not continuous at $t = 8/3$. The same must therefore hold for f_1 at the point $t = 4/3$.

The analysis of the first-order difference equations in the next section gives an insight into the reason for this phenomenon.

12.4 First-Order Difference Equations and Interpolation from $\mathcal{M}(\mathbf{a}^1, \mathbf{a}^2)$

The major result of this section is that we cannot interpolate from the space $\mathcal{M}(\mathbf{a}^1, \mathbf{a}^2)$ on three (or more) straight lines.

Theorem 12.9 *Assume we are given linearly independent directions* $\mathbf{a}^1, \mathbf{a}^2$ *in* $\mathbb{R}^n$, *and three distinct straight lines*

$$\ell_j := \{ t\mathbf{b}^j + \mathbf{c}^j : t \in \mathbb{R} \}, \qquad j = 1, 2, 3.$$

Then for almost all g_1, g_2, g_3 *defined on* $\mathbb{R}$ *there does not exist a* $G \in \mathcal{M}(\mathbf{a}^1, \mathbf{a}^2)$ *satisfying*

$$G(t\mathbf{b}^j + \mathbf{c}^j) = g_j(t), \qquad t \in \mathbb{R}, \ j = 1, 2, 3.$$

There is a different approach to a proof of Theorem 12.6 that we now explain. Assume (a) and (b) do not hold, and if Condition Z holds then $g_1(t_1) = g_2(t_2)$, where t_1, t_2 are defined as previously in the statement of Theorem 12.6. We want to solve the equations

$$f_1(tB_{1j} + C_{1j}) + f_2(tB_{2j} + C_{2j}) = g_j(t), \qquad j = 1, 2. \qquad (12.11)$$

We start with the simpler case where we assume that at least one of the $B_{ij} = 0$. As all these cases are the same we assume, without loss of generality, that $B_{11} = 0$. Since (a) and (b) do not hold, we must have $B_{12}, B_{21} \neq 0$. Solving (12.11) for $j = 1$ with the change of variable $s = tB_{21} + C_{21}$ we obtain

$$f_2(s) = g_1((s - C_{21})/B_{21}) - f_1(C_{11}).$$

Substituting this into (12.11) with $j = 2$ and setting $tB_{12} + C_{12} = C_{11}$ gives us

$$g_1\left(\frac{(C_{11} - C_{12})B_{22} + (C_{22} - C_{21})B_{12}}{B_{12}B_{21}}\right) = g_2\left(\frac{C_{11} - C_{12}}{B_{12}}\right). \qquad (12.12)$$

That is, we have Condition Z with

$$t_1 = \frac{(C_{11} - C_{12})B_{22} + (C_{22} - C_{21})B_{12}}{B_{12}B_{21}}$$

and

$$t_2 = \frac{C_{11} - C_{12}}{B_{12}}.$$

Set $f_1(C_{11}) := \alpha$ for any $\alpha \in \mathbb{R}$. Then solving in (12.11) with $j = 1$ we obtain

$$f_2(s) = g_1((s - C_{21})/B_{21}) - \alpha. \qquad (12.13)$$

From (12.11) with $j = 2$ and a change of variable we get

$$f_1(s) = g_2((s - C_{12})/B_{12}) - g_1\left(\frac{(s - C_{12})B_{22} + (C_{22} - C_{21})B_{12}}{B_{12}B_{21}}\right) + \alpha.$$

This is well-defined since on setting $s := C_{11}$ we obtain, by (12.12), that we have $f_1(C_{11}) = \alpha$. Thus we have determined solutions f_1 and f_2 for (12.11) in this case.

Let us now assume that $B_{ij} \neq 0, i, j = 1, 2$. By a change of variable we rewrite (12.11) as

$$f_1(s) + f_2\left(\frac{(s - C_{1j})B_{2j}}{B_{1j}} + C_{2j}\right) = g_j\left(\frac{s - C_{1j}}{B_{1j}}\right), \qquad j = 1, 2. \quad (12.14)$$

Taking the difference between these equations we get

$$f_2\left(\frac{(s - C_{11})B_{21}}{B_{11}} + C_{21}\right) - f_2\left(\frac{(s - C_{12})B_{22}}{B_{12}} + C_{22}\right)$$

$$= g_1 \left(\frac{s - C_{11}}{B_{11}} \right) - g_2 \left(\frac{s - C_{12}}{B_{12}} \right). \qquad (12.15)$$

Note that if

$$\frac{(s - C_{11})B_{21}}{B_{11}} + C_{21} = \frac{(s - C_{12})B_{22}}{B_{12}} + C_{22} \qquad (12.16)$$

then the left-hand side of (12.15) is the zero function and we cannot solve for f_2. Furthermore, since g_1 and g_2 are arbitrarily given, this leads to a contradiction. However, (12.16) is equivalent to (b) which, by assumption, does not hold. We shall prove that we can solve (12.15) to obtain f_2. We then solve for f_1 from (12.14).

We have therefore reduced our problem, via (12.15), to that of solving

$$f_2(sD_1 + E_1) - f_2(sD_2 + E_2) = g(s)$$

for an almost arbitrary g where $D_1, D_2 \neq 0$ (since $B_{ij} \neq 0$, all i, j), $(D_1, E_1) \neq (D_2, E_2)$ (since (b) does not hold), and $D_1 \neq -D_2$ (since (a) does not hold). What about Condition Z as it applies to g? If $D_1 = D_2$ there is no condition on g. Otherwise we must have $g((E_2 - E_1)/(D_1 - D_2)) = 0$. By the change of variable $u = sD_1 + E_1$ and writing f in place of f_2 we obtain the more easily stated difference equation

$$f(u) - f(uD + E) = g(u), \qquad (12.17)$$

where $D \neq 0, -1$, and $(D, E) \neq (1, 0)$. For $D \neq 1$ we have arbitrary g that must satisfy

$$g(E/(1 - D)) = 0. \qquad (12.18)$$

From Theorem 12.6 we know that there exist solutions. We will now exhibit solutions to the equations (12.17) and (12.18), and also discuss their continuity properties and the extent to which these solutions are unique. We will then have the tools to prove Theorem 12.9. We refer the interested reader to Buck [1972] and Kuczma [1968] for related results. We highlight the main results as propositions.

We start with the case $D = 1$, i.e.,

$$f(u) - f(u + E) = g(u) \qquad (12.19)$$

with $E \neq 0$. By the change of variable $v = u + E$, if necessary, we may assume $E > 0$.

Proposition 12.10 *Given any $c \in \mathbb{R}$ and arbitrary h defined on $[c, c + E)$, there is a unique f satisfying $f(u) = h(u)$ for $u \in [c, c + E)$ and equation (12.19).*

This function f is given by

$$f(u) = h(u - kE) - \sum_{r=1}^{k} g(u - rE)$$

for $u \in [c + kE, c + (k + 1)E)$, $k = 1, 2, \ldots$, and by

$$f(u) = h(u + kE) + \sum_{r=0}^{k-1} g(u + rE)$$

for $u \in [c - kE, c - (k - 1)E)$, $k = 1, 2 \ldots$ In addition, if g is continuous on $\mathbb{R}$, h is continuous on $[c, c + E]$ and

$$h(c) - h(c + E) = g(c),$$

then f is continuous on all of $\mathbb{R}$.

Proof Set $f(u) := h(u)$ on $[c, c + E)$, any h and any $c \in \mathbb{R}$. We rewrite (12.19) as

$$f(u) = f(u + E) + g(u) \tag{12.20}$$

or

$$f(u) = f(u - E) - g(u - E). \tag{12.21}$$

From (12.21) we have for $u \in [c + E, c + 2E)$

$$f(u) = h(u - E) - g(u - E),$$

and for $u \in [c + 2E, c + 3E)$

$$f(u) = h(u - 2E) - g(u - 2E) - g(u - E).$$

Thus for $u \in [c + kE, c + (k + 1)E)$, $k = 1, 2, \ldots$,

$$f(u) = h(u - kE) - \sum_{r=1}^{k} g(u - rE).$$

For $u < c$ we use (12.20). From (12.20) we have for $u \in [c - E, c)$

$$f(u) = h(u + E) + g(u),$$

and thus for $u \in [c - 2E, c - E)$

$$f(u) = h(u + 2E) + g(u + E) + g(u).$$

This gives us, for $u \in [c - kE, c - (k-1)E)$, $k = 1, 2, \ldots,$

$$f(u) = h(u + kE) + \sum_{r=0}^{k-1} g(u + rE).$$

From the above equations defining f it easily follows that if g is continuous on $\mathbb{R}$, h is continuous on $[c, c + E]$ and

$$h(c) - h(c + E) = g(c),$$

then f is continuous on all of $\mathbb{R}$. $\square$

Remark 12.11 Note that if g is bounded, then f is not necessarily bounded no matter what the choice of h. (Take, for example, $g(u) = 1$ for all u.)

Remark 12.12 In the above and in the next propositions we will have uniqueness of the form "given arbitrary h and assuming $f = h$ on an interval(s)" then f is uniquely defined on all $\mathbb{R}$. Considering an interval is convenient for us, but it can be replaced by any set for which the orbits of the points u under the mapping $uD + E$ and its inverse mapping exactly cover $\mathbb{R}\backslash\{E/(1 - D)\}$.

We now consider the case where $D \neq 1, -1, 0$. By the change of variable $v = uD + E$, if necessary, we may assume that $|D| > 1$. We first assume that $D > 1$.

Proposition 12.13 *Assume $D > 1$ in (12.17). Given c_1 such that $c_1 D + E > c_1$, and c_2 such that $c_2 D + E < c_2$, an arbitrary h_1 defined on $[c_1, c_1 D + E)$, and an arbitrary h_2 defined on $[c_2 D + E, c_2)$, then there exists a unique f satisfying (12.17) on $\mathbb{R}\backslash\{E/(1 - D)\}$, where $f(u) = h_1(u)$ for $u \in [c_1, c_1 D + E)$, and $f(u) = h_2(u)$ for $u \in [c_2 D + E, c_2)$. In addition, if g is continuous on $(E/(1 - D), \infty)$, h_1 is continuous on $[c_1, c_1 D + E]$ and*

$$h_1(c_1) - h_1(c_1 D + E) = g(c_1),$$

then f is continuous on $(E/(1 - D), \infty)$. Similarly, if g is continuous on the interval $(-\infty, E/(1 - D))$, h_2 is continuous on $[c_2 D + E, c_2]$ and

$$h_2(c_2) - h_2(c_2 D + E) = g(c_2),$$

then f is continuous on $(-\infty, E/(1 - D))$.

Proof We rewrite (12.17) as

$$f(u) = f((u - E)/D) - g((u - E)/D). \tag{12.22}$$

Set $f(u) := h_1(u)$ on $[c_1, c_1 D + E)$. Thus for $u \in [c_1 D + E, (c_1 D + E)D + E)$ we have

$$f(u) = h_1((u - E)/D) - g((u - E)/D).$$

Continuing, for $u \in [c_1 D^2 + E(1 + D), c_1 D^3 + E(1 + D + D^2))$ we have

$$f(u) = h_1((u - E(1 + D))/D^2) - g((u - E(1 + D))/D^2) - g((u - E)/D),$$

etc. At the nth stage of this process the right endpoint of the interval of definition equals

$$c_1 D^n + E(1 + D + \cdots + D^{n-1}),$$

which tends to infinity as $n \uparrow \infty$. To see this, note that it equals

$$c_1 D^n + E\left(\frac{D^n - 1}{D - 1}\right) = \frac{D^n(c_1 D + E - c_1)}{D - 1} - \frac{E}{D - 1}$$

and, by assumption, $c_1 D + E - c_1 > 0$ and $D > 1$. Thus the above process defines f on all of $[c_1, \infty)$. We now go in the reverse direction, i.e., write (12.17) as

$$f(u) = f(uD + E) + g(u). \tag{12.23}$$

Thus for $u \in [(c_1 - E)/D, c_1)$ we then have

$$f(u) = h_1(uD + E) + g(u).$$

For $u \in [(c_1 - E - DE)/D^2, (c_1 - E)/D)$ we have

$$f(u) = h_1(uD^2 + DE + E) + g(uD + E) + g(u),$$

etc. After the nth stage of this process we are considering the interval whose left endpoint is

$$\frac{c_1 - E(1 + D + \cdots + D^{n-1})}{D^n}.$$

Since this equals

$$\frac{c_1(D - 1) - E(D^n - 1)}{(D - 1)D^n}$$

it follows that this decreases monotonically to

$$\frac{E}{1 - D}$$

as n tends to infinity. Thus we have determined f on $(E/(1 - D), \infty)$. We also easily see that if g is continuous thereon, h_1 is continuous on $[c_1, c_1 D + E]$ and

$$h_1(c_1) - h_1(c_1 D + E) = g(c_1)$$

then f is continuous on $(E/(1-D), \infty)$.

On the interval $(-\infty, E/(1-D))$ we apply the same analysis. Recall that c_2 satisfies $c_2 D + E < c_2$. Set $f(u) := h_2(u)$ on $[c_2 D + E, c_2)$. Thus for $u \in [(c_2 D + E)D + E, c_2 D + E)$ and by (12.22) we have

$$f(u) = h_2((u - E)/D) - g((u - E)/D).$$

Continuing, for $u \in [c_2 D^3 + E(1 + D + D^2), c_2 D^2 + E(1 + D))$ we have

$$f(u) = h_2((u - E(1 + D))/D^2) - g((u - E(1 + D))/D^2) - g((u - E)/D),$$

etc. Now

$$c_2 D^n + E(1 + D + \cdots + D^{n-1})$$

tends to minus infinity as $n \uparrow \infty$ since, by assumption, $c_2 D + E - c_2 < 0$ and $D > 1$. Thus the above process defines f on all of $(-\infty, c_2]$. We go in the reverse direction using (12.23). For $u \in [c_2, (c_2 - E)/D)$ we have

$$f(u) = h_2(uD + E) + g(u).$$

For $u \in [(c_2 - E)/D, (c_2 - E - DE)/D^2)$ we have

$$f(u) = h_2(uD^2 + DE + E) + g(uD + E) + g(u),$$

etc. After the nth stage of this process we are considering the interval whose left endpoint is

$$\frac{c_2 - E(1 + D + \cdots + D^{n-1})}{D^n},$$

that increases to

$$\frac{E}{1-D}$$

as n tends to infinity. Thus we have determined f on $(-\infty, E/(1-D))$. We also easily see that if g is continuous thereon, h_2 is continuous on $[c_2 D + E, c_2]$ and

$$h_2(c_2) - h_2(c_2 D + E) = g(c_2)$$

then f is continuous on $(-\infty, E/(1-D))$.　　　　　　　　　　□

There remains the case $D < -1$. This case is slightly different because the transformation u to $uD + E$ flips us back and forth. We have the following.

Proposition 12.14 *Assume $D < -1$ in (12.17). Choose any c satisfying $(cD + E)D + E > c$. For an arbitrary h defined on $[c, (cD + E)D + E)$, there exists a unique f defined on $\mathbb{R} \backslash \{E/(1-D)\}$ satisfying (12.17), where $f(u) = h(u)$ for*

$u \in [c, (cD + E)D + E)$. *In addition, if g is continuous on* $\mathbb{R}\backslash\{E/(1 - D)\}$, *h is continuous on* $[c, (cD + E)D + E]$ *and*

$$h(c) - h((cD + E)D + E) = g(c) + g(cD + E),$$

then f is continuous on $\mathbb{R}\backslash\{E/(1 - D)\}$.

Proof Note that $(cD + E)D + E > c$ if and only if $c > E/(1 - D)$, since $D < -1$. We will first use

$$f(u) = f((u - E)/D) - g((u - E)/D).$$

Since $f(u) = h(u)$ on $[c, (cD + E)D + E)$, we have

$$f(u) = h((u - E)/D) - g((u - E)/D)$$

for $u \in ((cD + E)D^2 + DE + E, cD + E]$. Continuing, for $u \in [(cD + E)D + E, (cD + E)D^3 + D^2E + DE + E)$ we have

$$f(u) = h((u - E(1 + D))/D^2) - g((u - E(1 + D))/D^2) - g((u - E)/D),$$

etc. These intervals flip from side to side under the above transformation since $D < 0$ and they also grow outwards. The right endpoints of the right-most intervals are of the form

$$(cD + E)D^{2n-1} + E(D^{2n-2} + \cdots + D + 1).$$

This equals

$$\frac{D^{2n-1}}{D-1}[(cD + E)(D - 1) + E] - \frac{E}{D-1} = \frac{D^{2n-1}}{D-1}[(cD + E)D - cD] - \frac{E}{D-1}.$$

Since $c > E/(1 - D)$ and $D < -1$ it follows that $(cD + E)D - cD > 0$. Furthermore $D^{2n-1} < 0$ and $D - 1 < 0$. Thus this value tends to infinity as $n \uparrow \infty$. The left endpoints of the left-most intervals are of the form

$$(cD + E)D^{2n} + E(D^{2n-1} + \cdots + D + 1).$$

This equals

$$\frac{D^{2n}}{D-1}[(cD + E)D - Dc] - \frac{E}{D-1}.$$

For the same reasons as above, except that the power $2n$ replaces $2n - 1$, this tends to minus infinity as $n \uparrow \infty$. Note that the two sets of intervals uniquely define f on $[c, \infty)$ and $(-\infty, cD + E]$.

We now go the other way using (12.17). We obtain

$$f(u) = h(uD + E) + g(u)$$

for $u \in (cD + E, c/D - E/D]$. Continuing we have for $u \in [c/D^2 - E/D^2 - E/D, c)$ that

$$f(u) = h(uD^2 + DE + E) + g(uD + E) + g(u).$$

We continue in this way. The left endpoints of the right-most intervals are of the form

$$\frac{c}{D^{2n}} - E\left(\frac{1}{D} + \frac{1}{D^2} + \cdots + \frac{1}{D^{2n}}\right).$$

This equals

$$\frac{c(D-1) + E}{D^{2n}(D-1)} - \frac{E}{D-1},$$

that, as $n \uparrow \infty$, tends to $E/(1 - D)$ from above. The right endpoints of the left-most intervals are of the form

$$\frac{c}{D^{2n-1}} - E\left(\frac{1}{D} + \frac{1}{D^2} + \cdots + \frac{1}{D^{2n-1}}\right).$$

This equals

$$\frac{c(D-1) + E}{D^{2n-1}(D-1)} - \frac{E}{D-1},$$

that, as $n \uparrow \infty$, tends to $E/(1 - D)$ from below. This uniquely defines f on $(E/(1 - D), c)$ and $(cD + E, E/(1 - D))$. Thus f is uniquely define everything except at $E/(1 - D)$.

If we want continuity of f on $\mathbb{R} \backslash \{E/(1-D)\}$, then we will attain it if we have the continuity g thereon, h on $[c, (cD + E)D + E]$ and

$$h(c) - h((cD + E)D + E) = g(c) + g(cD + E). \qquad \square$$

Remark 12.15 The value of f at $E/(1 - D)$ in the above two propositions is immaterial, nor do we know anything about the behavior of f near $E/(1 - D)$. In fact, from Example 12.1 it follows that there can exist continuous and bounded g for which every solution f is unbounded about $E/(1 - D)$.

Proof of Theorem 12.9 Consider the interpolation problem

$$f_1(tB_{1j} + C_{1j}) + f_2(tB_{2j} + C_{2j}) = g_j(t), \qquad j = 1, 2, 3. \qquad (12.24)$$

Assume that this interpolation problem can be solved for most g_1, g_2, g_3. Then it can also be solved on any two of the three lines, and thus Theorem 12.6 holds with respect to any two of these three lines. The analysis of this section therefore also holds for any two of these three lines. We claim that this leads us to a contradiction.

Assume some of the B_{ij} are equal to zero. Without loss of generality, assume $B_{11} = 0$. From (12.24) we obtain

$$f_2(s) = g_1((s - C_{21})/B_{21}) - \alpha$$

for some arbitrary constant α. Substituting into (12.24) with $j = 2$ and $j = 3$ we see that

$$f_1(tB_{1j} + C_{1j}) = g_j(t) - g_1((tB_{2j} + C_{2j} - C_{21})/B_{21}) + \alpha, \qquad j = 2, 3.$$

Obviously, for general g_2 and g_3 there is no f_1 that simultaneously satisfies both these equations.

Let us now assume that the B_{ij} are all non-zero, $i = 1, 2$, $j = 1, 2, 3$. Then by the previous analysis we are led to f_2 simultaneously satisfying the equations

$$f_2(u) - f_2(uD_j + E_j) = \widetilde{g}_j(u), \qquad j = 1, 2,$$

for some given D_j, E_j where $D_j \neq 0, -1$, and $(D_j, E_j) \neq (1, 0)$, $j = 1, 2$. Here $\widetilde{g}_1, \widetilde{g}_2$ are arbitrary functions. Start with $j = 1$. From Propositions 12.10, 12.13 and 12.14 we see that we can arbitrarily define f_2 on a finite interval (or pair of intervals) depending on D_1, E_1. But on the complement of this interval the function f_2 is uniquely determined by this arbitrary function and $\widetilde{g}_1$ in a very specific manner. But then for almost all $\widetilde{g}_2$ we cannot solve (12.24) for $j = 2$. There is simply insufficient freedom. This proves the result. $\qquad \square$

Question What happens when we have three or more directions? The difficulties become so much greater. However we conjecture that, paralleling Theorems 12.6 and 12.9, for given

$$\mathcal{M}(\mathbf{a}^1, \ldots, \mathbf{a}^r) = \left\{ \sum_{i=1}^{r} f_i(\mathbf{a}^i \cdot \mathbf{x}) : f_i : \mathbb{R} \to \mathbb{R} \right\},$$

with pairwise linearly independent directions $\mathbf{a}^1, \ldots, \mathbf{a}^r$ in $\mathbb{R}^n$, it should be possible, except in certain specific cases, to interpolate along r straight lines. And it should be impossible to interpolate arbitrary data on any $r + 1$ or more straight lines.

References

Aczél, J. [1966]: *Functional Equations and their Applications*, Academic Press, New York.

Adams, R. A. [1975]: *Sobolev Spaces*, Academic Press, New York.

Aumann, G. [1959]: Über approximative Nomographie. II, *Bayer. Akad. Wiss. Math.-Nat. Kl. S.-B.* **1959**, 27–34.

Aumann, G. [1963]: Approximation by step functions, *Proc. Amer. Math. Soc.* **14**, 477–482.

Bauschke, H. H. [1996]: The approximation of fixed points of compositions of nonexpansive mappings in Hilbert space, *J. Math. Anal. Appl.* **202**, 150–159.

Bauschke, H. H., Borwein, J. M. [1996]: On projection algorithms for solving convex feasibility problems, *SIAM Review* **38**, 367–426.

Białynicki-Birula, A., Schinzel, A. [2008]: Representation of multivariate polynomials by sums of univariate polynomials in linear forms, *Colloq. Math.* **112**, 201–233.

Biermann, O. [1903]: Über Näherungsweise Cubaturen, *Monat. Math. Phys.* **14**, 211–225.

Boij, M., Carlini, E., Geramita, A. V. [2011]: Monomials as sums of powers: the real binary case, *Proc. Amer. Math. Soc.* **139**, 3039–3043.

Boman, J. [1984]: On the closure of spaces of sums of ridge functions and the range of the X-ray transform, *Ann. Inst. Fourier (Grenoble)* **34**, 207–239.

de Boor, C. [2005]: Divided differences, *Surveys in Approximation Theory* **1**, 46–69. [Online article at] http://www.math.technion.ac.il/sat

Brachat, J., Comon, P., Mourrain, B., Tsigaridas, E. [2010]: Symmetric tensor decomposition, *Lin. Alg. Appl.* **433**, 1851–1872.

Braess, D., Pinkus, A. [1993]: Interpolation by ridge functions, *J. Approx. Theory* **73**, 218–236.

Browder, F. E. [1967]: Convergence theorems for sequences of nonlinear operators in Banach spaces, *Math. Zeitschr.* **100**, 201–225.

Bruck, R. E., Reich, S. [1977]: Nonexpansive projections and resolvents of accretive operators in Banach spaces, *Houston J. Math.* **3**, 459–470.

de Bruijn, N. G. [1951]: Functions whose differences belong to a given class, *Nieuw Arc. Wisk.* **23**, 194–218.

de Bruijn, N. G. [1952]: A difference property for Riemann integrable functions and for some similar classes of functions, *Nederl. Akad. Wetensch. Proc. Ser. A.* **55** = *Indagationes Math.* **14**, 145–151.

Buck, R. C. [1972]: On approximation theory and functional equations, *J. Approx. Theory* **5**, 228–237.

Buhmann, M. D., Pinkus, A. [1999]: Identifying linear combinations of ridge functions, *Adv. Appl. Math.* **22**, 103–118.

Candès, E. J. [1998]: *Ridgelets: Theory and Applications*, Ph. D. dissertation, Dept. Statistics, Stanford University.

Candès, E. J. [1999]: Harmonic analysis of neural networks, *Appl. Comput. Harmonic Anal.* **6**, 197–218.

Candès, E. J., Donoho, D. L. [1999]: Ridgelets: a key to higher-dimensional intermittency?, *Philos T. Royal Soc. A* **357**, 2495–2509.

Cheney, E. W. [1966]: *Introduction to Approximation Theory*, McGraw-Hill, New York.

Chlebowicz, A., Wołowiec-Musial, M. [2005]: Forms with a unique representation as a sum of powers of linear forms, *Tatra Mt. Math. Publ.* **32**, 33–39.

Chung, K. C., Yao, T. H. [1977]: On lattices admitting unique Lagrange interpolations, *SIAM J. Numer. Anal.* **14**, 735–743.

Cohen, A., Daubechies, I., DeVore, R. A., Kerkyacharian, G., Picard, D. [2012]: Capturing ridge functions in high dimensions from point queries, *Constr. Approx.* **35**, 225–243.

Comon, P., Golub, G., Lim, L.-H., Mourrain, B. [2008]: Symmetric tensors and symmetric tensor rank, *SIAM J. Matrix Anal. Appl.* **30**, 1254–1279.

Courant, R., Hilbert, D. [1962] *Methods of Mathematical Physics, Vol. II*, Interscience Publishers, New York.

Dahmen, W., Micchelli, C. A. [1987]: Some remarks on ridge functions, *Approx. Theory and its Appl.* **3**, 139–143.

Deutsch, F. [1979]: The alternating method of Von Neumann, in *Multivariate Approximation Theory*, ISNM **51**, 83–96, eds. W. Schempp, K. Zeller, Birkhäuser, Basel.

Deutsch, F., Hundal, H. [1997]: The rate of convergence for the method of alternating projections, II, *J. Math. Anal. Appl.* **205**, 381–405.

Deutsch, F., Hundal, H. [2010]: Slow convergence of sequences of linear operators II: arbitrary slow convergence, *J. Approx. Theory* **162**, 1717–1738.

Diaconis, P., Shahshahani, M. [1984]: On nonlinear functions of linear combinations, *SIAM J. Sci. Stat. Comput. Applications* **5**, 175–191.

Diliberto, S. P., Straus, E. G. [1951]: On the approximation of a function of several variables by the sum of functions of fewer variables, *Pacific J. Math.* **1**, 195–210.

Donoho, D. L., Johnstone, I. M. [1989]: Projection-based approximation and a duality method with kernel methods, *Ann. Statist.* **17**, 58–106.

Dyn, N., Light, W. A., Cheney, E. W. [1989]: Interpolation by piecewise-linear radial basis functions, *J. Approx. Theory* **59**, 202–223.

Edwards, R. E. [1965]: *Functional Analysis, Theory and Applications*, Holt, Rinehart & Winston, New York.

Ellison, W. J. [1971]: Waring's problem, *Amer. Math. Monthly* **78**, 10–36.

Erdélyi, A. (Ed.) [1953]: *Higher Transcendental Functions*, Vol. 2, Bateman Manuscript project, McGraw-Hill, New York.

Falconer, K. J. [1979]: Consistency conditions for a finite set of projections of a function, *Math. Proc. Camb. Phil. Soc.* **85**, 61–68.

Fornasier, M., Schnass, K., Vybíral, J. [2012]: Learning functions of few arbitrary linear parameters in high dimensions, *Found. Comput. Math.* **12**, 229–262.

Franchetti, C., Light, W. [1986]: On the von Neumann alternating algorithm in Hilbert space, *J. Math. Anal. Appl.* **114**, 305–314.

Friedman, J. H., Stuetzle, W. [1981]: Projection pursuit regression, *J. Amer. Statist. Assoc.* **76**, 817–823.

Garkavi, A. L., Medvedev, V. A., Khavinson, S. Ya. [1995]: On existence of a best uniform approximation of a function in two variables by the sums $\phi(x) + \psi(y)$, *Sibirsk. Mat. Zh.* **36**, 819–827; English translation in *Siberian Math. J.* **36**, 707–713.

Golomb, M. [1959]: Approximation by functions of fewer variables, in *On Numerical Approximation*, 275–327, ed. R. Langer, University of Wisconsin Press, Madison.

Halperin, I. [1962]: The product of projection operators, *Acta Sci. Math. (Szeged)* **23**, 96–99.

Hamaker, C., Solmon, D. C. [1978]: The angles between the null spaces of X-rays, *J. Math. Anal. and Appl.* **62**, 1–23.

Hamel, G. [1905]: Eine Basis aller Zahlen und die unstetigen Lösungen der Funktionalgleichung $f(x + y) = f(x) + f(y)$, *Math. Ann.* **60**, 459–462.

Hardy, G. H., Littlewood, J. E., Pólya, G. [1952]: *Inequalities*, 2nd edn, Cambridge University Press.

Helgason, S. [1980]: *The Radon Transform*, Progress in Mathematics 5, Birkhäuser.

Hilbert, D. [1909]: Beweis für die Darstellbarkeit der ganzen Zahlen durch eine feste Anzahl $n$ter Potenzen (Waringsches Problem), *Math. Ann.* **67**, 281–300.

Horn, R. A., Johnson, C. R. [1991]: *Topics in Matrix Analysis*, Cambridge University Press.

Huber, P. J. [1985]: Projection pursuit, *Ann. Statist.* **13**, 435–475.

Iarrobino, A. [1995]: Inverse system of a symbolic power II. The Waring problem for forms, *J. Algebra* **174**, 1091–1110.

Ismailov, V. E. [2007a]: A note on the best L_2 approximation by ridge functions, *Appl. Math. E-Notes* **7**, 71–76.

Ismailov, V. E. [2007b]: Characterization of an extremal sum of ridge functions, *J. Comput. Appl. Math.* **205**, 105–115.

Ismailov, V. E. [2008a]: On the representation by linear superpositions, *J. Approx. Theory* **151**, 113–125.

Ismailov, V. E. [2009]: On the proximinality of ridge functions, *Sarajevo J. Math.* **5**, 109–118.

Ismailov, V. E. [2014]: Approximation by ridge functions and neural networks with a bounded number of neurons, to appear in *Appl. Anal.*

Ismailov V. E., Pinkus, A. [2013]: Interpolation on lines by ridge functions, *J. Approx. Theory* **175**, 91–113.

John, F. [1955]: *Plane Waves and Spherical Means Applied to Partial Differential Equations*, Interscience Publishers, Inc., New York.

Jones, L. K. [1987]: On a conjecture of Huber concerning the convergence of projection pursuit regression, *Ann. Statist.* **15**, 880–882.

Jones, L. K. [1992]: A simple lemma on greedy approximation in Hilbert space and convergence rates for projection pursuit regression and neural network training, *Ann. Statist.* **20**, 608–613.

Kemperman, J. H. B. [1957]: A general functional equation, *Trans. Amer. Math. Society*, **86**, 28–56.

Khavinson, S. Ya. [1997]: *Best Approximation by Linear Superpositions (Approximate Nomography)*, Transl. Math. Monographs, **159**, AMS, Providence, RI.

Kroó, A. [1997]: On approximation by ridge functions, *Constr. Approx.* **13**, 447–460.

Kuczma, M. [1968]: *Functional Equations in a Single Variable*, PWN – Polish Scientific Publishers, Warszawa.

Lang, H. [1984]: On sums of subspaces in topological vector spaces and an application in theoretical tomography, *Appl. Anal.* **18**, 257–265.

Leshno, M., Lin, V. Ya., Pinkus, A., Schocken, S. [1993]: Multilayer feedforward networks with a non-polynomial activation function can approximate any function, *Neural Networks* **6**, 861–867.

Light, W. A., Cheney, E. W. [1985]: *Approximation Theory in Tensor Product Spaces*, LNM 1169, Springer-Verlag, Berlin.

Light, W. A., Holland, S. M. [1984]: The L_1-version of the Diliberto–Straus algorithm in $C(T \times S)$, *Proc. Edinburgh Math. Soc.* **27**, 31–45.

Light, W. A., McCabe, J. H., Phillips, G. M., Cheney, E. W. [1982]: The approximation of bivariate functions by sums of univariate ones using the L_1-metric, *Proc. Edinburgh Math. Soc.* **25**, 173–181.

Lin, V. Ya., Pinkus, A. [1993]: Fundamentality of ridge functions, *J. Approx. Theory* **75**, 295–311.

Logan, B. F., Shepp, L. A. [1975]: Optimal reconstruction of a function from its projections, *Duke Math. J.* **42**, 645–659.

Maiorov, V. E. [1999]: On best approximation by ridge functions, *J. Approx. Theory* **99**, 68–94.

Maiorov, V. E. [2010a]: Best approximation by ridge functions in L^p-spaces, *Ukr. Math. J.* **62**, 452–466.

Maiorov, V., Meir, R., Ratsaby, J. [1999]: On the approximation of functional classes equipped with a uniform measure using ridge functions, *J. Approx. Theory* **99**, 95–111.

Maiorov, V. E., Oskolkov, K. I., Temlyakov, V. N. [2002]: Gridge approximation and Radon compass, in *Approximation Theory*, 284–309, ed. B. D. Bojanov, DARBA, Sofia.

Marshall, D. E., O'Farrell, A. G. [1979]: Uniform approximation by real functions, *Fund. Math.* **104**, 203–211.

Medvedev, V. A. [1991]: On the sum of two closed algebras of continuous functions on a compactum, *Funk. Anal. i Pril.* **27**, 33–36; English translation in *Func. Anal. Appl.* **27**, 28–30.

Medvedev, V. A. [1992]: Refutation of a theorem of Diliberto and Straus, *Mat. Zametki* **51**, 78–80; English translation in *Math. Notes* **51**, 380–381.

Mordashev, V. M. [1969]: Best approximations of functions of several variables by sums of functions of fewer variables, *Mat. Zametki* **5**, 217–226; English translation in *Math. Notes* **5**, 132–137.

Murata, N. [1996]: An integral representation of functions using three-layered networks and their approximation bounds, *Neural Networks* **9**, 947–956.

Natterer, F. [1986]: *The Mathematics of Computerized Tomography*, John Wiley & Sons.

von Neumann, J. [1950]: *Functional Operators – Vol. II. The Geometry of Orthogonal Spaces*, Annals of Math. Studies #22, Princeton University Press, Princeton, NJ. (This is a reprint of mimeographed lecture notes first distributed in 1933.)

Oskolkov, K. I. [1997]: Ridge approximation, Fourier–Chebyshev analysis, and optimal quadrature formulas, *Tr. Mat. Inst. Steklova* **219**, *Teor. Priblizh. Garmon. Anal.*, 269–285; English translation in *Proc. Steklov Inst. Math.* **219**, 265–280.

Oskolkov, K. I. [1999a]: Linear and nonlinear methods for ridge approximation, metric theory of functions and related problems in analysis, 165–195, *Izd. Nauchno-Issled. Aktuarno-Finans. Tsentra (AFTs)*, Moscow, (Russian).

Oskolkov, K. I. [2002]: On representations of algebraic polynomials by superpositions of plane waves, *Serdica Math. J.* **28**, 379–390.

Petersen, B. E., Smith, K. T., Solmon, D. C. [1979]: Sums of plane waves, and the range of the Radon transform, *Math. Ann.* **243**, 153–161.

Petrushev, P. P. [1998]: Approximation by ridge functions and neural networks, *SIAM J. Math. Anal.* **30**, 155–189.

Pinkus, A. [1999]: Approximation theory of the MLP model in neural networks, *Acta Numerica* **8**, 143–195.

Pinkus, A. [2013]: Smoothness and uniqueness in ridge function representation, *Indagationes Mathematicae* **24**, 725–738.

Pinkus, A. [2015]: The alternating algorithm in a uniformly convex and uniformly smooth Banach space, *J. Math. Anal. Appl.* **421**, 747–753.

Radon, J. [1948]: Zur mechanischen Kubatur, *Monatsh. der Math. Physik* **52**, 286–300.

Reich, S. [1982]: Nonlinear semigroups, accretive operators, and applications, in *Nonlinear Phenomena in Mathematical Sciences*, 831–838, ed. V. Lakshmikantham, Academic Press, New York.

Reich, S. [1983]: A limit theorem for projections, *Linear and Multilinear Alg.* **13**, 281–290.

Reznick, B. [1992]: Sums of even powers of real linear forms, *Memoirs A. M. S.* **463**.

Rudin, W. [1973]: *Functional Analysis*, McGraw-Hill Inc., New York.

Schinzel, A. [2002a]: On a decomposition of polynomials in several variables, *J. Théor. Nom. Bordeaux* **14**, 647–666.

Schinzel, A. [2002b]: On a decomposition of polynomials in several variables, II, *Colloq. Math.* **92**, 67–79.

Schwartz, L. [1944]: Sur certaines familles non fondamentales de fonctions continues, *Bull. Soc. Math. France* **72**, 141–145.

Smith, K. T., Solmon, D. C., Wagner, S. I. [1977]: Practical and mathematical aspects of the problem of reconstructing objects from radiographs, *Bull. Amer. Math. Soc.* **83**, 1227–1270.

Stahl, D., de Boor, C. [2011]: On Radons recipe for choosing correct sites for multivariate polynomial interpolation, *J. Approx. Theory* **163**, 1854–1858.

Stein, E. M., Weiss, G. [1971]: *Introduction to Fourier Analysis on Euclidean Spaces*, Princeton University Press, Princeton.

Stridsberg, E. [1912]: Sur la démonstration de M. Hilbert du théorème de Waring, *Math. Ann.* **72**, 145–152.

Sun, X. [1993]: Ridge function spaces and their interpolation property, *J. Math. Anal. Appl.* **179**, 28–40.

Svensson, L. [1989]: Functional analytic approach to stability problems in three-dimensional theoretical tomography, *J. Math. Anal. Appl.* **139**, 303–310.

Sylvester, J. J. [1886]: Sur une extension d'un théorème de Clebsch relatif aux courbes du quatrième degré, *C. R. Math. Acad. Sci. Paris* **102**, 1532–1534.

Temlyakov, V. N. [2000]: Weak greedy algorithms, *Adv. Comput. Math* **12**, 213–227.

Temlyakov, V. N. [2011]: *Greedy Approximation*, Cambridge Monographs on Applied and Computational Math., Vol. 20, Cambridge University Press.

Tyagi, H., Cevher, V. [2014]: Learning non-parametric basis independent models from point queries via low-rank methods, *Appl. Comput. Harmonic Anal.* **37**, 389–412.

Usevich, K. [2014]: Decomposing multivariate polynomials with structured low-rank matrix completion, in *21st International Symposium on Mathematical Theory of Networks and Systems, July 7–11, 2014*, Groningen, The Netherlands, 1826–1833.

Vostrecov, B. A. [1963]: Conditions for a function of many variables to be representable as a sum of a finite number of plane waves traveling in given directions, *Dokl. Akad. Nauk SSSR* **153**, 16–19; English translation in *Soviet Math. Dokl.* **4**, 1588–1591.

Vostrecov, B. A., Ignat'eva, A. V. [1967]: The existence of best approximation of functions by sums of a finite number of plane waves of given directions in the L_p metric, *Dokl. Akad. Nauk SSSR* **176**, 1225–1228; English translation in *Soviet Math. Dokl.* **8**, 1288–1291.

Vostrecov, B. A., Kreines, M. A. [1961]: Approximation of continuous functions by superpositions of plane waves, *Dokl. Akad. Nauk SSSR* **140**, 1237–1240; English translation in *Soviet Math. Dokl.* **2**, 1326–1329.

Vostrecov, B. A., Kreines, M. A. [1962]: Approximation of a plane wave by superpositions of plane waves of given directions, *Dokl. Akad. Nauk SSSR* **144**, 1212–1214; English translation in *Soviet Math. Dokl.* **3**, 875–877.

Weinmann, A. [1994]: The interpolation problem for ridge functions, *Numer. Funct. Anal. Optim.* **15**, 183–186.

Supplemental References

The following is a supplemental list of references on ridge functions. These works are not referenced in this book.

Babayev, M.-B. A. [2004]: On estimation of the best approximation by ridge polynomials, *Proc. Inst. Math. Mech. Natl. Acad. Sci. Azerb.* **20**, 3–8.

Babayev, M.-B. A., Novruzova, N. A. [2003]: On de la Valle-Poussin type theorem, *Proc. Inst. Math. Mech. Natl. Acad. Sci. Azerb.* **19**, 45–48.

Babenko, V. F., Levchenko, D. A. [2013]: Uniformly distributed ridge approximation of some classes of harmonic functions, *Ukrainian Math. J.* **64**, 1621–1626.

Candès, E. J. [2002]: New ties between computational harmonic analysis and approximation theory, in *Approximation Theory, X* (St. Louis, MO, 2001), 87–153, eds. C. K. Chui, L. L. Schumaker, J. Stöckler, Innov. Appl. Math., Vanderbilt University Press, Nashville, TN.

Candès, E. J. [2003]: Ridgelets: estimating with ridge functions, *Ann. Statist.* **31**, 1561–1599.

Cheney, E. W. [1992]: Approximation by functions of nonclassical form, in *Approximation Theory, Spline Functions and Applications (Maratea, 1991)*, 1–18, ed. S. P. Singh, NATO Adv. Sci. Inst. Ser. C Math. Phys. Sci., 356, Kluwer Academic Publishers, Dordrecht.

Cheney, E. W., Xu, Y. [1993]: A set of research problems in approximation theory, in *Topics in Polynomials of One and Several Variables and their Applications*, 109–123, eds. Th. M. Rassias, H. M. Srivastava, A. Yanushauskas, World Scientific Publishing.

Chui, C. K., Li, X. [1992]: Approximation by ridge functions and neural networks with one hidden layer, *J. Approx. Theory* **70**, 131–141.

Davison, M. E., Grunbaum, F. A. [1981]: Tomographic reconstruction with arbitrary directions, *Comm. Pure and Applied Math.* **34**, 77–120.

DeVore, R. A., Oskolkov, K. I., Petrushev, P. P. [1997]: Approximation by feed-forward neural networks, *The heritage of P. L. Chebyshev: a Festschrift in honor of the 70th birthday of T. J. Rivlin*, in *Ann. Numer. Math.* **4**, 261–287.

Donoho, D. L. [2001]: Ridge functions and orthonormal ridgelets, *J. Approx. Theory* **111**, 143–179.

Garkavi, A. L. [1996]: On the problem of best approximation of a function $f(x, y)$ by sums $\phi(ax + by) + \psi(cx + dy)$ (on a question of S. B. Stechkin), *Proceedings of the XX Workshop on Function Theory (Moscow, 1995)* in *East J. Approx.* **2**, 151–154.

Garkavi, A. L., Medvedev, V. A., Khavinson, S. Ya. [1996]: Existence of the best possible uniform approximation of a function of several variables by a sum of functions of fewer variables, *Mat. Sb.* **187**, 3–14; English translation in *Sb. Math.* **187**, 623–634.

Gordon, Y., Maiorov, V., Meyer, M., Reisner, S. [2002]: On the best approximation by ridge functions in the uniform norm, *Constr. Approx.* **18**, 61–85.

Hemmat, A. A., Dehghan, M. A., Skopina, M. [2005]: Ridge wavelets on the ball, *J. Approx. Theory* **136**, 129–139.

Ismailov, V. E. [2006]: On the approximation by linear combinations of ridge functions in L_2 metric, *Proc. Inst. Math. Mech. Natl. Acad. Sci. Azerb.* **24**, 101–108.

Ismailov, V. E. [2007c]: Representation of multivariate functions by sums of ridge functions, *J. Math. Anal. Appl.* **331**, 184–190.

Ismailov, V. E. [2008b]: On the approximation by weighted ridge functions, *An. Univ. Vest Timis,. Ser. Mat.-Inform.* **46**, 75–83.

Ismailov, V. E. [2011]: Approximation capabilities of neural networks with weights from two directions, *Azerb. J. Math.* **1**, 122–128.

Ismailov, V. E. [2013]: A review of some results on ridge function approximation, *Azerb. J. Math.* **3**, 3–51.

Jones, L. K. [2009]: Local minimax learning of functions with best finite sample estimation error bounds: applications to ridge and lasso regression, boosting, tree learning, kernel machines, and inverse problems, *IEEE Trans. Inform. Theory* **55**, 5700–5727.

Kazantsev, I. G. [1998]: Tomographic reconstruction from arbitrary directions using ridge functions, *Inverse Problems* **14**, 635–645.

Kolleck, A., Vybíral, J. [2015]: On some aspects of approximation of ridge functions, *J. Approx. Theory* **194**, 35–61.

Konovalov, V. N., Kopotun, K. A., Maiorov, V. E. [2010]: Convex polynomial and ridge approximation of Lipschitz functions in R^d, *Rocky Mountain J. Math.* **40**, 957–976.

Konovalov, V. N., Leviatan, D., Maiorov, V. E. [2008]: Approximation by polynomials and ridge functions of classes of s-monotone radial functions, *J. Approx. Theory* **152**, 20–51.

Konovalov, V. N., Leviatan, D., Maiorov, V. E. [2009]: Approximation of Sobolev classes by polynomials and ridge functions, *J. Approx. Theory* **159**, 97–108.

Kozarev, R. [2004]: The greedy ridge algorithm in Gaussian weighted L^2, *East J. Approx.* **10** (2004), 419–440.

Levesley, J., Sun, X. [1995]: Scattered Hermite interpolation by ridge functions, *Numer. Funct. Anal. Optim.* **16**, 989–1001.

Li, W., Padula, S. [2005]: Approximation methods for conceptual design of complex systems, in *Approximation Theory XI: Gatlinburg 2004*, 241–278, eds. C. K. Chui, M. Neamtu, L. L. Schumaker, Modern Methods Math., Nashboro Press, Brentwood.

Light, W. [1993]: Ridge functions, sigmoidal functions and neural networks, in *Approximation Theory VII (Austin, TX, 1992)*, 163–206, eds. E. W. Cheney, C. K. Chui, L. L. Schumaker, Academic Press, Boston.

Lin, V. Ya., Pinkus, A. [1994]: Approximation of multivariate functions, in *Advances in Computational Mathematics*, 257–266, eds. H. P. Dikshit, C. A. Micchelli, World Scientific Publishing.

Madych, W. R., Nelson, S. A. [1985]: Radial sums of ridge functions: a characterization, *Math. Methods Appl. Sci.* **7**, 90–100.

Maiorov, V. [2010b]: Geometric properties of the ridge function manifold, *Adv. Comput. Math.* **32**, 239–253.

Maiorov, V., Pinkus, A. [1999]: Lower bounds for approximation by MLP neural networks, *Neurocomputing* **25**, 81–91.

Marshall, D. E., O'Farrell, A. G. [1983]: Approximation by a sum of two algebras. The lightning bolt principle, *J. Funct. Anal.* **52**, 353–368.

Mayer, S., Ullrich, T., Vybíral, J. [2014]: Entropy and sampling numbers of classes of ridge functions, arXiv:1311.2005.

Oskolkov, K. I. [1999b]: Approximation by ridge functions and the Nikol'skii-Kolmogorov problem, *Dokl. Akad. Nauk* **368**, 445–448; English translation in *Dokl. Math.* **60**, 209–212.

Park, M. G., Sun, J. [1998]: Tests in projection pursuit regression, *J. Statist. Plann. Inference* **75**, 65–90.

Pelletier, B. [2004]: Approximation by ridge function fields over compact sets, *J. Approx. Theory* **129**, 230–239.

Pinkus, A. [1995]: Some density problems in multivariate approximation, in *Approximation Theory: Proceedings of the International Dortmund Meeting IDOMAT 95*, 277–284, eds. M. W. Muller, M. Felten, D. H. Mache, Akademie Verlag.

Pinkus, A. [1997]: Approximating by ridge functions, in *Surface Fitting and Multiresolution Methods*, 279–292, eds. A. Le Mehaute, C. Rabut, L. L. Schumaker, Vanderbilt University Press, Nashville.

Reid, L., Sun, X. [1993]: Distance matrices and ridge function interpolation, *Canad. J. Math.* **45**, 1313–1323.

Sanguineti, M. [2008]: Universal approximation by ridge computational models and neural networks: a survey, *Open Appl. Math. J.* **2**, 31–58.

Sproston, J. P., Strauss, D. [1992]: Sums of subalgebras of $C(X)$, *J. London Math. Soc.* **45**, 265–278.

Sternfeld, Y. [1978]: Uniformly separating families of functions, *Israel J. Math.* **29**, 61–91.

Sun, X., Cheney, E. W. [1992]: The fundamentality of sets of ridge functions, *Aequationes Math.* **44**, 226–235.

Wang, Z., Qin, X., Wei, G., Su, L., Wang L. H., Fang, B. Y. [2010]: Meshless method with ridge basis functions, *Applied Math. Comp.* **217**, 1870–1886.

Wu, W., Feng, G., Li, X. [2002]: Training multilayer perceptrons via minimization of sum of ridge functions, *Adv. Comput. Math.* **17**, 331–347.

Xu, Y., Light, W. A., Cheney, E. W. [1993]: Constructive methods of approximation by ridge functions and radial functions, *Numer. Algorithms* **4**, 205–223.

Zhang, L. W. [2005]: Error estimates for interpolation with ridge basis functions, (Chinese) *J. Fudan Univ. Nat. Sci.* **44**, 301–306.

Author Index

205

Subject Index